THE PSYC
OF INTERPERSON

Michael Argyle, D.Sc., is Reader in Social Psychology at Oxford University and a Fellow of Wolfson College. He was born in Nottingham in 1925; went to Nottingham High School and Emmanuel College, Cambridge, and was a navigator in the R.A.F. He has been teaching social psychology at Oxford since 1952. He has been engaged in research in various aspects of social psychology and is particularly interested in the experimental study of social interaction and its application to wider social problems. In recent years he has been greatly helped by his very active research group. During sabbatical terms and long vacations, he has been a Fellow at the Center for Advanced Study in the Behavioral Sciences, Stanford, and has been visiting professor at the Universities of Michigan, British Columbia, Ghana, Delaware, the State University of New York at Buffalo, the University of Leuven, the Hebrew University, Jerusalem, the University of Adelaide, York University, Ontario, the University of Nevada and the University of Kansas.

Michael Argyle is the author of *The Scientific Study of Social Behaviour*, *Psychology and Social Problems*, *Social Interaction*, *The Social Psychology of Work*, *Bodily Communication*, *Gaze and Mutual Gaze* (with Mark Cook), *The Social Psychology of Religion* (with B. Beit-Hallahmi), *Social Skills and Mental Health* (with P. Trower and B. Bryant), and *Social Situations* (with A. Furnham and J. A. Graham), and has written numerous articles in British, American and European journals. He helped to found the *British Journal of Social and Clinical Psychology* and was Social Psychology Editor (1961–7). He is the editor of the Pergamon Press *International Studies in Experimental Social Psychology*. He was Chairman of the Social Psychology Section of the British Psychological Society (1964–7 and 1972–4).

He is married and has four children; his hobbies are travel, interpersonal behaviour, Scottish country dancing, Utopian speculation, theological disputation and playing the goat.

MICHAEL ARGYLE

THE PSYCHOLOGY
OF INTERPERSONAL
BEHAVIOUR

THIRD EDITION

PENGUIN BOOKS

Penguin Books Ltd, Harmondsworth, Middlesex, England
Penguin Books, 625 Madison Avenue, New York, New York 10022, U.S.A.
Penguin Books Australia Ltd, Ringwood, Victoria, Australia
Penguin Books Canada Ltd, 2801 John Street, Markham, Ontario, Canada L3R 1B4
Penguin Books (N.Z.) Ltd, 182–190 Wairau Road, Auckland 10, New Zealand

—

First published 1967
Reprinted 1967, 1968, 1970, 1971 (twice)
Second edition 1972
Reprinted 1973, 1974, 1975, 1976, 1977
Third edition 1978
Reprinted 1979, 1981, 1982

—

—

Set, printed and bound in Great Britain by
Cox & Wyman Ltd, Reading
Set in Monotype Imprint

CONTENTS

LIST OF FIGURES AND TABLES

9

LIST OF FIGURES AND TABLES

TABLES

ACKNOWLEDGEMENTS

Acknowledgement is gratefully made to the following:

The University of Illinois Press, Urbana, Illinois, for Figure 3 (copyright *American Journal of Psychology*, 1969); Mouton & Co., The Hague, Netherlands, for Figures 14 and 15; Duke University Press, Durham, North Carolina, for Figure 16 (copyright 1963 by Duke University Press); Addison-Wesley Publishing Co. Inc., Reading, Massachusetts, for Figure 19; John Wiley & Sons, Chichester, for Figure 20.

EDITORIAL FOREWORD

IT is often argued that modern psychology has become out of touch with the realities of everyday life. There is some truth in the argument. The rigorously controlled experiments which are required in scientific work must usually be carried out in artificial laboratory settings, and in the last decades psychologists have often been more interested in devising experiments to test hypotheses than in making and systematizing observations on everyday behaviour of ordinary people. This book comes as a refreshing change. It is about one particular aspect of social psychology – the ways in which people behave to each other. It is difficult to think of anything which has more relevance to everything one does while not actually asleep or unconscious. Although the findings of research on this subject have great generality, readers of this book will discover that the subject can be treated with scientific rigour.

The author, Michael Argyle, is a leading British social psychologist. He has contributed to his subject at all levels, in his writing on social psychology in general, in theoretical contributions – for instance in his development of the concept of introjection – and through empirical studies of industrial life and also in the laboratory, as in his studies of the part played by eye-to-eye contact during conversation.

In this book Argyle surveys the whole field of the psychological study of behaviour between people, but he chooses several topics to discuss in depth. Some people say that psychology is mainly common sense dressed up in fancy language. For such people this book will be full of surprises because many of the research findings could not have been anticipated by a thoughtful person sitting in an armchair and analysing what happens when people meet. The reason is that we all spend much of our time interacting with other people, with the result that the habits we use in such interaction have been practised over and over again and become automatic. We are no longer aware of what we do. In this way, as well as in others, social interaction resembles many skills, and one of Argyle's most stimulating and original ideas comes from this analogy.

The book opens with an analysis of the social motives which energize and direct social behaviour. It is in this chapter that there is the closest tie with the psychology of the individual, but even here the author uncovers certain motives which are purely social in origin and which would not be discovered by a psychologist studying the individual in a non-social setting. The author then goes on to discuss the actual behaviour of people in social settings, the social techniques which they use, varying from bodily contact to the persuasive use of language, and he looks at the various styles which people employ in using these techniques. Then there are sections on the way people perceive each other and themselves, on the different kinds of bond which can exist between people and on the determinants of friendship. Other sections are concerned with the relations between interpersonal behaviour and the group and the culture in which people live. Particular attention is given to the importance to the individual of the way other people react to him. The last chapters are concerned with applications of the topic, in the study of mental disorder; in professional social skills such as in interviewing, public speaking, and in teaching; and finally there is a section on methods of teaching social skills.

For the student of psychology this book will be valuable because of the author's survey of relevant work and because of his original ideas. For others it will provide an illustration of one of the values of psychology, which is that it helps one to think objectively about difficult subjects. The difficulty lies in the fact that these subjects are normally talked about imprecisely or that the observer himself is so involved in what is going on that he cannot see actions for words, or principles for detail.

B. M. FOSS

PREFACE TO THE FIRST EDITION

MAN is a social animal: he collaborates with others to pursue his goals and satisfy his needs. It is well known that relations with others can be the source of the deepest satisfactions and of the blackest misery. Moralists, novelists and others have written about these things, but the detailed analysis of social interactions and relationships has been lacking. Recent research by social psychologists has made these phenomena very much clearer. In particular there have been important advances in the experimental analysis of social encounters at the level of such things as eye-movements, the timing of speech, and non-verbal communication.

This research has a number of possible applications. The work of many people consists of dealing with people, rather than with things – teachers, psychologists, air hostesses, managers, and many others: research has been done into the social techniques which are most effective, and into how such skills can be taught. Many people are lonely and unhappy, some are mentally ill, because they are unable to establish and sustain social relationships with others. Many everyday encounters are unpleasant, embarrassing, or fruitless, because of inept social behaviour. Conflicts between different social classes and different cultural groups are partly due to the difficulties of interaction. Many of those difficulties and frustrations could be eliminated by a wider understanding, and better training in the skills of social interaction.

This book reflects the activities of the Social Skills research group at Oxford. I am grateful to Professor A. B. Cherns and the Social Science Research Council for financing this research, and to all those who have been associated with the group, especially to Dr Adam Kendon, who has collaborated over this work and made valuable comments on most of the MS., and to Dr E. R. F. W. Crossman, Douglas Seymour, Nicholas Bateson,

Janet Dean, Professor J. Ex, Mansur Lalljee, Mary Lydall, Peter McPhail, Euan Porter and Emma Shackle. I am also indebted to Professor Brian Foss, Professor Ralph Exline, Corinne Hutt, Dr Peter Robinson, Dr H. Tajfel, Dr A. Yates and Penguin Books for their valuable comments on parts of the MS.

Institute of Experimental Psychology   MICHAEL ARGYLE
South Parks Road
Oxford   October 1965

PREFACE TO THE SECOND EDITION

THERE have been dramatic and far-reaching developments in research into interpersonal behaviour since the first edition of this book was written in 1965. Details of some of this work can be found in my book *Social Interaction* (London: Methuen; New York: Atherton Press, 1969). I have done my best to report most of these developments, within the same framework as before. The main areas which have been added or modified are:

The biological roots of social behaviour
Non-verbal communication in animals and humans
Research at Oxford on gaze and other aspects of two-person interaction
Social behaviour and personality
Social performance of mental patients
Research on identity
Cultural rules and social behaviour .

I am indebted to the following for stimulation and collaboration – Florisse Alkema, Chris Brand, Bridget Bryant, Philip Burgess, Peter Collett, Mark Cook, Ralph Exline, Roger Ingham, Brian Little, Robert McHenry, Hilary Nicholson, Veronica Salter, Elizabeth Sidney, Mary Sissons, Jerry Tognoli, Ederyn Williams, Marylin Williams.

Department of Experimental Psychology   MICHAEL ARGYLE
South Parks Road
Oxford   March 1971

PREFACE TO THE THIRD EDITION

IT is very gratifying to see how much has been added to our knowledge of interpersonal behaviour during the last six years. I have incorporated in this edition the main findings of the social psychology group at Oxford, and of our friends and colleagues elsewhere. The main areas which have been extended or modified are:

Gaze
Interpersonal attraction
Non-verbal communication
Person perception
Person–situation interaction
Rules of social behaviour
Social skills training
Sequences of social events
Verbal interaction

I am extremely grateful to the following for their collaboration and ideas – John Breaux, Bridget Bryant, Anne Campbell, David Clarke, Peter Collett, Mark Cook, Joe Forgas, Gerry Ginsburg, Jean Ann Graham, Rom Harré, Roger Ingham, Mansur Lalljee, Luc Lefebvre, Peter Marsh, Kimiko Shimoda, Peter Trower. And once again Ann McKendry made a splendid job of the typing.

Department of Experimental Psychology   MICHAEL ARGYLE
South Parks Road   June 1977
Oxford

CHAPTER I

SOCIAL MOTIVATION

MOST people spend a great deal of their time engaging in some kind of social interaction. They live together, work together, and spend spare time with their friends. Why do they do this? Why don't we all behave like hermits, living and working alone? In fact for most individuals solitary confinement, or other forms of isolation for more than short periods, are very unpleasant indeed. Loss of 'face' in the Far East is a cause of suicide, and rejection by friends in our own society is a common source of distress. The explanation given by earlier thinkers was that humans (and most animals) have a 'herd instinct' or 'gregarious instinct' which draws them together. It is now realized that people seek a number of more specific goals in social situations – help with work or other activities, friendship, guidance, power, admiration, and so on.

Different people seek different things in social situations. In the present state of knowledge it looks as if social behaviour is the product of at least seven different drives. A 'drive' can be defined as a persistent tendency to seek certain goals. As well as directing people towards goals, a drive is a source of energy; when the drive is operating there is a general increase of vigour. Much the same is true of biological drives such as hunger: when a person is hungry he will seek food with increased effort. Furthermore the drive can be subdivided into a number of more specific ones for salt, sugar, and so on: animals deprived of one of these substances will select a diet which makes good the deficit. It is necessary to postulate these various forms of motivation to account for variations in the behaviour of the *same* person on different occasions, e.g. when hungry and not, and to describe differences between *different* people in the goals they pursue, and the energy with which they do it.

There is as yet no final agreement on how social motivation should be divided up. What will be done here is to offer a provisional list of motivational sources of interpersonal behaviour. These are sufficient to account for the phenomena described in this book, and each has been extensively studied by psychologists and others. Later in this chapter, some account will be given of how these drives function, and of their origins in childhood experience or innate tendencies. Here, then, is the provisional list, together with a note of the goals which are sought in each case. These goals are either responses which are sought from others, or types of relationships with other people.

1. *Biological needs* – hunger and thirst, eating and drinking, cooperation and competition, and emergence of other drives.

2. *Dependency* – acceptance, help, protection and guidance, especially from people in positions of power and authority.

3. *Affiliation* – physical proximity, eye-contact, warm and friendly responses and acceptance by peers and groups of peers.

4. *Dominance* – acceptance by others, and groups of others, as the task-leader, being allowed to talk most of the time, take the decisions, and be deferred to by the group.

5. *Sex* – physical proximity, bodily contact, etc., eye-contact, warm, friendly and intimate social interaction, usually with attractive peers of the opposite sex.

6. *Aggression* – to harm other people physically, verbally or in other ways.

7. *Self-esteem and ego-identity* – for other people to make approving responses and to accept the self-image as valid.

8. *Other motivations which affect social behaviour* – needs for achievement, money, interests and values.

This list is provisional, but moderately well established: drives 1–6 have all been studied in animals, and their biological and evolutionary basis is understood; they have also been studied in humans, and we know how they are affected by childhood experiences, how they are aroused, and how they affect social behaviour.

The biological functions of social behaviour in animals. During the last few years studies have been carried out on apes and monkeys in the wild; these studies have shown clearly how their social behaviour is important for the biological survival of these animals. A set of partly innate social drives has emerged during the course of evolution; these drives produce a pattern of partly instinctive social behaviour that enables groups of apes and monkeys to eat and drink, defend themselves against enemies, reproduce themselves, care for and train their young.

1. Apes and monkeys need access to water, and to suitable vegetables and fruits to eat. They occupy a territory which contains these resources, and may defend it against rivals. The patterns of social behaviour described below vary considerably between species. They also vary between groups of the *same* species, depending on the ecology, e.g. the availability of food and nesting sites; such 'cultural' patterns are perpetuated by socialization (Crook, 1970).

2. Most species live in groups, with a fairly stable dominance hierarchy which is established by aggressive displays between adult males. Certain adult males provide leadership in defending the territory and keeping internal order.

3. There is a definite family structure, which is different in different species. Opposite sex pairs mate, in order to continue the species, adult males look after their females for a time, and act as generalized fathers to the infants in the group.

4. Mothers feed and look after their young, and provide socialization experiences which complete the partly 'open' instinctive systems. Mothers have maternal patterns of behaviour which are aroused by the sight of young; the young have dependent patterns of behaviour which are aroused by the sight, feel and sound of the mother.

5. Aggressive behaviour is used to defend group and territory; it may also occur between males of the same group who are competing for dominance or for access to the same female. However, such aggression is usually limited to ferocious displays in which the most terrifying animal wins – it would not be in the interests of the group for much real fighting to take place.

6. Young apes and monkeys engage in play, adults in grooming; these are two examples of affiliative behaviour which

probably have the functions of restraining aggression inside the group, and making cooperation easier.

Social behaviour in lower animals is almost entirely instinctive: the entire pattern of social behaviour is innate and has emerged during evolution because of its biological survival value. The apes and monkeys are different in that their instinctive systems are more 'open', and remain to be completed during socialization experiences. There are also components of culture, perpetuated in particular groups of animals; these include washing food in sea water, in one group of Japanese macaques, and swimming in another.

The behaviour of apes and monkeys is quite illuminating for understanding human social behaviour – they are certainly more helpful than rats. However, there are some very important differences between men and monkeys: we use language, and our behaviour is more affected by plans and social rules. In men innate factors are less important, and there is a longer period of socialization. Human groups build up a far more elaborate culture, which is passed on to later generations, so that we live in an environment which is not only physically constructed by us, but has been given meanings by us – as in the case of clothes, cars, and everything else around us.

Biological and other drives. The best-understood drives are hunger and thirst. There seems to be a bodily self-regulating system which keeps the levels of food and water in the body at an equilibrium level. For example, when there is a shortage of water, thirst is experienced and this drive is aroused, leading to behaviour which makes good the deficit and restores the equilibrium. Most of the other drives do not work like this. Sex is an interesting intermediate case: in lower animals sexual arousal depends on the level of sex hormones in the blood stream – though there is no deficit here; in higher mammals and in man there is little connection between hormones and sexual arousal and activity; castration after puberty leads to no loss of sexual desire.

In the case of other drives, such as those for affiliation and money, the contents of the bloodstream are not involved; whatever physiological basis they have must be in the brain. There is no deficit, so that satisfaction of the need does not lead to a cessation of activity: it may lead to more. These drives resemble hunger and thirst in that relevant internal states and external stimuli result in autonomic arousal and the direction of behaviour towards the goals in question.

Arousal and satiation. People are not hungry all the time; the momentary strength of any drive depends on how far it has been aroused or satiated. It is now known that the activation of any drive system involves a similar pattern of physiological 'arousal'. This consists of electrical activity originating in the hypothalamus, and of activity in the sympathetic nervous system, producing higher blood pressure, a faster heart-beat and perspiration – though the physiological pattern varies between individuals.

A well-known law in psychology states that increasing arousal has an energizing effect, which first improves performance, but later leads to deterioration, as emotionality disrupts the pattern of behaviour. The optimum level of arousal for most effective performance is lower the more complex the task.

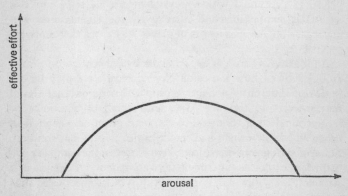

Figure 1. The relation between motivational arousal and effective effort.

Arousal is stronger when the expected reward or 'incentive' is larger, when it is greatly desired, and when its probability of being attained appears to be greater. The effect of incentives varies with the drive strength, and may vary between different cultural groups. For instance working-class children are aroused more by cash incentives, while middle-class children are more affected by hopes of 'success'.

We turn now to the conditions under which needs are satisfied. The hungry person is made less hungry by eating; the hunger drive builds up gradually with time until it is satisfied again. The drives behind social behaviour do not seem to work quite like this. A person who seeks money, or fame, does not cease to do so when he receives some gratification. Indeed the reverse is more likely: a person who seeks fame and never receives any is likely to give up, and seek different goals instead. In other words gratification seems to reinforce rather than satiate the goal-seeking tendency. There may still be some parallel to biological drives in that there may be temporary satiation, before further goals of the same type are sought.

Emotions and motivations are different aspects of the same states. The main emotions are happiness, fear, anger, disgust/contempt, sadness, surprise and interest; these are conscious experiences combined with a physiological condition, and also with facial expressions and other non-verbal signals. Fear and anger also appear on our list of drives – as states that motivate behaviour.

An ingenious series of experiments by Schachter and Singer (1962) showed how the same physiological state may be experienced differently, and how physiological and external stimuli may interact to produce a particular kind of emotional or motivational state. Some subjects were given an injection of adrenalin, while others had neutral injections of salt solution. Some of each group of subjects were placed in the company of a confederate of the experimenter, who generally behaved in a wild and crazy manner. Further groups of subjects were subjected to an insulting interview, in the company of a confederate of the experimenter, who became very angry with the interviewer. The main finding was that the adrenalin-injected subjects became very euphoric in the first situation, and aggressive in the second – more so than those injected with salt solution. Thus emotion depends partly on the operation of cognitive factors.

There is also a close connection between emotions and facial expression. Studies by Paul Ekman and others (1972) have demonstrated that the seven emotions listed above are shown by similar facial expressions in very different parts of the world, and Eibl-Eibesfeldt (1972) has found that some of them are used by blind infants. So they are probably innate, though there are cultural rules about when one is supposed to laugh or cry.

The measurement of motivation. People vary in the energy with which they pursue the goals of sex, dominance, affiliation and so on. How can these individual differences be assessed? We need to distinguish between their normal or typical level of anxiety, anger, etc., and their state at a particular moment. Questionnaires have been constructed by Spielberger (1966) for *state anxiety* and *trait anxiety*, using rather different questions. Like other questionnaires there is the problem that they can get only at the conscious part of motivation, and errors are caused by people trying to give a favourable impression. Nevertheless, some questionnaire measures have been successfully validated against behaviour.

Another means of measuring drive-states has been devised which can probably assess unconscious as well as conscious aspects of motivation. In 'projection tests' subjects are asked to tell a story about people shown in rather vaguely-drawn pictures. Their answers are scored to show the amount of affiliative, aggressive or other imagery, and this is used to predict the overt behaviour of the subject. There is considerable doubt over the validity of such projection tests, and they cannot be said to provide very good predictions. In the case of aggression and sex, there may even be a reverse prediction – some of the people who write the most aggressive stories display the least actual aggression in their behaviour; this is because fantasy may become a substitute for the real thing if that has been heavily punished.

Conflict. In the cases of sex, aggression and probably affiliation, there are restraining forces which often prevent the goal being attained. When the drive is aroused, there is also arousal of inner restraints, probably because of punishment in the past. These are cases of approach–avoidance conflict – where the same object is both desirable and undesirable. It is found that as the goal gets nearer, its desirability increases, but fear or other avoidance forces increase even more. The anxiety induced by the prospect of parachute jumping, for example, increases rapidly as the time approaches. A small child who wants to stroke a horse finds that her fear increases as she gets closer to the horse, and she vacillates at a short distance from it. Rats who are both fed and shocked at the end of a maze stop part of the way down it. Miller (1944) presented a theoretical analysis in terms of approach and avoidance 'gradients', where the avoidance gradient is steeper, and the crossing point shows where they balance (Fig. 2).

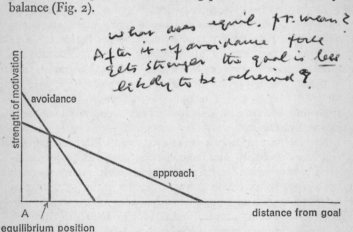

what does equil. pr. mean?
After it – if avoidance force
gets stronger the goal is less
likely to be achieved ?

Figure 2. Analysis of approach–avoidance conflicts.

A further part of the theory states that increased drive raises the whole gradient, so that increased prospects of punishment will raise the avoidance gradient and alter the equilibrium point.

Darwin maintained that emotional expression was part of a behavioural response, for example, showing the teeth in anger. A number of psychologists have argued that we know what emotion to experience through awareness of our own reactions, especially our facial expressions (Izard, 1971). Several experiments have shown that if subjects are asked to assume a certain facial expression for a time, then they come to experience the corresponding emotion (see p. 98).

The origins of drives. Hunger and thirst are innate bodily needs, though the way that they are satisfied is partly learnt from the culture. Sex, aggression and affiliation also have an instinctive basis; in other words all human beings have an innate tendency to pursue these goals when aroused. However, particular environmental conditions may be necessary for the drive to develop.

Some social drives may be wholly learnt, as the need for money is. Drives may be acquired in childhood in a number of ways. There may be something like 'imprinting' during the first year of life: the infant becomes attached to the dominant moving object in its environment, and does its best to follow that object. This has been observed in birds and other species and there is evidence that something similar occurs with human infants. A pattern of behaviour may become a drive because it consistently leads to other kinds of satisfaction: the origin of the need for money is probably that it leads to gratification of hunger and then becomes a goal which is sought for its own sake. Drives may be acquired through other learning processes, such as identification with parents: a child who takes a parent as a model is likely to acquire the parental pattern of motivation. There are great variations between cultures in the typical strength of these drives. Some cultures are very aggressive, some are greatly concerned about status and loss of face. These variations can sometimes be traced to the environmental setting – tribes which are constantly having to defend themselves against enemies need to have aggressive members, and so aggression is encouraged in children (Zigler and Child, 1969).

The origins of restraints. It is now believed by many biologists that although animals are basically selfish, some aspects of altruistic behaviour have emerged in the course of evolution, because they result in improved chances of survival of genes. Animals look after their own immediate relations, because they share a proportion of genes, which are thus helped to survive – 50 per cent for children, brothers and sisters, 25 per cent for cousins and grandchildren, etc. And a tendency towards generalized reciprocal altruism will lead to survival, since those who have it will benefit when they in turn are in need (Dawkins, 1976a). However, the main sources of restraints on selfish behaviour in man come from cultural learning. As well as biological evolution, there is also social evolution, whereby the elements of culture which help a society to survive are retained. And some of the most important aspects of culture are the moral values, and other norms of behaviour, which keep aggressive, sexual and selfish behaviour in check. There is thus a conflict in man between the egoistic desires resulting from biological evolution, and the restraints derived from social evolution (Campbell, 1975).

THE ROOTS OF SOCIAL BEHAVIOUR

In this section we shall give a brief account of each of the motivational systems listed earlier. It must be emphasized that this is a provisional list which will probably have to be revised in the light of future research.

1. *Biological drives affecting social behaviour.* Basic biological drives, such as the need for food, may lead to various kinds of interaction. They may result in drawing together the members of a primitive group in a cooperative task which none could accomplish alone. This happens with animals and leads to the formation of cooperative agricultural and pastoral groups in primitive communities. In modern societies work leads to the satisfaction of biological needs less directly. In other situations

biological needs can lead to intense competition or hostility, as when there is a limited amount of food to be shared out. It is possible for such cooperative and competitive situations to be set up experimentally by manipulating the way in which rewards are to be shared out. More important for us, these drives are the basis for other motivational systems: any pattern of behaviour that leads to food may become a new drive.

2. *Dependency*. This is the first form of social motivation and behaviour. Infants are physically dependent on their mother (or whoever is looking after them). There is an innate tendency to respond to pairs of eyes and to female voices; both are in range during feeding, and this is part of the rather complex process whereby the infant develops an early attachment to the mother.

It is not clear how similar human infant–mother bonding is to imprinting in animals. Infants can't walk, and perhaps following the mother with the eyes is the equivalent of following physically. There may also be learning by reward here: the important reward appears to be not so much food as the reduction of anxiety brought about by physical and visual contact with the mother. The critical period for the development of visual dependence on the mother is probably between six weeks and six months. The earliest forms of social behaviour are repeated rituals with mother, for example at bath-time and feeding-time, such as 'peek-a-boo', which involve interactive sequences of bodily contact, visual contact and vocalization (Bruner, 1975).

During the period of one to five years, children can bear greater physical distance from mother, and longer periods of separation. They may have to be trained to be more independent, if younger children appear on the scene. Dependent behaviour is stronger when the mother has been most responsive to the child's crying and there has been a lot of interaction between them (Schaffer and Emerson, 1964). It is found that dependency is also greater in first-born and only children; the reason for this is that their mothers interfere more, have stronger emotional reactions, but are more inconsistent.

Dependency may be aroused in adults in situations which are new and frightening, and where others know the ropes. Dependence, or submission, is closely related to its opposite, dominance, in that some people may show both types of behaviour on different occasions. The so-called 'authoritarian personality' is submissive to people of greater power or status, and dominant to those of less. He can be found displaying these alternating styles of behaviour in organizations with many levels in the hierarchy, and where little authority is delegated to those in lower ranks. Authoritarians come from homes where parents have been very dominating and strict. One explanation of their behaviour is that in their dependent role they are continuing the relationship which they had with their parents while in their dominant role they are imitating their parents.

3. *The need for affiliation.* This need leads to bodily contact, eye-contact, friendly social interaction, and other forms of intimacy with others. Only an intermediate degree of intimacy is sought with most people, for reasons which will be given below. In laboratory situations it is found that subjects strong in affiliation spend time establishing personal relationships with other people, rather than getting on with the appointed task. This dimension is closely related to 'social extraversion', in that both describe the people who are strongly motivated to interact with others. In particular they are keen to interact with other people of similar age, position, etc. to themselves. It probably leads to interaction with members of the opposite sex as well, and at present we are unable to disentangle its effects from those of the sexual drive – with which it appears to be rather closely related.

There is probably an innate basis to affiliative motivation, but it is mainly acquired from early experiences in the family. It has long been believed that affiliative behaviour develops in some way out of dependency. There is quite a lot of evidence to support this theory – the Harlows' monkeys showed no later affiliative behaviour if they had been reared in isolation, and affectionless psychopaths often have a history of maternal deprivation. One version of the theory is that anxiety reduction through contact with mothers reinforces social contacts in general. Schachter (1959) found that college girls who had been made anxious by the prospect of receiving electric shocks from 'Dr Zilstein' chose to wait with other subjects rather than alone: this was especially the case for those who were made most anxious, and for first-born and only children, who we have seen are more dependent. However, it is very difficult to see how a dependency pattern of behaviour becomes 'transformed' into an affiliative one. Human infants need mothers during the first year of life, but interaction with peers is important during the next few years in the development of affiliative motivation.

Under what conditions is affiliative motivation aroused? If affiliation is to be regarded as a drive in some way similar to hunger and thirst, it should be aroused by deprivation, in this case by isolation. A number of experiments have been conducted in which subjects have been isolated for periods up to four days. It has been found that periods of isolation as short as twenty minutes make children more responsive afterwards to social rewards. However, other experiments suggest that isolation does not arouse affiliative motivation unless it creates anxiety (Walters and Parke, 1964), and Schachter's experiment showed that anxiety alone can arouse it. Probably affiliative motivation is also aroused by anticipation of parties and other social events. Affiliative behaviour may bring a number of benefits – reducing anxiety, providing a means of checking opinions against those of others, inhibiting aggression, and making cooperation easier. However, affiliation appears to act as an autonomous drive, quite apart from such consequences.

The analysis of approach–avoidance conflicts described earlier can be applied to affiliative behaviour. Suppose that people are attracted towards one another physically, as a result of past rewarding experiences, and also repelled physically, as a result of punishing experiences. If the avoidance gradient is steeper than the approach, it follows that people will move together until the equilibrium is reached, and then stop. We can extend this theory and postulate that people move towards an equilibrium degree of 'intimacy' with others, where:

Intimacy is a function of:
$$\begin{cases} \text{physical proximity} \\ \text{eye-contact} \\ \text{facial expression (smiling)} \\ \text{topic of conversation (how} \\ \quad \text{personal)} \\ \text{tone of voice (warm), etc.} \end{cases}$$

Experimental support for this theory is given on p. 86.

4. *Dominance*. This refers to a very important group of motivations, including needs for power – to control the behaviour or fate of others, and for status or recognition – to be admired and looked up to by others. We shall be mainly concerned with its effect in face-to-face situations, such as small groups. Dominant people want to talk a lot, have their ideas attended to, and to be influential in decisions. People strong in dominance take part in a struggle for position, the winner emerging as the 'task leader', i.e. the person responsible for decisions (see Chapter 8). The same is true in groups of monkeys: dominance here is usually established by threat displays or actual fighting, and the winner receives deference from the others, and most access to the females. The need for dominance can be assessed by questionnaires or projection tests, which will give a prediction about how hard a person will struggle for position – though not about how successful he will be.

There may be innate, instinctive origins of dominative behaviour: dominance is thought to have developed during evolution since it has the biological function of providing leaders who can keep order in the group, and repel enemies. Males are more dominant than females in every human society, and among monkeys and other mammals (Wilson, 1975). It has been shown that injecting male monkeys or other male animals with male sex hormones produces more aggression and dominance.

Dominance is also affected by childhood experiences, such as identifying with a dominant parent; the male sex-role is mainly acquired by identification with the father. However, this appears to be a need which is only aroused at certain times and in relation to certain groups. Once a hierarchy has been established it is fairly stable, and struggling for position ceases. Dominance is also aroused during elections to office in groups, when the struggle for power becomes salient.

5. *Sex.* In the lower animals sexual motivation is instinctive; arousal is controlled by sex hormones and leads to the fulfilment of the biological purpose of reproduction. In man sex seems to have become a pleasurable end in itself, and is controlled by the cortex rather than by sex hormones. For present purposes sexual motivation can be looked at as a social approach drive similar to the need for affiliation, but which is usually directed towards members of the opposite sex. We shall not be concerned with the specific consummation to which sexual motivation is directed: in social situations it is similar to affiliation in leading to physical proximity, eye-contact, and other aspects of intimacy. Perhaps the most important difference is that rather greater degrees of arousal are generated, and this will occur when presentable members of the opposite sex come together, especially if they are within the fifteen to forty age-group.

Sexual motivation is wholly instinctive in lower animals, partly so in primates. As with affiliation, sexual motivation is affected by childhood experiences. Harlow and Harlow (1965) found that monkeys reared in isolation for the first six months did not engage in sexual behaviour in later life. Human beings apparently need a lot of instruction, elaborate cultural rules are built up governing sexual behaviour, and special social skills are needed to negotiate it.

Among monkeys and other animals sexual behaviour tends to be unrestrained; in civilized society it is possible only under very restricted conditions. It is continually being aroused. The normal stimuli which arouse sex are the sight, touch, smell or sound of an appropriate mate, especially one of high physical attractiveness (see p. 109f.). In addition, erotic pictures and films are very arousing – as measured by subjective reports or penis expansion; the most arousing are films of intercourse, genital petting, and oral sex (Baron and Byrne, 1977). Humans can also be aroused by a wide range of stimuli which have become associated with sex.

However, there are difficulties in the easy satisfaction of sexual needs. This is partly due to external restraints – the potential partner is unwilling, or others would disapprove. It is partly due to internal restraints in the personality. These are based on parental discipline of early manifestations of sexuality, such as playing with the genitals; sexual behaviour in later life comes to be associated with anxiety. There are great individual differences between the very inhibited, who fear and avoid sex, and those who seek it without any feelings of guilt. However, these restraints are greatly weakened by alcohol. There is probably a biological basis for such restraints – human beings need a long period of care and socialization, which means that there must be some kind of enduring family, which imposes certain restraints on sexuality in adults.

Sexual motivation thus affects social behaviour in many situations. This is another example of approach–avoidance conflict, in which the equilibrium consists of various forms of sexual behaviour short of intercourse, and often without physical contact at all, such as conversation and eye-contact. We suggested earlier that sexual motivation may be closely related to affiliative motivation: both may derive from early dependency on the mother.

6. *Aggression.* This is behaviour which is intended to hurt people (or objects), physically or verbally. It includes *angry* aggression and *instrumental* aggression – to gain another goal such as escape or approval.

Aggression in animals is biologically useful – in defending territory and group, and in giving individuals priority over food and (for males) access to females. Aggression in animals occurs when they are frustrated, i.e. when goal-directed activity is blocked and expected rewards are not obtained. This happens in humans, if the frustration is fairly severe, if there is no good reason for the frustration, and if there is no great danger of punishment or disapproval for aggressive behaviour. Animals fight when attacked (unless they run away); for humans, insults provoke more aggression than frustration. Aggression appears to be an innate response to frustration and attack in animals and men, but it is not a drive, since aggression does not occur in the absence of these stimuli, and it is not a need which must be satisfied. It is heightened by certain physiological conditions – heat, physiological arousal, and male sex hormones. It is also affected by seeing violence on TV; Berkowitz and Geen (1966) found that a stooge would be given more shocks by an experimental subject if the stooge had a similar name to that of a person just seen in an aggressive role in a film.

Patterns of aggressive behaviour are learnt in childhood: fighting may be encouraged or discouraged, and parents may present models of aggressive behaviour; physical punishment results in more aggression.

Aggression is prevented in animals if the other gives appeasement signals – looks away, adopts a submissive posture, etc. It has been found in experiments that human subjects will give lower electric shocks to a victim if they can see his signs of pain. Aggression often results in punishment, so that for most people there is a strong avoidance component, partly internalized as part of the conscience, partly due to fear of retaliation. The conflict analysis predicts that an indirect form of aggression will occur, which may consist of verbal rather than physical attacks, displacement of aggression on to weaker people, or mere aggression in fantasy, such as watching western films or wrestling matches. Like sex, aggression is constantly aroused and restrained in social situations, and may be manifested very indirectly. Aggressive behaviour can be cathartic, that is it can reduce the initial level of anger. Hokanson and Burgess (1962) found that subjects who were allowed to give electric shocks or give negative ratings on a questionnaire to someone who had insulted them were less aggressive afterwards, but only if the other was of lower status. In another experiment, a smaller amount of catharsis occurred if the experimenter gave the shocks instead (Doob and Wood, 1972). On the other hand, anger is not discharged by attacking physical objects or watching aggressive scenes on TV.

7. *Self-esteem and self-consistency*. Many psychologists have thought it necessary to postulate a need for self-esteem, i.e. a

need to have a favourable evaluation of the self (e.g. Rogers, 1942).

Concern with the self-image is aroused under certain conditions – being in front of audiences, TV cameras and mirrors, and being assessed, in particular. Individuals differ in their level of self-esteem, and in their degree of confidence in what they are worth.

The origin of the need for self-esteem may be in the favourable evaluations made by most parents about their children. Children accept or partly accept these valuations, and seek to make later experiences and evaluations consistent with them (Secord and Backman, 1974). If the parents gave negative evaluations, in later life the child may accept this view of himself and show no sign of a need for self-esteem. There seem to be cultural differences in the extent to which self-esteem is important. In the East 'loss of face' is a much more serious matter than in the West.

A second type of motivation in this area which must be postulated is the need for a clear, distinct and consistent self-image. Part of this is a desire to regard oneself as a unique person, distinct from others. It will be shown later that adolescents often behave in deviant ways, or rebel against their families, simply in order to be able to see themselves as separate individuals. In addition to this there are pressures to establish a self-image that is consistent and integrated. There is plenty of evidence that people develop attitudes and beliefs that are consistent, and this is particularly true of attitudes towards the self. There are a number of processes involved – social pressure to conform to occupational, class and other roles, the effort to avoid motivational conflicts within the personality, and the effort to establish a clear and meaningful picture of the self and its ideals and goals. This affects social behaviour in much the same way as self-esteem – attempts are made to get others to accept and bolster up the self-image, and to avoid them or change their attitude if they do not (see Chapter 9).

8. *Other motivations which affect social behaviour*. Achievement motivation leads to attempts to attain higher and higher stand-

ards of excellence, whether at examinations, competitive sports, or in other ways. In many social situations there is a task to be completed, as in committee work, or in research groups. People high in achievement motivation are found to be most concerned with the task, while those in whom affiliative motivation is stronger are more concerned about getting on well with others. Achievement motivation is higher in first-born children, those who have been encouraged to be independent, and children with achieving parents. Weiner (1974) has produced evidence that high achievers differ mainly in attributing the likelihood of success to their own efforts, rather than to external factors. Achievement is unlike a drive in that it doesn't seem to satiate – the high-jumper who jumps as high as he hoped to simply revises his target upwards, and the same applies to other fields of achievement. Women have special problems; they are often found to have a fear of success, consisting of fear of social rejection, or concern for their femininity or 'normality' (Horner, 1970). Since many forms of achievement are felt to be incompatible with the female role, they may seek achievement in feminine domains, which often involves competence in social skills.

There are also a number of acquired needs which affect social behaviour – for money, and needs related to interests, values, work or career.

In particular social situations, certain drives are likely to be aroused and satisfied. The immediate goals and plans which are formed are a complex product of a person's needs and the nature of the situation. Thus a dinner party may become the occasion primarily for sexual activity, affiliation, self-esteem, social contacts related to work or other interests, and so on.

Some of the social situations with which we shall be concerned later can be regarded as exercises of professional social skill – for example interviewing, teaching or selling. Here the performer of the skill is trying to affect the behaviour of others, not primarily because of his social needs but for professional reasons. He wants the others to learn, or buy, just as a person strong in affiliation wants others to respond in a warm and friendly manner. Of course the social-skill performer has other motivations – for achievement, money, etc. – which make him keen to do well at his job, but the *immediate* goals for him are those of getting the client to respond in the specific ways required by the situation. The social-skill performer will also in most cases be affected by social drives, and the client may be primarily affected by these.

FURTHER READING

Argyle, M., *Social Interaction*, London: Methuen, 1969, Chapter 2.

Atkins, A. L., and Hilton, I., 'Social motivation', in B. Seidenberg and A. Snadowsky (eds.), *Social Psychology*, London: Collier-Macmillan, 1976.

Atkinson, J. W. (ed.), *Motives in Fantasy, Action and Society*, New York: Van Nostrand, 1958.

Baron, R. A., and Byrne, D., *Social Psychology*, Boston: Allyn and Bacon, 1977, Chapters 9 and 10.

Cofer, C. N., and Appley, M. H., *Motivation: Theory and Research*, New York: Wiley, 1964.

DeVore, I. (ed.), *Primate Behavior*, New York: Rinehart and Winston, 1965.

CHAPTER 2

VERBAL AND NON-VERBAL COMMUNICATION

In Chapter 1 the goals which people seek in social interaction were discussed, and it was argued that these goals are satisfied by certain behaviour on the part of others. In order to get these responses people make use of a variety of verbal and non-verbal elements of behaviour. In conversation, for example, there are alternating utterances, together with continuous facial expressions, gestures, shifts of gaze and other non-verbal acts on the part of both speaker and listener. We shall start with the non-verbal elements, which communicate attitudes and emotions, as well as supplementing the verbal interchange in various ways.

The reader may feel that he is in the position of Molière's Monsieur Jourdain, who discovered that he had been speaking prose all these years. However, it is necessary to categorize and label the whole range of social acts, of different types and degrees of complexity, in order to move towards a scientific analysis of social behaviour.

NON-VERBAL COMMUNICATION

NVC (as it is usually called) is the only means of communication amongst animals. Similar signals are used by man, and the evolutionary origins of some of them have been traced. Showing the teeth by animals in anger, for instance, is derived from the act of attacking, but is now used when there is no intention of actually biting. This is an example of a non-verbal signal having meaning, by being similar to or part of another act. Van Hooff (1972) has suggested the origins of human smiling and laughter: the lower primates have an expression known as the 'bared-teeth scream face', used in fear and submission, which has gradually evolved into our smile. Young primates also use a 'play-gnaw' accompanied by a kind of barking, which has become the human laugh.

All social signals are encoded and decoded by a sender and a receiver.

Often the sender is unaware of his own NVC, though it is plainly visible to the decoder. Sometimes neither is aware of it; an example is dilation of the pupils of the eyes in sexual attraction, which affects the receiver though he doesn't know why he likes the sender. Social skills training or reading this book will increase sensitivity to the NVC of others, and control over the NV signals which are emitted. We turn now to the main forms of NVC.

1. *Facial expression.* As we have just seen, facial expressions have developed in the course of evolution, and are an important means of communication in apes and monkeys. Izard (1975) cut the facial muscles of some infant monkeys and their mothers, and found that the pairs failed to develop any relationship with each other.

One of the main functions of facial expression is to communicate emotional states, and attitudes such as liking and hostility. Paul Ekman and others (1972) have found that there are seven main facial expressions for emotion:

Happiness
Surprise
Fear
Sadness
Anger
Disgust, contempt
Interest

Each involves a configuration of the whole face, though the mouth and eyebrows carry a lot of the information.

Descriptions	Blank	Control Neutral	Neutral	Happy	Sad1	Angry1	Fiendish	Angry2	Sad2	Happy Sheepish	Sad3
1 Elated				o3			o3			o3	
2 Happy	89 (5)	11	33 (2)	81 (4)						36 (3)	
3 Neutral		38 (4)	39 (3)						o6		
4 Sad		22 (2)	o8		42 (3)			o3	50 (3)		61 (5)
5 Angry					13	58 (4)		53 (5)			
6 Furious						17		33 (4)			
7 Amused		o6	o3	o8		o3				19 (3)	
8 Sheepish		o6	o3		o3				o3	25 (3)	
9 Mischievous				o8			16			o6	
10 Fiendish						11	75 (5)	11	o3		
11 Depressed					17	o3			o8		24
12 Apprehensive		o6			19	o3			22 (3)	12	o6
13 Afraid		o3			o3	o3			o3		o6
14 Horrified		11				o3			o6		
15 Other			o3								o3

Figure 3. Emotions perceived in schematic faces (from Thayer and Schiff, 1969). Per cent (rounded) responses to faces in each descriptive response category and modal intensity rating of predominant judgement (in parentheses).

The seven emotions can be discriminated quite well, though similar ones can be confused such as anger and fear, or surprise and happiness. And, unlike monkeys, we often conceal our true feelings: it is not always easy to decode a smiling face, for example. These facial expressions seem to be much the same in all cultures, though Ekman has shown that there are 'display rules' which specify when an emotion may be shown – whether to cry at funerals, or to show pleasure when you have won. Shimoda, Ricci Bitti and Argyle (1978) found that Japanese could decode British and Italian facial expressions *better* than Japanese ones (Table 1), probably because the Japanese are not supposed to display negative emotions like anger and sadness. The Japanese were probably helped by having seen Western films.

| | Performers | | |
Judges	English	Italian	Japanese
English	63	58	38
Italian	53	62	28
Japanese	57	58	45

Table 1. Cross-cultural recognition of emotions (percentages correct; Shimoda, Ricci Bitti and Argyle, 1978).

Of the emotions listed above, surprise and interest are not really emotions, but cognitive reactions. The face gives a fast-moving display of reactions to what others have said or done, and a running commentary on what the owner of the face is saying. The eyebrows are very expressive in this way:

Fully raised   – disbelief
Half raised   – surprise
Normal   – no comment
Half lowered   – puzzled
Fully lowered – angry

The area round the mouth adds to the running commentary by varying between being turned up (pleasure) and turned down (displeasure). These facial signals lead to reactions from others; for example, looking puzzled may lead to clarification, and a smile acts as a reinforcement, encouraging the kind of act which led to it.

However, facial signals are used differently on different occasions, and situations may be associated with a particular set of expressions. For example, Kendon (1975) studied a couple kissing on a park bench: detailed analysis of the sequence of events showed that the girl used two different smiles, one of which led to her being kissed while the other led to withdrawal. It is generally true that non-verbal signals form systems, and each signal gains meaning partly from the other signals with which it is contrasted.

People are recognized by their faces, and impressions of personality are partly derived from faces. There are a number of common stereotypes here but most of them have little foundation (p. 108). We can learn something from a person's habitual facial expression – which may affect the shape of the face; and we can learn something from grooming – which shows the image which is being presented. There is some association between physique and personality (p. 121), and physique is partly displayed in the face – thin, fat or muscular.

2. *Gaze*, i.e. looking at other people in the area of their faces, is primarily a means of collecting information about visible aspects of NVC, but it is also a signal itself – about direction of attention, attitudes to others, and the synchronizing of speech (see Chapter 4).

3. *Gestures and other bodily movements*. While a person speaks he moves his hands, body and head continuously; these movements are closely coordinated with speech, and form part of the total communication. He may (1) display the structure of the utterance by enumerating elements or showing how they are grouped, (2) point to people or objects, (3) provide emphasis, and (4) give illustrations of shapes, sizes or movements, particularly when these are difficult to describe in words. Kendon (1972) found that these movements are synchronized with speech, the larger movements corresponding with larger verbal units like long utterances.

Other gestures have conventional meanings, like our hitch-hike sign, nodding and shaking the head, clapping, beckoning, various rude signs, religious signs, and so on. These signs do not resemble their objects as closely as illustrative gestures do, and they have complex histories in the local culture. Italy is particularly rich in them; Desmond Morris and Peter Collett have listed over 200 in use in Naples.

Head-nods are a rather special kind of gesture, and have two distinctive roles. They act as 'reinforcers', i.e. they reward and encourage what has gone before, and can be used to make another talk more, for example. Head-nods also play an important role in controlling the synchronizing of speech – in Britain a nod gives the other permission to carry on talking, whereas a rapid succession of nods indicates that the nodder wants to speak himself.

Gestures also reflect emotional states. When a person is emotionally aroused he produces diffuse, apparently pointless, bodily movements. People often touch themselves during certain emotions – fist-clenching (aggression), face-touching (anxiety), scratching (self-blame), forehead-wiping (tiredness) etc. These 'autistic' gestures are not normally used to communicate, since they are also used in private, and appear to express attitudes to the self such as shame and self-comforting.

4. *Bodily posture*. Attitudes to others are indicated, in animals and men, by posture. A person who is trying to assert himself stands erect, with chest out, squaring the shoulders, and perhaps with hands on hips. A person in an established position of power or status, however, adopts a very relaxed posture, for example leaning back in his seat, or putting his feet on the table. Positive attitudes to others are expressed by leaning towards them (together with smiling, looking, etc.). Posture doesn't show specific emotions very clearly, and mainly shows how tense or relaxed someone is. Some postures which do communicate fairly clearly are shown in Fig. 4.

People also have general styles of expressive behaviour, as shown in the way they walk, stand, sit and so on. This may reflect past or present roles – as in the case of a person who is or

Figure 4. Some postures with clear meanings (from Sarbin and Hardyk, 1953).

has been a soldier; it also reflects a person's self-image, self-confidence, and emotional state. It is very dependent on cultural fashions:

In a street market I watched a working-class mum and her daughter. The mother waddled as if her feet were playing her up. Outside a Knightsbridge hotel I watched an upper-class mum and her daughter come out from a wedding reception and walk towards Hyde Park Corner, the mother on very thin legs slightly bowed as though she had wet herself. She controlled her body as if it might snap if moved too impulsively. Both daughters walked identically [Melly, 1965].

43

This last example shows the effect of cultural norms on expressive behaviour; style of walking may give information in this case about social class.

5. *Bodily contact* is the most primitive kind of social behaviour, and is a very powerful signal. There are many ways of touching

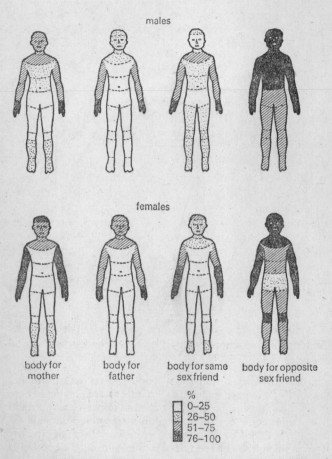

Figure 5. Male and female 'bodies-for-others', as experienced through the amount of touching received from others (Jourard, 1966).

people, but only a few are used in any one culture – in ours, for example, shaking hands, patting on the back, kissing, etc. Jourard (1966) has surveyed who has been touched by whom and where, and his results for American students are shown in Fig. 5. It can be seen that there are great differences in who is touched by whom, and on which parts of their anatomy.

Bodily contact in our culture is controlled by strict rules, and is used mainly in the family, and by courting couples. Doctors, tailors and other professionals use it, but not as a *social* act. There is bodily contact with strangers in crowds, but in the absence of a social relationship. Bodily contact plays an important part in greetings and other ceremonies, and probably helps to bring about the changed relationship that such rituals achieve. Distinctive forms of bodily contact occur in some of the most basic relationships – sexual, nurturant, aggressive and affiliative.

Anthropologists distinguish between contact cultures (e.g., North Africa) and non-contact cultures (e.g., Europe, India, North America). In Britain we use touch very little, but there has been some interest in 'encounter groups' in the USA and Britain during recent years. The greater use of bodily contact here is found to be exciting and disturbing – but it must be remembered that those concerned have been brought up in cultures in which there are strong restraints against bodily contact, and will have internalized these restraints.

6. *Spatial behaviour. Physical proximity* is one of the cues for intimacy, both sexual and between friends of the same sex. The normal degree of proximity varies between cultures, and every species of animal has its characteristic social distance. The significance of physical proximity varies with the physical surroundings – proximity to the point of bodily contact in a lift has no affiliative significance, and it is noteworthy that eye-contact and conversation are avoided here. If A sits near B, it makes a difference whether there are other places where A could have sat, whether he is directly facing B or at an angle, and whether there is any physical barrier. Closer distances are adopted for more intimate conversations: at the closest distances, different

sensory modes are used – touch and smell come into operation, and vision becomes less important (Hall, 1966). It is found that people sit or stand closer to people they like. There are also large cross-cultural differences – Arabs and Latin Americans stand very close, Swedes and Scots are the most distant (Lett *et al.*, 1969).

Orientation also signals interpersonal attitudes. If person A is sitting at a table, as shown in Fig. 6, B can sit in several different

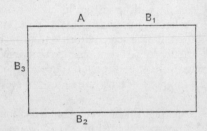

Figure 6. Orientation in different relationships.

places. If he is told that the situation is cooperative he will probably sit at B_1; if he is told he is to compete, negotiate, sell something or interview A, he will sit at B_2; if he is told to have a discussion or conversation he usually chooses B_3 (Sommer, 1965). This shows (a) that one can become more sensitive to the cues emitted, often unintentionally, by others, and (b) that one can control non-verbal as well as verbal signals.

Dominance, however, is signalled neither by proximity nor orientation, but by the symbolic use of space – sitting in the largest chair, or at the high table, for example. Movement in space is also important – to start or end an encounter, or to invade territory. Movements in space show attitudes to other people – of friendship, dominance, and so on. See if you can work out the four relationships in the scenes in Fig. 7.

Manipulating the physical setting itself is another form of spatial behaviour – placing a desk to dominate the room, or arranging seats for intimate conversation.

Territorial behaviour is found in men as well as animals.

46

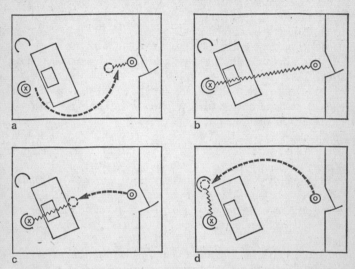

Figure 7. Key movements between men in an office indicating their relationship (Burns, 1964).

There is the space immediately round the body, which we like to keep free – except in lifts and buses. Pairs or groups of people establish a claim to the space they are occupying, and others will keep out, or in the street will walk round them.

7. *Clothes and appearance* are also part of social behaviour, and they communicate information about the self. Clothes, badges, hair, skin, and physique can all be manipulated to a considerable degree. The information that is conveyed includes social status, occupation, attractiveness, attitudes to other people like rebelliousness or conformity, and other aspects of personality. These signals are different from the others we have been considering, in that the code keeps changing as fashions change – long and short hair in males has had different significance at different dates. This will be discussed further in Chapter 8.

8. *Non-verbal aspects of speech.* Emotional states, and attitudes to others, are conveyed by tone of voice. Davitz studied this by getting actors to read out an emotionally neutral passage to express different emotional states (see p. 96). The author has used this method as a means of sensitivity training. Some people are much better at making a judgement of the emotional state than others.

Other non-verbal signals are closely linked to speech, and should perhaps be regarded as part of it. Timing is used to indicate punctuation, and short pauses (under $\frac{1}{5}$ sec.) to give emphasis. The pattern of pitch indicates whether a question is being asked, and also 'frames' an utterance, to show, for instance, whether 'Where are you going?' is a friendly inquiry or a threat. Variations in loudness place stress on particular words or phrases – for example on 'where' or 'you' in the question above. It can make clear which possible meaning an otherwise ambiguous sentence has, as in 'They are hunting *dogs*'.

People speak in different accents, which are related to and convey information about their geographical origins and social class. Experiments by Lambert in Canada and Giles in Britain (see Giles and Powesland, 1975) show that if the same person records a passage in two different accents, he is rated by different judges as possessing the stereotyped properties of the two cultural or social groups in question. It is also found that speakers often accommodate to one another – shifting to a style of speech and accent similar to that of the other, perhaps in order to be approved of by him.

There are non-linguistic aspects of the conversation as a whole – the patterns of speech and silence – how much of the time each person talks, how fast, how soon after the other stops, and so on. Chapple (1956) has shown that people have characteristic ways of reacting to interruption and silence on the part of another. In his 'standard interview' the subject is first interviewed in a relaxed manner; later follows a period in which the interviewer fails to respond to twelve successive utterances by the subject, and another period during which the interviewer interrupts twelve successive speeches by the subject. Some people yield at once if interrupted, while others try to talk the interrupter down. Some people cannot tolerate silence, and will speak again if the interviewer is silent.

Sequences of NVC. We have seen that NV signals come in combinations – a smile is commonly combined with a gaze and a friendly tone of voice, for example. They also occur in sequences of interaction between two or more people. Most social behaviour consists of verbal as well as non-verbal signals, and we shall see shortly how NVC operates in conversation. When there is little speech we can look at the NV sequences separately. For example, in greetings the following sequence has been found, by Kendon and Ferber (1973) and others:

1. Person A waves, smiles, looks and says something like 'Hi'. B probably responds, and there is a brief mutual gaze.

2. A moves nearer to B, looks away, grooms himself, frees his right hand.

3. A and B shake hands, or make other bodily contact, second smile, second mutual gaze, second verbal greeting.

4. A and B stand at an angle, and conversation begins.

Scheflen (1965) and Kendon (op. cit.) have studied the 'gestural dance' during conversation, whereby people move in a coordinated way. One person mirrors the movements of the other; he gives head-nods, glances and other attentive signals, and reacts with appropriate facial expressions while the other speaks, reacting to the other's verbal and non-verbal communication. At the end of the conversation they get up and move apart in a finely coordinated way.

When a third person approaches two others, if they are willing to talk to him, they open up to give him the third side of a triangle to make what Kendon calls a 'facing formation'. The three move about, but maintain an equilibrium level of distance and orientation to each other. When one leaves he starts by a move away, revealing his intentions; this is followed by a move *in*, and then by his departure (Kendon, 1977).

DIFFERENT ROLES OF NON-VERBAL COMMUNICATION

Non-verbal communication functions in four rather different ways (Argyle, 1975).

1. *Communicating inter-personal attitudes and emotions.* Animals conduct their entire social life by means of NVC – they make friends, find mates, rear children, establish dominance hierarchies, and cooperate in groups, by means of facial expression, postures, gestures, grunting and barking noises, etc. It looks as if much the same is true of humans too. Argyle *et al.* (1970) carried out an experiment in which superior, equal and inferior verbal messages were delivered in superior, equal and inferior non-verbal styles, nine combinations in all, by speakers recorded on video-tapes. Two of the verbal messages were as follows:

(1) It is probably quite a good thing for you subjects to come along to help in these experiments because it gives you a small glimpse of what psychological research is about. In fact the whole process is far more complex than you would be able to appreciate without a considerable training in research methods, paralinguistics, kinesic analysis, and so on.

(2) These experiments must seem rather silly to you and I'm afraid they are not really concerned with anything very interesting or important. We'd be very glad if you could spare us a few moments afterwards to tell us how we could improve the experiment. We feel that we are not making a very good job of it, and feel rather guilty about wasting the time of busy people like yourselves.

Some of the results were as shown in Figure 8. It can be seen that the non-verbal style had more effect than the verbal contents, in fact about five times as much; when the verbal and non-verbal messages were in conflict, the verbal contents were virtually disregarded. Much the same results were obtained in another experiment on the friendly-hostile dimension.

The explanation of these results is probably that there is an innate biological basis to these NV signals, which evoke an immediate and powerful emotional response – as in animals. In

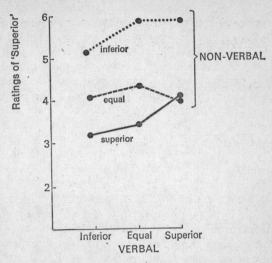

Figure 8. Effects of verbal and non-verbal cues (Argyle *et al.*, 1970).

human social behaviour it looks as if the NV channel is used for negotiating interpersonal attitudes, while the verbal channel is used primarily for conveying information.

2. *Self-presentation.* As we have seen, clothes and other aspects of appearance, and accent, convey information about the self; the general style of behaviour also does this. In Britain and a number of other countries there is something of a taboo on the use of speech to convey many kinds of information about the self, especially favourable information, so this can only be done non-verbally, or very indirectly by speech. What is conveyed is not always true, of course, i.e. self-presentation may be partly bogus. This will be pursued further in Chapter 9.

3. *Rituals* and ceremonies are repeated patterns of behaviour which have no instrumental function, but which have certain social consequences. They include 'rites of passage' like weddings and graduations, and greetings and farewells, where a

change of status or relationship is brought about. Other ceremonies appear to have the function of confirming social relationships, like drill parades; others are intended to heal, though by symbolic rather than medical methods, while others express religious beliefs and hopes. In these events, 'ritual work' is accomplished, i.e. a change of state or relationship is brought about by the ritual. The French anthropologist Van Gennep (1908) maintained that rituals all have three main phases – separation–transition–incorporation – which fit rites of passage quite well. Greetings, on the other hand, could be said to have a different structure – of moving towards and away from a climax. Exactly how the ritual work is done is not known, but it is clear that NVC plays an important part in it. Some NV signals here work by similarity or analogy – wine stands for blood; in some primitive rites to cure barrenness, red paint represents menstrual blood. Other signals have meaning through arbitrary associations, as in the case of flags, totem animals, or other objects representing social groups. Rituals are usually conducted by a priest or other official; at the height of the ceremony he usually looks at and touches those who are being processed, which probably heightens the social impact of his work. The elements used may symbolize the state of affairs being brought about – putting on a chain of office, and the red paint which stands for menstrual blood, for example.

4. *Supporting verbal communication.* Linguists recognize that timing, pitch and stress are integral to the meaning of utterances, e.g. by providing punctuation. A few linguists recognize that NVC plays a more extensive part – 'We speak with our vocal organs, but we converse with our whole body' (Abercrombie, 1968).

Completing the meaning of utterances. In addition to the *vocal* signals of timing, pitch and stress, *gestural* signals also add to meaning – by illustrating, pointing, displaying structure, etc. Jean Graham and the author (1975) found that shapes could be conveyed much better, in one minute of speech, if hand movements were allowed. The effect was greater for those shapes for which there were no obvious words, and more information was conveyed in gestures by Italian than British subjects. The fine pattern of pitch, timing and stress elaborates and comments on the verbal message, and frames it, as described above.

Controlling synchronizing. When two or more people are conversing they must take it in turns to speak, and usually achieve a fairly smooth pattern of synchronizing. This is done by the use of non-verbal signals such as shifts of gaze, head-nods, and grunts (p. 70).

Obtaining feedback. When a person is speaking he needs feedback on how the others are responding, so that he can modify his remarks accordingly. He needs to know whether his listeners understand, believe him, are surprised or bored, agree or disagree, are pleased or annoyed. This information could be provided by *sotto voce* muttering, but is in fact obtained from careful study of the other's face, especially his eyebrows and mouth (p. 40).

Signalling attentiveness. For an encounter to be sustained, those involved must provide intermittent evidence that they are still attending to the others. They should not fall asleep, look out of the window, or read the paper; they should be at the right distance, in the right orientation, look up frequently, nod their heads, adopt an alert, congruent posture, and react to the speaker's bodily movements.

Replacing speech. When speech is impossible, gesture languages develop. This happens in noisy factories, the army, racecourses, and underwater swimming. Some of these languages are complex and enable elaborate messages to be sent, as in deaf languages, and the sign language used by some Australian aborigines. Some examples are given in Fig. 9.

It has been suggested by some psychiatrists that the symptoms of certain mental patients are a kind of NVC used when speech has failed – in pursuit of attention or love (p. 217).

Why do we use NVC? Animals use it because it is the only means of communication they have, but why do we? There are several reasons. (1) NV signals are more powerful for communicating emotions and interpersonal attitudes; they put the recipient in a

Warning : You
are on the air

F. finger
inscribes a ring
in the air
(Symbol for
red light)

Start

Not loud enough
Get the
microphone
nearer

F. finger
makes a ring
round the ear

Stretch it a bit.
You are
ahead of time

You are behind time
Quicker !

Pointing
F. fingers
brought
together

Two minutes
left

You have five
minutes left

R.F. finger
forms a big
Z-line – or
C-line – in the
air

You have
$\frac{1}{2}$-minute left

F. fingers form
an X

You have
$\frac{1}{4}$-minute left

One F. finger
'chops off' tip
of the other

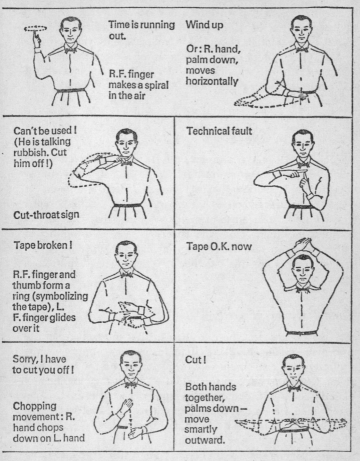

Time is running out.

R.F. finger makes a spiral in the air

Wind up

Or: R. hand, palm down, moves horizontally

Can't be used! (He is talking rubbish. Cut him off!)

Cut-throat sign

Technical fault

Tape broken!

R.F. finger and thumb form a ring (symbolizing the tape), L. F. finger glides over it

Tape O.K. now

Sorry, I have to cut you off!

Chopping movement: R. hand chops down on L. hand

Cut!

Both hands together, palms down — move smartly outward.

Figure 9. Non-verbal signals used in broadcasting (from Brun, 1969).

state of immediate biological readiness, to deal with aggression, love or whatever. The power of ritual to change relationships is probably due to the NV components. (2) Some messages are more easily conveyed by gesture than by words – shapes, for example – especially if we don't know the language well enough to describe things. (3) The verbal channel is often full, and it is useful to use another channel for feedback and synchronizing signals. (4) It would be disturbing to focus attention on some messages by putting them into words – such as certain aspects of self-presentation, or partly negative attitudes to others.

VERBAL COMMUNICATION

Speech is the most complex, subtle and characteristically human means of communication. Most animal noises simply communicate emotional states. Human speech is different in that it is learnt, can convey information about external events, has a grammatical structure and sentences that can convey complex meanings. However, speech is used in a number of rather different ways, it is supported and elaborated by NVC, and utterances are put together in a sequence to form conversations.

The different uses of speech.

1. *Asking questions*. These lead to further interaction, and to information being supplied. Some forms of encounter, such as the interview, consist entirely of questions and the answers to them. Questions vary in the extent to which they are open or closed – an open-ended question requires a lengthy explanation rather than a choice between alternatives; the best way to get someone to talk is to ask this kind of question.

2. *Conveying information*. This may be in answer to questions, part of the work of committees or work-teams, in lectures, and elsewhere. The speaker may be reporting facts, giving his opinions, or arguing on the basis of these. Such communications are often imperfectly received, because the speaker has not made himself sufficiently clear, or because the hearer attaches different meanings to words or phrases. Ideally, both should speak exactly the same language, i.e. where every sentence carries the

identical penumbra of meanings and implications for each of them.

3. *Giving orders, instructions, etc.* Speech is used to influence the behaviour of others, by means of instructions or orders, persuasion and propaganda, as well as by aggressive remarks – which may be used when all else fails. Aggressive speech occurs in a variety of forms, of which the milder ones are gentle ridicule and teasing, and the more severe are direct insults.

4. *Informal conversation.* A lot of speech is not primarily intended to communicate anything very serious, or to solve any problems. Informal speech is more concerned with establishing, sustaining and enjoying social relationships – chat, idle gossip, and joke-telling between friends or family members, or during coffee breaks at work. It has been found that about half of the very expensive conversation over the trans-Atlantic telephone is of this kind. Formal speech, as in a well-delivered lecture, is more concise, conveys information clearly, and is more like written language in structure.

5. *Performative utterances.* This is the name which Austin (1962) gave to those utterances which are actions in themselves – like naming a ship, declaring a conference open, voting, giving a verdict, and making a promise. Such utterances are not true or false, but are items of social behaviour. All utterances have such performative aspects, but they can also be looked at as meaningful sentences.

6. *Utterances with latent meanings.* Here the speaker reveals something additional to the main message. This may be unintended, as with the speaker who was asked if he had ever been to Nigeria and replied 'That's a place I've not been to' (Brown, 1965). Or it may be intentional as when a schoolboy says 'Please Sir, the board's shining' (when it isn't).

7. *Talk about the interaction.* This is when a person says 'There's an awkward pause, isn't there?', or comments on the behaviour

of others, or of himself, in the situation. This happens in psychotherapy, T-groups, and social skills training, and is acceptable there, but it is usually very disrupting on other occasions. Words may be used to provide rewards and punishments; in fact this happens continually in the course of interaction, but is largely unintended. Experiments will be described later in which reinforcements have been deliberately manipulated.

8. *Social routines and rituals.* Greetings, farewells, apologies, requests for help, and so on involve standard sets of words like 'How do you do?' and 'Thank you', which have almost no meaning in the usual sense, but function, like a series of performative utterances, in a well-understood way.

Speech is also used to express emotions and attitudes towards others; but as we have seen this is done better by NVC. The joke is a special kind of verbal utterance, which has the effect of relieving tension and creating euphoria in social situations. In particular social situations, special types of utterances are used, like 'interpretation' in psychotherapy, 'proposing a motion' at a committee meeting, and 'bidding' at an auction sale. Speech varies in a number of ways; it can be intimate or impersonal, easy, abstract or technical, interesting or boring to the hearer. There are great individual differences in the skill of using language, mainly associated with intelligence, education and training, and social class. A large part of most social skills lies in putting together utterances which are tactful, persuasive, or whatever is required. Some examples of the subtleties and nuances involved in selecting the most effective combination of words are given in Chapter 11 in connection with various professional skills.

FURTHER READING

Argyle, M., *Bodily Communication*, London: Methuen, 1975.
Harper, R. G., Wiens, A. M., and Matarazzo, J. D., *Non-verbal Communication*, New York: Wiley, 1978.
Robinson, W.P., *The Social Psychology of Language*, Harmondsworth: Penguin Books, 1972.

CHAPTER 3

SOCIAL SKILL

In the last chapter we introduced the elements, verbal and non-verbal, of social interaction. The next problem is how to analyse this stream of events. We make a start by introducing a simple conceptual model. And we shall find that understanding social behaviour leads at once to an understanding of what one has to do in order to be socially competent. For example, as was shown in the last chapter, attitudes to other people, such as friendliness and hostility, are communicated mainly by non-verbal signals. In our work with mental patients who have inadequate social skills we have found that they are often unable to use the normal signals for friendliness, in the face or voice. The social behaviour problems of mental patients will be discussed in Chapter 10, and the special skills of interviewers, teachers and other professionals, in Chapter 11. We shall bring the latest research on social interaction to bear on these practical problems.

Social interaction is a fascinating and baffling object of study: on the one hand it is immediate and familiar, on the other it is mysterious and inexpressible – there do not seem to be the words to describe it, or the concepts to handle it. An attempt has been made to dispel some of the mystery in previous chapters by describing the goals of social interaction (Chapter 1), and the elements of social behaviour which people use to attain these goals (Chapter 2).

In this chapter we shall try to break through the conceptual barriers which have held up the study of social interaction by introducing a theoretical model, and its associated language, for describing these events. The model is simply this: that the sequence of individual behaviour which occurs during social interaction can usefully be looked at as a kind of motor skill. By motor skills are meant such things as cycling, skating, driving a

, playing the piano, typing, sending and receiving morse, erforming industrial tasks, playing tennis and other games. These have been extensively studied in the field and in laboratory experiments, and their psychological components are now well understood. Social interaction has many resemblances to other motor skills: the point of our suggestion is to pursue the basic psychological similarities in more detail, to see if the same processes operate.

We shall give a brief account of motor skills, and show the parallels in social behaviour. This will direct attention to certain important aspects which might otherwise be overlooked, such as the perception of the right cues, the need for timing and anticipation, and the development of larger units of response. However, there are aspects of social behaviour which have no immediate parallel in motor skills, and which need special attention – such as seeing the other person's point of view, and the projection of a self-image. This analysis enables us to handle the matter of degrees of social skill or competence. In later chapters we shall consider the closely related issues of training for social skills, and of the breakdown of skill – both of which have suggestive parallels in the case of motor skills (Argyle and Kendon, 1967).

SOME COMMON SEQUENCES OF BEHAVIOUR IN SOCIAL INTERACTION

Before presenting the social skill model, we need to describe some common sequences of social behaviour on which it depends.

1. *The effects of reinforcement.* If Joan smiles, nods her head, and agrees, whenever George talks about politics, he will talk about politics more. If she wants him to talk about something else, she should frown and yawn whenever politics is mentioned. This process has been demonstrated in social situations by experiments on 'operant verbal conditioning'. A subject is interviewed by the experimenter; first there are ten minutes of

relaxed, non-directive questioning on the part of the inter-viewer; for the second ten minutes the interviewer system-atically rewards certain types of behaviour on the part of the client. For example, every time the client offers an opinion, the interviewer smiles, nods his head, agrees, looks him in the eye, or makes approving noises. For the third ten minutes the inter-viewer responds negatively to opinions – by disagreeing, looking away, looking at his watch, or by making disapproving noises. The subject increases the frequency of giving opinions in the second period, and decreases it in the third period; this response is extremely rapid, and happens with a variety of types of social behaviour; the reinforcement may be any of the agreeable and agreeing social responses listed above. Some laboratory ex-periments have found that this process works only if the subject becomes aware of what the experimenter wants him to do; how-ever experiments conducted under more natural conditions have found that the effect occurs without awareness – for ex-ample, during telephone conversations, where reinforcement is given and the effect on the other's conversation studied. Other experiments suggest that the person who delivers the rewards and punishments is not usually aware of what he is doing – he is merely reacting spontaneously to behaviour that pleases or dis-pleases him. During social interaction each person is constantly reinforcing others and being reinforced himself, without either being aware of it (Argyle, 1969).

A large number of variations on this experiment have now been carried out, and the results are consistent with the idea that such conditioning occurs fastest when the subject is highly motivated to be accepted by the experimenter. Thus the subject should be anxious and compliant, and the experimenter should be prestigious, an attractive person of the opposite sex, or rewarding in other ways. Middle-class children condition well to 'correct', working-class children to 'good', reflecting child-rearing and motivational patterns (Krasner, 1958).

2. *Imitation.* If Joan smiles, nods or folds her arms, it is likely that George will do the same – interactors tend to copy each other's styles of behaviour. This has been found for long and

short utterances, the use of interruptions and silences, telling jokes and asking questions, the use of words like 'I', 'we', 'the', 'a', etc., smiles and head-nods, bodily posture, and revealing information about the self (e.g. Rosenfeld, 1967). This is probably a special kind of imitation, in which case we would expect it to occur under the normal conditions for imitation – B will imitate A when A is similar to B but of somewhat higher status, when A is found to be rewarding, when A rewards B for imitating him, and when B is uncertain how he should behave. Again, this process is normally spontaneous and unplanned, but it can be deliberately controlled – in order to put a nervous person at his ease, for example, one should avoid catching his nervousness, and adopt a visibly calm manner which he is likely to copy.

3. *The effect of non-verbal signals*. As we showed earlier, non-verbal signals for friendly and hostile, superior and inferior, have a much greater impact than their verbal equivalents (p. 50f). We showed that the relationship between two or more people is negotiated, established and sustained mainly by signals of this kind, normally in a spontaneous manner; those concerned do not usually attend to this process and are barely conscious of what is going on. Nevertheless N V signals are used in a highly skilled way, and social relationships may be negotiated by a series of small, tentative and ambiguous moves which can be withdrawn and disowned if necessary. A move to establish greater dominance, for example, could consist of a slightly raised voice level combined with a slight backward tilt of the head. Normally these moves are not the result of conscious planning, but they can be controlled in this way by those who know how N V signals work.

THE SOCIAL SKILL MODEL

We have said that interactors seek goals, consisting of desired responses on the part of others, and have shown that one social act leads to another. We have seen that social behaviour consists of a certain range of verbal and non-verbal signals.

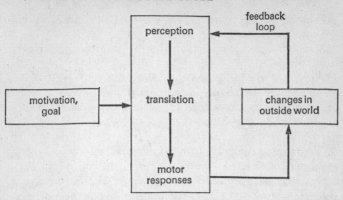

Figure 10. Motor skill model.

I want to suggest that there is a useful analogy between motor skills, like riding a bicycle, and social skills, like making friends, conducting conversations, and interviewing. In each case the performer seeks certain goals, makes skilled moves which are intended to further them, observes what effect he is having, and takes corrective action as a result of feedback. Let us explore the parts of this model in more detail.

1. *The aims of skilled performance.* The motor-skill operator has quite definite immediate goals – to screw a nut on to a bolt, to guide a car along the road by turning the steering wheel, and so on. He also has further goals, under which the immediate ones are subsumed: to make a bridge, or to drive to Aberdeen. He knows when each goal is attained by the appearance of certain physical stimuli. These goals in turn are linked to basic motivations; for example, he may be paid for each unit of work completed. In much the same way, a 'social-skill' operator may have quite definite goals; for example:

Conveying knowledge, information or understanding (teaching)
Obtaining information (interviewing)
Changing attitudes, behaviour or beliefs (salesmanship, canvassing, disciplinary action)

Changing the emotional state of another (telling joke, dealing with hostile person)

Changing another's personality (psychotherapy, child-rearing)

Working at a cooperative task (most industrial work)

Supervising the activities of another (nursing)

Supervision and coordination of a group (chairmanship, foremanship, arbitration)

These aims are linked in turn to more basic motivations in the performer, connected with his work. In everyday non-professional social situations the actors are motivated too, but this time simply by basic social motivations of the kind discussed in Chapter 1. Each person wants the other person to respond in an affiliative, submissive, or dominant manner, according to his own motivational structure. In professional situations the social-skill operator will, in fact, be motivated by a combination of professional and social motivations – he may for example want the client both to learn and to be impressed by his knowledge.

2. *The hierarchical structure of social acts.* Commands go from the brain to the appropriate muscles, producing a pattern of movements, of feet, hands, and face. In fact there is a hierarchy of commands, so that larger goals are linked to larger patterns of movements, in a hierarchical structure. There is also a series of sub-goals: when one sub-goal has been reached the sequence leading to the next sub-goal begins, until the main goal is attained. Driving a car from Oxford to Cambridge has sub-goals like starting the car, getting into the Banbury Road, and getting to Bicester and Buckingham. One of the interesting findings about motor skills is that the series of responses leading to sub-goals become more or less automatic, and can be regarded as larger response units; for example, words rather than letters become the units for morse or typing. When a motor skill has been perfected, it is faster, movements are more accurate, unnecessary movements are eliminated, conscious awareness is much reduced, tension is reduced or sometimes focused at

points of difficulty, there is less need for feedback together with a danger of becoming mechanical, and the whole operation is smoother, effortless and more effective.

The pattern of motor responses has a hierarchical structure, where the larger, high-level units consist of integrated sequences and groupings of lower-level units. An interview has a number of phases (p. 147), each with a certain sequence of questions, each question consisting of a number of words, and accompanying non-verbal signals. The sequences making up smaller units tend to become habitual and 'automatized', i.e. independent of external feedback; more attention is given to the performance of the larger units on the other hand – they are carefully planned, and are controlled by rules and conventions. Even quite large units may become habitual; a lecturer reported that he could 'arise before an audience, turn his mouth loose, and go to sleep'.

Harré and Secord (1972) have argued persuasively that much of human social behaviour is the result of conscious planning, often in words, with full regard for the complex meanings of behaviour and the rules of situations. This is an important correction to earlier social psychological views, which often failed to recognize the complexity of individual planning and the different meanings which may be given to stimuli, for example in laboratory experiments. However, it must be recognized that much social behaviour is *not* planned in this way: the smaller elements of behaviour and longer automatic sequences are very often outside conscious awareness, though it is possible to attend to patterns of gaze, shifts of orientation, or the latent meanings of utterances. The social skill model, in emphasizing the hierarchical structure of social performance, can incorporate both kinds of behaviour.

Scheflen's analysis (1965) of verbal and bodily behaviour during psychotherapy is useful in this connection. He distinguishes two main kinds of behavioural unit. *Positions* refer to whole phases of an encounter, for example establishing rapport, or answering questions on some topic; Scheflen finds that the same bodily postures are held throughout a position. Positions consist of *points*, which consist for example of single utterances and are usually accompanied by a particular orientation of the head. The verbal and non-verbal hierarchies are closely coordinated; examples of some of the ways in which the two sequences are linked were given earlier (p. 52f.).

3. *The perception of the other's reactions.* An experienced motorist concentrates his attention on certain stimuli: outside the car he attends to the movement of other traffic and the position of the edge of the road, rather than the architecture of the houses; while inside he is aware of the speedometer rather than the upholstery of the seats. He knows where to look for the cues, and what they mean; he can interpret road signs and can anticipate what is going to happen next. Part of the training for some industrial skills consists in teaching performers to make finer discriminations, to learn the significance of cues, concentrating on particular cues and suppressing irrelevant ones.

The selective perception of cues is an essential element in serial motor skills. The performer learns which cues to attend to and becomes highly sensitive to them. Vision is the most important channel. The performer makes a rapid series of fixations, each lasting a fraction of a second – as, for instance, in reading. The pattern of fixation is itself part of the skill; ideally, information should be collected just before it is needed. The performer also learns where to look at each point, in order to obtain the necessary information: perception is highly selective. The incoming data are actively organized into larger units which are recognized as objects, signals, or cues. These in turn are interpreted, i.e. used to predict future events, as with dial-readings or road signs. In Chapter 5 it will be shown how people learn to perceive and interpret the relevant cues, and how some people are more sensitive than others, especially in areas about which they are personally concerned. In Chapter 12 methods of training in social sensitivity will be described, and in Chapter 10 it will be shown that some kinds of mental patient are seriously deficient in it.

The perceptual channels used in social interaction include hearing the literal content of speech, hearing the paralinguistic, emotive aspects of speech, observing the other's facial expression and other bodily cues. It seems likely that the more skilled performer can make more use of the last two channels. A rare fourth channel is touch – used in parts of the world where inter-action often involves bodily contact. Hearing the emotive aspects of speech is very important, but it appears that many people fail to make use of this part of the message. Visual per-ception of the other consists mainly of scanning his face with a series of short glances in the area of the eyes. This area not only provides information about the other's emotional reactions, but also about the direction of his attention, for which his direction of gaze is a cue. Visual attention is finely timed and coordinated with speech, so that perceptual information, for example, to immediate reactions to what has just been said, is received when it is needed. Failure of social performance can result from not looking in the right place at the right time, or not being able to interpret what is seen or heard.

The motor-skill performer gets quite a lot of information from perceiving his own movements, either by sound, vision, or by kinaesthetic sensations. Do social interactors receive any direct feedback in a similar way? As we shall show in Chapter 9, people are very interested in the image they are projecting: one of the goals of interaction is to present oneself in a certain light to others. The main source of direct feedback is the sound of one's own voice. Some people are said to be very fond of this sound, but the sound they hear is quite different from what other people hear, since they hear the sound as transmitted through their bones. Many people fail to recognize tape-recordings of their voices, and are very startled the first time they hear one. People are often quite unaware of the emotive, paralinguistic aspects of their speech – they do not realize how cross they sound, for instance. They may also be unaware of the timing aspects of their speech – such as how often they interrupt. Posture, gestures and facial expression cannot be perceived visually by the actor: it is very difficult to *see* ourselves as others see us. The only way to do this is to have a lot of mirrors, or to study films of oneself. There are however kinaesthetic, mus-cular cues to bodily movements. People have a fairly definite body image, and do have some idea of their posture.

4. *Feedback and corrective action.* The information obtained by perception is transferred to more central regions of the brain and is converted into an appropriate plan of action. If someone is steering a boat he must learn which way to turn the rudder to go in the desired direction. There has to be some central store of 'translation' processes in the brain, which prescribe what to do about any particular perceptual information. This may be in the form of verbalized information, e.g. 'pull the rope on the side you want to turn towards', in the case of a rudder. Often the translation processes are completely unverbalized and lead to automatic sequences of behaviour with little conscious awareness – as in riding a bicycle. Or they may start as conscious rules and deliberate decisions but become automatic later, as with changing gear in a car. The output consists of a plan, i.e. the decision to make a particular series of motor responses, which has been selected from a range of possible alternatives. This involves some prediction about how external events are likely to develop while the response is being organized – as when a tennis or squash player, while he is shaping his shot, anticipates exactly where the ball will be.

Social interaction also depends on the existence of a learnt store of central translation processes. In the course of socialization people learn which social techniques will elicit affiliative or other responses from those they encounter. Research has shown how these can be improved upon in many cases. For example, to get another person to talk more the best techniques are (1) to talk less, (2) to ask open-ended questions, (3) to talk about things he is interested in, and (4) to reward anything he does say. In Chapter 11 an account will be given of the rather specialized styles of response for professional social skills.

A curious feature of the central system is that it can only handle one piece of information at a time – it has limited capacity. The effects of limited channel capacity are seen in social interaction as in motor-skill performance: during periods of hesitating and unfluent speech speakers do not scan the faces of the others present – presumably to avoid overloading the system.

It is in a continuous skill or 'tracking' task that feedback can be seen most clearly. A beginner motorist tries to steer the car down the road, he sees that he is about to hit the kerb, so he corrects the steering to the right. When he is more competent the same process takes place with greater speed and accuracy. The social-skill performer corrects in a similar way. A teacher who sees that her pupils have not understood the point will repeat it slowly in another way; a person who realizes that he is annoying someone by his behaviour will usually change his style of behaviour.

Special techniques, verbal or non-verbal, may be needed to control emotional states. If a candidate is being interviewed for a job, he is usually very anxious and it is important to reduce this anxiety before proceeding with the interview. To do this, rather subtle techniques are needed. Perhaps the most important is the adoption of a very relaxed manner on the part of the interviewer – in tone of voice, gestures, and facial expression.

Turning to a quite different social situation, it is interesting to study Goffman's description of the way in which a surgeon will keep down the level of anxiety among his assistants during an operation.

Thus at a point of high tenseness, when a large renal tumour had been completely exposed and was ready to be pierced by a draining needle, a chief surgeon lightly warned before he pierced, 'Now don't get too close'.

Since the surgeon's own self-control is crucial in the operation and since a question concerning it could have such a disquieting effect upon the other members of the team, he may feel obliged to demonstrate that he is in possession of himself.

During quite delicate tasks, he may softly sing incongruous undignified tunes such as 'He flies through the air with the greatest of ease'. [Goffman, 1961, pp. 124–7.]

5. *The timing of responses*. An important feature of motor skills is the achieving of correct timing, and often of rhythm. Without correct anticipation of when a response will be required the performance is jerky and ineffective. This can be seen in the intermediate motor/social skill of tennis: each player moves alternately in a regular rhythm, all the time adjusting to the

reactions of the other. The same is true of the simplest type of interaction – a conversation between two people. They must speak in turns, and there must be synchronizing of tempo, as described later (p. 136f.). There must be some adjustment of each person's characteristic tempo, length of speeches, speed of reaction, and tendency to interrupt, for a synchronized set of responses to develop. We now know the signals which are used to manage the synchronizing of speech. If George wants to carry on talking, he doesn't pause at the end of sentences, or look at Joan, for these are 'full-stop signals'; he keeps a hand in mid-air – this is a suppressor signal. If Joan gets fed-up and interrupts, George can respond by speaking more loudly; if this does not work, he should speak louder than Joan. If Joan wants him to carry on talking, on the other hand, when he comes to the end of a sentence and looks up, she simply nods, smiles and says 'Uh-huh', in an encouraging tone of voice. By such signals the 'battle for the floor' is conducted, and a smoothly timed sequence of speech attained (Kendon, 1967; Duncan and Fiske, 1977). Not all interruptions are intended to shut the other person up: some are to help him finish a sentence, some are intended as simultaneous speech – 'How interesting' – others are due to incorrect anticipation of the other coming to the end of an utterance. Thus one aspect of verbal behaviour, and of gaze-direction and other bodily movements, is the control of who shall hold the floor. Silences and interruptions become rare as the two become more adjusted to one another, and an equilibrium pattern develops.

What is the use of the social skill model? It makes some rather general predictions – e.g. that feedback is essential for effective performance, and that social behaviour depends on a set of learned responses to different situations. It provides an analogy with motor skills, which provides another set of hypotheses – that the empirical laws governing motor skills will apply to social skills. For example there may be one or more 'plateaux' in acquiring social skills, i.e. periods of training where there is no improvement, and periods of sudden improvement. This and other more specific theories or hypotheses about social performance can be stated in the language provided by the model.

It also provides us with a conceptual map of social behaviour and a list of the main components and processes involved – this will be used later as a guide to methods of training, and a means of classifying failures of social performance in mental patients.

One objection which has been made to the social skill model is that when people are engaged in relaxed, informal chat they do not appear to be trying to influence or control the others. My analysis of this kind of situation is that those concerned are trying to sustain a certain type of interaction, and that this *does* involve the control of others' behaviour – keeping them relaxed and happy, preventing them from leaving, or getting too serious, keeping the intimacy level right, and so on.

However the social skill model does require some amplification, since there are several features of social performance which are absent from the performance of a motor skill. These are discussed in the next section.

SPECIAL FEATURES OF SOCIAL SKILLS

We have considered social skills on the analogy of serial motor skills. We will now look at what appear to be special features of social skills, which are not obviously present in manual skills.

1. *The independent performance of the other(s)*. A car or bicycle may have unique idiosyncrasies, but it does not exercise independent initiative in an attempt to control the driver. In social situations however the influence of A on B is not a one-way affair, and can better be represented as a system in which each accommodates to the other:

Sometimes one person can direct operations – teachers, interviewers, therapists and doctors; the dominant person has a plan which he follows, and the other reacts to his series of moves. The social skill model fits this kind of situation very well – though sometimes pupils and patients exercise some initiative, in which case things become more complicated. We shall discuss the problems of interaction where *both* parties have plans in Chapter 7.

2. *Taking the role of the other*. A cyclist is not constantly wondering how the bicycle is feeling, or whether it thinks he is riding it nicely. Interactors, however, are concerned with what others are thinking, and to a greater or lesser degree imagine how the others are reacting. An interactor may be worried about what sort of impression he is making (if being interviewed or assessed), what the other person really wants (if he is a salesman), or what the other's problems are (if he is a psychiatrist). He may do this in an external, calculating way, or he may find himself identifying with the other and sharing his emotions and problems (Turner, 1956). A selection interviewer or social worker may start by doing the first, and end up by crossing over to the client's side, and trying to get him the job, or defending him against all comers. In many social skills a balance has to be kept between sympathy and some degree of detached objectivity.

There are tests for the ability to 'take the role of the other'. In the 'As-if' test, subjects are asked to describe how their life would have been different if they had (1) been born a member of the opposite sex, and (2) if they had been born a Russian (Sarbin and Jones, 1956). It is found that people who do well on such tests also perform better at laboratory interaction tasks. It is supposed that one will interact better with another person X if one can imagine correctly what X's point of view is – the problems he faces, the pressures he is under, etc. On the other hand most people seem able to deal perfectly well with the opposite sex, and with older people – roles of which they have no experience, and which they probably imagine very inaccurately.

Taking the role of the other is one source of 'altruism', and of helping others. It has been found that a child is more likely to help a second child in distress if the first child has experienced this state of distress himself (Lenrow, 1965). There is no doubt that people often do help each other, especially members of their family, friends, and people that they like. To a more limited extent people are willing to help certain members of the public in public places (Krebs, 1970). In one of these experiments it was arranged for a stooge to collapse on the New York underground. Strangers came forward to help more rapidly if (1) the stooge was white rather than black, (2) he was not drunk, and (3) if there were not many people present (Piliavin *et al.*, 1969). Other studies show that helping behaviour is more likely to occur if another person has just been seen giving help in a similar situation.

3. *Self-presentation.* The presenting of information about the self is a normal and essential part of our social behaviour. This information is needed by others in order to know how to deal with us appropriately. We have seen that the desire to have self-image and self-esteem confirmed by others is a common form of social motivation, and that it has to be done in a way that is acceptable in the culture. In social skill situations where there is a more specific task, such projection of images may be a distraction from the proper task – the teacher should be concerned with getting his pupils to learn rather than with impressing them.

On the other hand, it may be important that the client should have the right attitudes towards and perception of the performer: it has certainly been found that learning takes place more readily when pupils respect and trust the teacher – and the same is true of clients in all social skill situations. Perhaps the answer is that skilled social performers should provide subtle evidence of their competence and expertise, but particularly by their expert performance in the role. Self-presentation can go wrong in a number of ways – by putting too much effort into it, by revealing too little, or by presenting an image which is false or misleading (See p. 198f.).

4. *Rewardingness.* We described above how small rewards and punishments during the course of interaction are able to increase or reduce the behaviour reinforced. However, the overall balance of rewards and punishments which is emitted has a

73

second effect – attracting the other person, and keeping him in the situation. A person can be rewarding in a large variety of ways – by being warm and friendly, taking an interest in the other, admiring him, being submissive, showing sexual approval, helping with his problems, or by being interesting and cheerful. What is rewarding to one person may not be rewarding for another. However if B is to be kept in the situation at all, A must keep it sufficiently rewarding for him. While A is free to use any social techniques he likes on B, in fact he is constantly restricted by what B will put up with. If A is not extremely careful, B will either withdraw from the situation entirely, e.g. by slamming the door on a political canvasser, or he may become sullen and uncooperative. If Joan can talk to David or Peter at a party, she drifts towards the one who is more rewarding to her.

We shall show later that rewardingness is the key to popularity – the main way in which popular people differ from others is in being more rewarding. Rewardingness is also the key to effective social influence: if A is sufficiently rewarding to B, he has more influence over B, because there is the possibility that the rewards may be withdrawn (see p. 149f.).

5. *The rules of social behaviour*. When we think of the skills involved in playing tennis, or any other game, it is obvious that the performer has to keep to the rules of the situation. The same is true of social situations. Some rules are 'intrinsic' – if broken, interaction is completely disrupted: for instance, playing cricket with a football, bidding less than the last person at an auction sale, or saying goodbye at the beginning of an encounter. Other rules are matters of fashion and convention, like what clothes are worn (see p. 144f.).

6. *The sequence of social events*. In social behaviour there is a flow of verbal and non-verbal events which proceeds in an orderly and understandable way. In Chapter 7 we give examples of unacceptable utterance sequences ('How do you do?', 'No thank you', etc.). So in social behaviour one has to take due account of what the other has just done, as in A's response, R_3, to B's move R_2:

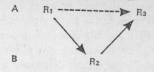

In producing R_3, A has to respond properly to R_2, as well as pursuing his plans in an R_1–R_3 sequence. Not only must A respond properly to B's last move, but there must be proper continuity in his own behaviour, or it will be incomprehensible. In this and other ways, a social event affects not only the next one, but it affects acts several moves later, intervening ones being 'bracketed'. This is what is meant by saying there may be 'grammatical' rules of sequence.

SOCIAL COMPETENCE

Performers of manual skills improve with practice until they attain a certain level of skill. For many skills it is possible to measure a person's degree of competence, so that his progress can be studied and he can be compared with others. For industrial skills the quantity and quality of output can be assessed, for performance at sport people can be directly compared with each other, and at laboratory tasks some numerical score is available. In the case of social behaviour, what exactly is meant by an 'effective' performance? For professional social skills it is at first sight clear what is meant: an effective teacher teaches better and an effective salesgirl sells more. When we look more closely, it is not quite so simple: examination marks may be one index of a teacher's effectiveness, but usually more is meant than just this. A salesgirl should not simply sell a lot of goods, she should make the customer feel she would like to go to that shop again. The general idea is clear, however: an effective performer of a professional skill is one who gets better results of the kinds relevant to the task.

Attempts have been made to assess 'social intelligence' and competence at particular tasks such as foremanship by means of paper-and-pencil tests. There appears to be a rather poor correlation between these and more direct measures of performance. High scorers in the tests tend to be people who are intelligent rather than socially competent: it is a commonplace that highly intelligent people are not always socially skilled, while some less intelligent people often are. A better method of measuring competence at particular tasks is to assess actual effectiveness: a salesgirl's sales over a period in relation to those of others in the same department; the output, absenteeism, labour turnover, accidents, etc., of a foreman's work-group. Also, individuals can be rated by observers, who watch their performance on the job, or during laboratory encounters. These ratings can include detailed aspects of behaviour, such as facial expression, and other non-verbal signals, as well as details of verbal performance.

People who are socially inadequate. For everyday, non-professional situations, it is more difficult to give the criteria of success. We can partly define them by listing the criteria of failure. Clearly many mental patients, as will be described in Chapter 10, are *not* effective – they fail to communicate with other people, they annoy and cannot sustain friendly cooperative behaviour with others, they find social situations stressful and unrewarding. The same is true of many people who are not mental patients, and of many people at work, who are found to be very difficult to deal with, and are avoided if possible. They are very unrewarding, and this is because of their lack of appropriate social skills.

The processes which have been described in this chapter enable us to understand the different ways in which people can be socially inadequate. In addition, a number of different kinds of training can be used. First, it is important to find out which are the situations which an individual finds 'difficult', i.e. feels anxious in, perhaps avoids, or simply feels he is not making a success of. On the opposite page is a list of common situations: rate yourself on how difficult you find each of them.

The next step is to find out what an individual is getting wrong. The different processes which we have described in this

Rate according to degree of difficulty	a lot	a little	none
1 Going into shops			
2 Going into pubs			
3 Going to parties			
4 Mixing at work			
5 Making friends of your own age			
6 Going out with someone of the opposite sex			
7 Dealing with awkward members of the family			
8 Being in a group			
9 Making decisions in a group			
10 Entertaining at home			
11 Dealing with a noisy neighbour			
12 Attending a formal dinner			
13 Going into a crowded room			
14 Meeting strangers			
15 Dealing with unsatisfactory service at a shop, laundry, garage, etc.			
16 Getting to know someone more intimately			
17 Seeing doctors, solicitors or bank managers			
18 Appearing in front of an audience, e.g. giving a talk			
19 Being interviewed			
20 Being chairman at a committee or other meeting			
21 Dealing with people who are older or of higher status			
22 Reprimanding a subordinate (e.g. for being late)			

chapter each correspond to common forms of social inadequacy, which we will elaborate further in later chapters.

FURTHER READING

Argyle, M., *Social Interaction*, London: Methuen, 1969.
Argyle, M., *Bodily Communication*, London: Methuen, 1975.
Trower, P., Bryant, B., and Argyle, M., *Social Skills and Mental Health*, London: Methuen, 1978.

CHAPTER 4

EYE-CONTACT AND THE DIRECTION OF GAZE

WE began studying gaze because the social skill model suggested the importance of feedback – much of which appeared to be visual. The study of gaze is closely linked with NVC – because most NVC is received by looking at face, hands, and so on. Gaze is a non-verbal signal itself, but a rather special one, since it does two things at once – it is a signal for the person looked at, but it is a channel for the person doing the looking.

During conversation, and other kinds of interaction, individuals look at each other, mainly in the region of the eyes, intermittently and for short periods – this will be referred to as 'gaze', or 'looking at the other'. For some of the time, two people are doing this simultaneously – this will be called 'mutual gaze' or 'eye-contact' (EC). Fig. 11 shows how these phenomena can be studied.

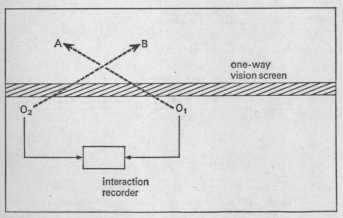

Figure 11. Laboratory arrangements for studying gaze-direction.

Two subjects A and B are seated, perhaps at a table, and are asked to discuss some topic. A's gaze is recorded by observer 1, B's gaze by observer 2; the observers press buttons which activate some kind of interaction recorder. The observers may also record periods of speaking. One kind of interaction recorder marks periods of looking or speaking as deflections of inked lines on a paper tape, as shown in Fig. 12. It is also possible to record electronically, on equipment that summates periods of button-pressing and number of presses. A and B may both be real subjects, or one of them may be a trained confederate, whose behaviour has been programmed by the experimenter.

Instead of observers, video cameras may be used, the pictures

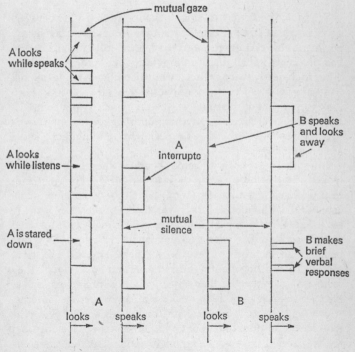

Figure 12. Record of looking and speaking (Argyle, 1969).

being combined in a split screen by a video-mixer; the video-tapes are analysed later by observers, who can play them through several times if necessary.

Several different aspects of gaze can be recorded, and typical figures from one of our experiments are given below.

Total individual gaze	61%
Looking while listening	75%
Looking while talking	41%
Average length of glances	2·95 secs
Mutual gaze	31%
Average length of mutual glances	1·18 secs

(From Argyle and Ingham, 1972.)

When two people are talking, they look at each other between 25 per cent and 75 per cent of the time (61 per cent in the experiment above), though we have seen the full range from 0 to 100 per cent; I shall discuss these individual differences later. They look nearly twice as much while listening as while talking. Mutual gaze is shorter than individual gaze; if two people both look 50 per cent of the time, we should expect 25 per cent EC. Individual glances can be anything up to 7 seconds or so (average 2·95 seconds in the above experiment), and mutual glances are rather shorter.

Interactors can tell with some accuracy when they are being looked at, as can observers of the interaction. On the other hand, Von Cranach and Ellgring (1973) have found that interactors cannot tell with much accuracy which part of their face is being looked at. What is being recorded as gaze is really gaze directed to the face; studies with eye-movement recorders show that people scan each other's faces with repeated cycles of fixation, each fixation being about a third of a second long, though they fixate on the eyes more than anywhere else. Interactors look at the eyes because there is an innate interest in eye-like patterns, which leads to early focusing on the mother's eyes; eyes provide crucial information about where the other is looking, and the area round the eyes is extremely expressive. The main exception to this is that deaf people focus on another person's mouth while he is speaking. When not looking at the face most people look right away – either at objects under discussion, or blankly into space.

In addition to the amount and timing of gaze, the eyes are expressive in other ways.

Pupil dilation (from 2–8 mm. in diameter)
Blink rate (typically every 3–10 seconds)
Direction of breaking gaze, to the left or right
Opening of eyes, wide-open to lowered lids
Facial expression in area of eyes, described as 'looking daggers', 'making eyes', etc.

GAZE DURING CONVERSATION

There is more gaze in some kinds of conversation than others. If the topic is difficult, people look less – to avoid distraction. If it is intimate, they look less – to avoid undue overall intimacy, as explained below. If there are other things to look at, inter-actors look at each other less, especially if there are objects present which are relevant to the conversation. Argyle and Graham (1977) found that gaze at the other fell from 77 per cent to 6·4 per cent if a pair of subjects were asked to plan a European holiday and there was a map of Europe in between them; 82 per cent of the time was spent looking at the map. Even a very vague, outline map was looked at for 70 per cent of the time, suggesting that they were keeping in touch by looking at and pointing to the same object, instead of looking at each other. There was little gaze at the map if it was irrelevant to the topic of con-versation.

It is found that glances are synchronized with speech in a special way. Kendon (1967) found that long glances were made, starting just before the end of an utterance, as shown in Fig. 13, while the other person started to look away at this point.

The main reason why people look at the end of their utterances is that they need feedback on the other's response. This may be of various kinds. A wants to know whether B is still attending –

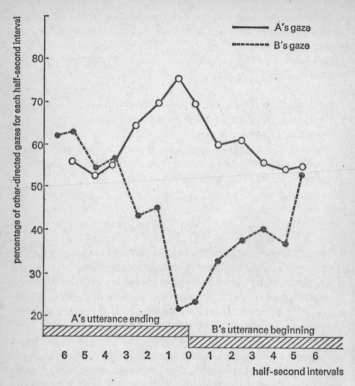

Figure 13. Direction of gaze at the beginning and end of long utterances (Kendon, 1967).

his direction of gaze shows if he is asleep, or looking at someone else. A also wants to know how his last message was received – whether B understood, agreed, thought it was funny. At pauses in the middle of long speeches, A will look for continued permission to carry on speaking, and B will nod or grunt if he is agreeable to this.

In another experiment strong support was obtained for the hypothesis that looking is used to gain information on the other's response. Vision between A and B was interfered with in various ways, e.g. B wore (1) dark glasses, (2) a mask with only eyes showing, (3) was behind a one-way screen. In these conditions A was increasingly uncomfortable, was increasingly less clear about how B was reacting, and expressed a desire for more information about B's responses. The experiment shows that it is more useful to see the face than the eyes, though it was necessary to see the eyes themselves for signals about synchronizing (Argyle, Lalljee and Cook, 1968).

Gaze is also used to *send* information, though this is not usually done with conscious intent. An experiment was carried out at Oxford in which pairs of subjects were separated by a one-way screen (Argyle, Ingham, Alkema and McCallin, 1973). A could see but not be seen, while B could be seen but not see. The person who could see looked directly at the other 65 per cent of the time, compared with 23 per cent for the other. This study confirms the obvious but very important point that people look at each other in order to receive information, mainly non-verbal signals. However, the act of looking is itself a signal. In the experiment above, when those who could not see through the screen looked directly at their partner (23 per cent of the time), they looked at certain points to give emphasis, and to indicate interest or approval – evidently to *send* information. In other situations a glance may be deliberately used to catch someone's eye, or to indicate the direction of attention.

In the Kendon study it was found that the terminal glance conveyed information to the other, that the speaker was about to stop speaking; if this glance were omitted, a long pause followed. In the one-way screen experiment there was much less gaze when subjects were asked to exchange monologues – where no signals for synchronizing speech were required.

So gaze does three main jobs during conversation – it enables non-verbal reactions to be seen, it sends information, and it helps with synchronizing of utterances.

We can also observe which direction a person looks away. Ask someone a question and he will look away – either to left or right. There is a tendency for people to look right (and downwards) if asked a question about words, spelling, etc., and to look left (and upwards) if asked a spatial question such as asking the way. This is because verbal processes take place primarily in the left hemisphere and produce a gaze shift in the opposite direction, while spatial issues are dealt with by the right hemisphere. There is some evidence that 'verbal' people tend to look right, while 'spatial' people like artists look left (Bakan, 1971).

SEQUENCES OF GLANCES

We have just seen the main ways in which gaze is coordinated with speech. In any kind of encounter, gaze is also used to show interest in and involvement with the others present. It is used to start encounters – one person catches the other's eye, and receives a signal that the other is willing to have some conversation. Kendon and Ferber (1973) found, in their study of greetings, that there were two periods of mutual gaze – in the 'distant salutation' and the 'close phase' (see p. 49). Other studies suggest that gaze is used at boundaries of episodes, perhaps because it is necessary to monitor the other's reactions very carefully at these points.

During encounters, those present should show their continued involvement by looking frequently at the others – rather than at other people (during a party, for example), since the direction of gaze indicates the direction of attention. It is interesting that we can tell where someone is looking by looking at his eyes. Infants of 11–14 months can follow their mother's line of regard (Scaife, 1975). Shifts of gaze are sometimes used by adults as an alternative to pointing. Cycles of looking are used in most kinds of interaction. The earliest kinds of social behaviour between infants and their mothers consist of simple cycles like 'peek-a-boo' in which gaze is one of the main components (p. 27).

Gaze fits into the sequence of social behaviour in another way: it acts as a reinforcer. Like nods and smiles, glances act as reinforcers of what another person has just said or done – particularly if the person doing the looking is an attractive female or a high-status male. This is not exactly reinforcement like giving a rat a piece of cheese; glances also carry meaning, that the gazer is interested and attentive. People are found to make use of this principle. For example, if one individual is trying to extract a favour from another – 'ingratiation' – he smiles and looks more in the softening-up stage, where he is being nice preparatory to asking the favour (Lefebvre, 1975). Gaze is itself affected by reinforcement: if Joan smiles and nods whenever George looks at her, George will look at her more.

It is found that the synchronizing of speech is quite good without vision – there are longer pauses but *fewer* interruptions; conveying information and solving problems can be done just as well over the telephone, provided visual materials like maps or charts are not needed. These results are somewhat surprising in view of what has been discovered about the role of gaze in interaction. The explanation is probably that people learn a rather different kind of social behaviour in which visual signals are transferred to the vocal channel; for example, head-nods are replaced by approving noises. However, vision does make an important difference in certain kinds of interaction. People get to like and trust each other more if they can see one another, and cooperate more readily. If bargaining is done over the telephone, the person with the better case wins; when two people can see each other, they become concerned about being approved of by each other, and sustaining the relationship, with the result that the person with the weaker case sometimes wins (Short, Williams and Christie, 1976).

GAZE AS A SIGNAL FOR INTERPERSONAL ATTITUDES AND EMOTIONS

We have seen how gaze is used to collect information and do various jobs during interaction. It is also under the influence of more basic motivational forces, and comes to act as a signal for attitudes to other people, and for emotional states. For example, we look more at those we like. Exline and Winters (1965) arranged for subjects to talk to two confederates, and then to state their preference for one or the other; in subsequent interaction they looked much more at the one they preferred. Rubin

(1973) found that couples who were in love (as measured by his questionnaire) spent a higher proportion of time in mutual gaze. Although gaze and E C are pleasant, especially with those we like, E C is unpleasant and embarrassing if there is too much of it, and if mutual glances are too long. This may be because unpleasantly high levels of physiological arousal are generated. Or it may be because there are also avoidance components connected with E C. We have mentioned one of these already – the avoidance of distraction at certain points of the conversation. However, there is no doubt that it is more comfortable watching others from behind a one-way vision screen than watching others who can look back.

If there are forces both to engage in E C and also to avoid it, there will be a state of conflict of the kind described earlier (p. 24f.). It follows that there is an equilibrium level of looking for each person and of E C for any two people, and that when the approach forces are relatively strong there will be more E C. We will now consider some implications of this equilibrium when the positive forces for E C are mainly affiliative or sexual, as opposed to dominative or aggressive. It was suggested earlier that E C is one of several components of 'intimacy', along with physical proximity, intimacy of topic, smiling and tone of voice (p. 29f.). If we suppose that there is an overall equilibrium for intimacy, it follows that when one of the component elements is disturbed there will be some complementary change among the others to restore the equilibrium. Several examples of this have been observed.

Argyle and Dean (1965) tested the hypothesis that greater proximity would result in less E C. Subjects took part in three three-minute discussions with stooges trained to stare, at distances of two, six and ten feet. The amount of E C was recorded by observers in the usual way (Fig. 14). In later experiments it was found that the same results were obtained with pairs of genuine subjects. The effect is greatest for male–female pairs; the change is mainly in looking while listening, and changes of E C are due to amount of individual gaze, not changes in coordination.

The gaze-distance effect has been widely confirmed, as have

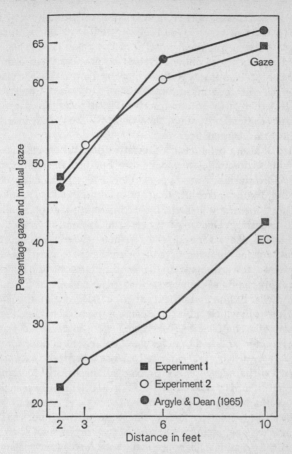

Figure 14. The effects of distance on gaze and mutual gaze
(from Argyle and Ingham, 1972).

a number of other derivations from the affiliative balance
theory. There is less gaze at the points where a person is smiling
and when intimate topics are discussed. The theory works best
for externally-imposed changes to an established relationship,
but it does not allow for changes of intimacy during an
encounter.

Under certain conditions another person's moves, e.g. towards greater proximity, are reciprocated – which is the very opposite of what the theory predicts. Patterson (1976) has extended the theory to allow for this: he proposes that a move towards greater intimacy leads to increased arousal in the target person; if the move is interpreted as a pleasant event (e.g. friendly) there will be reciprocity, if it is interpreted as unpleasant (e.g. embarrassing), then there will be withdrawal, i.e. equilibrium maintenance.

Gaze is also a product of other attitudes. When individuals are trying to dominate, they look more, but once the relationship is stabilized the lower-status person looks most, especially while listening. Exline and colleagues (1975) found that lower ranks in a military hierarchy looked 25 per cent more and particularly while listening; this may reflect the 'attention structure' whereby monkeys keep an eye on their leaders. Dislike may lead to 'cutting' another person, or to the 'hate stare' used by some whites towards blacks in the Southern states of the U.S.A.

In depression and embarrassment, people look away, usually downwards. Exline and others (1970) carried out an ingenious experiment in which subjects became implicated in cheating on the part of a confederate. When they were interviewed by the experimenter, and lied to defend the confederate, their level of gaze fell to nearly half what it had been before – except for subjects with high scores on 'machiavellianism' (cold, calculating manipulators), who looked frankly and fearlessly as before.

How much a person looks appears to depend on a balance of approach and avoidance forces. There are positive forces to look at those we like, at those with whom we are involved, and to collect information. There are avoidance forces to avoid seeing negative reactions, to avoid too much distracting input, and to avoid undue intimacy. The actual amount of gaze is a result of the balance between these two sets of forces.

How is gaze perceived? Very often it is not – we have found that many subjects do not notice variations of gaze level from 15 per cent to 85 per cent. If A becomes aware that B is looking at him, the main message received is that he is the object of B's attention. Some people find this a disturbing experience, that they are being transformed into objects, observed as if they were insects, and, for some psychotics, turned into stone. We shall discuss this experience further in Chapter 9. On the other hand mutual gaze is experienced as a special kind of intimacy. in which each is attending to and receptive to the other.

Gaze also conveys more specific meanings, indicating the nature of the other's interest. If A looks a lot at B, B often thinks (correctly) that A likes him, and B will like A in return. Argyle, Lefebvre and Cook (1974) found that people were liked if they looked more, up to the normal amount, but that too much gaze was liked less.

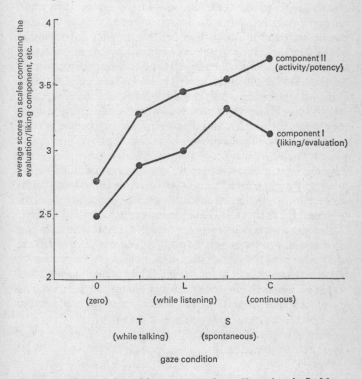

Figure 15. The meaning of five patterns of gaze (from Argyle, Lefebvre and Cook, 1974).

If A loves B, his or her pupils will dilate, and B will decode the signal correctly, though without awareness. In Italy, girls used to enlarge their pupils with drops of belladonna. The eyes are used a lot in courtship, and girls both make up their eyes and enlarge their eye display by dark glasses.

In animals gaze is often used as a threat signal. Exline and Yellin (1969) found that a monkey (in a strong cage) would attack or threaten an experimenter who stared at him, but would relax if the experimenter averted gaze – which is an appeasement signal. A number of experiments show that gaze can act as a threat signal for humans too. Ellsworth (1975) found that staring confederates on motorcycles caused motorists to move off more rapidly from stop lights; other studies found that people stared at in libraries either left or built barricades of books. Marsh, in recent studies of football hooligans, has found that a single glance at a member of the opposing group can be an occasion for violence, with cries of 'He looked at me!' (Marsh et al., 1978). As Fig. 15 shows, high levels of gaze are seen as dominating. However, a glance can have quite different consequences: Ellsworth found that a glance from a person in need of help increased the likelihood of help being given.

Gaze is also used as a cue for personality. Those who avoid gaze are seen as nervous, tense, evasive, and lacking in confidence; people who look a lot are seen as friendly and self-confident. In the next section we will examine the real relationships between personality and gaze.

Decoding gaze is a two-stage process, rather like deciding which emotional state one is in (p. 22f.). There is a general factor of awareness of the other's attention, heightened concern with the other, and readiness for action. The specific meaning and response, however, depends on other contextual cues, such as the other's facial expression and the nature of the relationship.

INDIVIDUAL DIFFERENCES

Some people look consistently more than others. Kendon and Cook (1969) studied the gaze of fifteen subjects who each met between four and eleven others; they found a high degree of consistency across different partners, though gaze was also affected by the partner. We have already seen that several aspects of the situation affect gaze, and we shall see that not everyone reacts to situations in the same way.

The most striking link between personality and gaze is found in autistic children – for whom gaze aversion is one of the defining symptoms. They look very little, in very short glances of up to 0·5 seconds, and have various ways of avoiding mutual gaze, such as turning other people round and pulling hats over their eyes; sometimes, however, they look with a blank and unresponsive stare. One theory is that they have a high level of arousal and find mutual gaze very arousing, for which there is some evidence, though it is not known how this comes about. Clancy and McBride (1969) suggest that autism is due to a failure to form the initial attachment to the mother, leading to the development of cut-off skills for maintaining isolation. Good results are reported for children treated to improve the mother–child relationship by feeding and play routines.

Schizophrenia will be discussed more fully in Chapter 10. It has often been noticed that schizophrenics seem to avert gaze, and this has been confirmed in a number of studies in which the gaze of schizophrenics was recorded while they talked to a psychologist, or a partner provided by him – they look on average about 65 per cent as much as normals. However, a recent study by Rutter (1976) has shown that when schizophrenics are talking to another person, whether a patient or a nurse, about impersonal problems, their gaze level is normal. It appears from this and other studies that schizophrenics avert gaze only when interviewed about personal matters by psychologists or their assistants. Depressive patients avoid gaze to about the same extent as schizophrenics when interviewed, and also look downwards; there is still some gaze aversion with neutral topics (Rutter, op. cit.). Neurotic patients sometimes avert gaze, and some of them stare; altogether nearly half of them show one abnormality or the other.

Turning now to variations in the normal population, it has often been found that extraverts look more than introverts.

Extraverts look more frequently, especially while talking; they also look for more of the time, and the effect is greater for females than males. Need for affiliation has some overlap with extraversion. Individuals high in need for affiliation look more – but only in non-competitive situations, and again the effect is stronger for females (Exline, 1963; see Fig. 16). The explanation

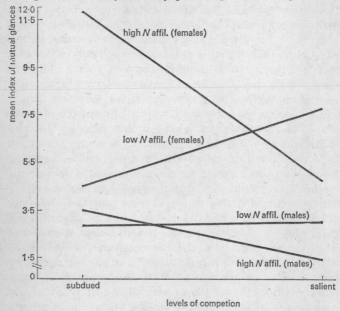

Figure 16. Gaze as a function of sex, affiliative motivation and cooperative–competitive situations (Exline, 1963).

of these findings is probably that gaze is part of a broader, affiliative pattern of behaviour, which establishes friendly relations with others.

Females look more than males, on all measures of gaze. A difference between the sexes has been found at the age of six months, but it increases up to adulthood, so is probably not innate. The experiment by Exline on affiliative motivation suggests that gaze is used more by females as an affiliative signal – though we don't know why. Mutual gaze, and being looked at, may be less disturbing for females, if they interpret this as affiliative rather than as threatening. And for a female to be looked at by a male may be seen as sexual choice: Argyle and Williams (1969) found that females often felt 'observed' by males, which is probably part of the normal relationship between the sexes in our culture.

Gaze is used as a social signal very early in life: mutual gaze with the mother first occurs at the age of four weeks. Visual interaction between mother and infant plays an important part in forming the bond between them; by six months, infants are upset when E C is broken, by eight months it plays an important part in games with the mother. During childhood the amount of gaze increases, falls during adolescence, and rises again in early adulthood; the pattern of looking at the ends of utterances and looking away at the beginning develops during childhood (Levine and Sutton-Smith, 1973).

There are some interesting cultural differences in gaze. In 'contact cultures', like those of the Arabs, Latin Americans and Southern Europeans, level of gaze is high; here, too little gaze is seen as insincere, dishonest, impolite, etc. The affiliative balance theory predicts *less* gaze in contact cultures. The reason that there is more is probably that a given level of gaze has a different meaning in these cultures, though it is possible that relationships are more intimate in contact cultures. In non-contact cultures, like Britain, Europe and Asia, too much gaze is seen as threatening, disrespectful, insulting, etc. There are often rules about gaze: not to look at your mother-in-law (Luo in Kenya), at a high-status person (Nigeria), not to look at the other but at outside objects during conversation (some South American Indians), or to look at the neck, not the face (Japan). In a number of Mediterranean countries there is still a belief in the Evil Eye – that priests or old women with squints or other facial abnormalities cast a curse on anyone they look at. This depends on an outmoded theory of vision – that the looker sends a radiation to the object, together with the often disturbing experience of being looked at.

We can summarize some of the main findings in this way: if A gazes at B a lot, this may be because:

they are placed far apart
they are discussing impersonal or easy topics
there is nothing else to look at
A is interested in B, and in B's reactions
A likes B
A loves B
A is of lower status than B
A is trying to dominate or influence B
A is an Arab, Latin American, etc.
A is an extravert
A is affiliative (and female, in a cooperative situation)
A is low in affiliation (and female, in a competitive situation).

When an interactor tries to decode the meaning of another's gaze pattern, he can recognize some of these factors, as we have seen. Others are more obscure, and were not recognized until the relevant research was done. The ways in which people perceive each other will be discussed in the next chapter.

FURTHER READING

Argyle, M., and Cook, M., *Gaze and Mutual Gaze*, Cambridge University Press, 1976.

CHAPTER 5

PERCEPTION OF OTHERS

IN order to 'perceive' other people and social events, interactors use visual and auditory signals, verbal as well as non-verbal. Sherlock Holmes was very good at it. He perceived that Watson had returned to his medical practice in this way:

If a gentleman walks into my rooms smelling of iodoform, with a black nitrate of silver upon his right forefinger, and a bulge on the side of his top hat to show where he has secreted his stethoscope, I must be dull indeed if I do not pronounce him to be an active member of the medical profession. [*A Scandal in Bohemia*]

It was shown in the last chapter that gaze is important because it opens the channel for receiving NVC. In fact we make use of auditory as well as visual information, verbal as well as non-verbal, to perceive events and other people. However, more than 'perception' is involved; I am referring to the whole process of interpreting and making sense of what is going on. This is important because the way in which a person perceives (and interprets) events affects how he will behave. In an experiment by Kelley (1950), subjects who expected a person who was presented by the experimenter to be 'warm' interpreted his behaviour differently from those who expected him to be 'cold', and members of the first group talked to him more. The 'perception' of people is quite different from the perception of physical objects: objects are seen as being pushed and pulled by physical laws, while people are seen as to some extent being responsible for events and initiating action; the perceiver does his best to understand why they do it. Inadequate social performance is often due to faulty perception – simply not attending enough, or making inaccurate interpretations. It is particularly important for interviewers, doctors, personnel officers and others, to avoid the various sources of error here.

THE PERCEPTION OF EMOTIONS

Apes and monkeys keep up a continuous running commentary on their emotional states, for other members of the group to see and hear. From their facial expressions and shrieks and grunts, it is clear whether they are angry, relaxed, want to play, want to copulate or are in fear of attack. In man, the face is the main source of information about emotional state. As we have seen, the face displays seven main emotions – happiness, surprise, fear, sadness, anger, disgust/contempt, and interest (p. 38f.). How accurately can these faces be decoded? If photographs of posed facial expressions are used, the success rate is about 60 per cent. Some emotions are more easily confused than others; for example, anger may be confused with fear or disgust, but not with happiness or surprise. Facial expressions can be recognized more readily when there is a word to describe them, like 'frown' or 'sneer'.

There is now evidence that the face plays a central part in the experience of emotion (see below). However, in most cultures there are restraints or 'display rules' on what may be shown in the face. This makes it difficult to tell what someone is really feeling, and we have to make use of other cues. Some of these are found in the face itself: an anxious person perspires at the temples, sometimes people smile with the lower half of the face only, and the area round the eyes has been found to convey curiously mixed emotions like pleasure and anger.

The second main cue to emotions is tone of voice. Davitz (1964) carried out experiments in which neutral statements were tape-recorded in different emotional styles. One of these statements was, 'I'm going out now. I won't be back all afternoon. If anyone calls, just tell them I'm not here.' The average accuracy score was 30–45 per cent, which is rather lower than the accuracy of judging faces. Some emotions are conveyed better by face (happiness, anger), others by voice (fear). The cues in the voice which convey emotions have been found; for example, sadness is conveyed by a low pitch and slow speed, anxiety by a breathy tone of voice, with many speech disturbances. These and other dimensions have been produced on a Moog synthesizer and the 'emotions' judged correctly (Scherer, 1974).

Some information about emotions is conveyed by the rest of the body below the head, but not very much. Graham, Ricci Bitti and Argyle (1975) showed video-tapes of people enacting emotional scenes, with different parts of the screen covered up. The body, including gestures, conveyed as much information about level of emotional intensity as the face, but was a poor source of information about specific emotions.

A further source of information is the situation the other person is seen to be in. If the other person has just been given a nice present, it is very likely that he will be pleased; if something very unexpected has happened, it is likely that he will be surprised. A number of experiments have tried to find out how facial expression is combined with information about the situation. In some situations, the situational cues may be more important than bodily signals. Early experiments used rather melodramatic situations; for example, a smiling person was said to be 'watching a hanging', in which case subjects would judge him to be tense rather than happy. Later studies suggest that it depends on the clarity and strength of the cues from each source – if facial expression is restrained, situational cues will presumably be relied upon. Lalljee, in an unpublished study found that people work out a sensible solution if confronted by conflicting information: for example, a sad face was thought to be more authentic than a happy one, or subjects reinterpreted the nature of the situation if the wrong facial expression was shown. This shows that perceiving emotions is quite a complex process, which may include inference and the application of principles acquired in the course of experience – for example, that people often pretend to be happy when they are not, but do not often pretend to be sad.

As well as interpreting the emotional states of others, we also interpret our own. The experiment by Schachter and Singer described earlier showed that people use situational cues to interpret a state of physiological arousal (p. 24f.). Izard (1971) has put forward the view that the face plays an important part in this process: a situation produces a biological response at lower

97

levels of the nervous system; this creates a facial expression, which provides information resulting in the subjective experience of emotions. This theory has been supported by a number of experiments in which subjects adopt a facial expression for a few minutes, and are then found to be experiencing the appropriate emotion (Laird, 1974) – 'Smile, and you will feel happy'!

The face tells us which emotion we are feeling, but we also need information on level of arousal. This can be learnt from the rate of the beating of the heart, perspiration, and similar bodily signals. Valins (1966) played amplified sounds of heart-beats to subjects, and found that he could influence how much young men thought they liked slides of nude females by speeding up the heart-beats they heard – making them think that they were more emotionally aroused than they were. In another experiment he made subjects feel less afraid of snakes, by the same method. Leventhal (1974) has carried out some amusing experiments on what makes people laugh, i.e. decide that they are amused. If funny films are accompanied by canned laughter, subjects find them funnier. However, it makes a difference which ear the laughter is administered to: for males the right ear, for females the left ear, is better; this suggests that males process jokes in a verbal way, since verbal activities are concentrated in the left brain hemisphere, which is activated more by the *right* ear. Females perhaps process jokes intuitively, using brain processes which are concentrated in the right hemisphere.

PERCEPTION OF INTERPERSONAL BEHAVIOUR

We have seen that animals establish their social relationships entirely by means of non-verbal signals, and that, to a surprising extent, so do human beings. There are two main dimensions of attitudes to others which are communicated (see opposite page). There are also combinations of these, such as friendly dominance, and friendly combined with sexual attraction – the difference between loving and liking will be discussed later (p. 153). These attitudes are expressed by a wide range of non-

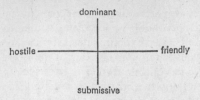

verbal signals. Thus, a *friendly* attitude may be shown by some or all of the following:

    bodily contact
    close proximity
    side-by-side orientation
    leans towards, open arm position
    high level of gaze
    smiling face
    soft tone of voice

We have done a number of experiments on the decoding of verbal and non-verbal cues for interpersonal attitudes, which were described on p. 5of. A number of other experiments have been carried out on the perception of conflicting cues for inter-personal attitudes. Shirley Weitz (1972) found that white American students sometimes used friendly words towards a black subject, but in an unfriendly tone of voice. These subjects chose less intimate joint tasks and less close proximity, showing that their tone of voice showed their real attitude, not their words. Daphne Bugenthal and her colleagues (1970) found that children placed more weight on a negative signal, whether in the verbal or non-verbal channel: a woman delivering a rebuke with a friendly face and voice was regarded as negative.

How accurate are these perceptions of others' attitudes to ourselves? Tagiuri (1958) surveyed likes and dislikes in sixty groups of people who knew each other well. He found that most people knew who liked them, but made quite a lot of mistakes about who did not like them – nine per cent of dislikes were seen as likes. The reason is that we very rarely make overt signals of rejection, so that politeness is mistaken for liking.

It is particularly difficult to interpret interpersonal attitudes

99

where the other person is in a dependent or subordinate position. In 'ingratiation', one person is nice to another and then asks for a favour. Experiments by Jones (1964) and others have found that ingratiators agree with the other, flatter him, look and smile more; they also do so strategically, such as disagreeing on unimportant matters. It is found that observers of these events interpret them as ingratiating if the actor is in a dependent position. In real life, the boss or other recipient of ingratiation may find it very difficult to tell whether his subordinates like and admire him or not. He can improve the accuracy of his judgements by using the strategies of inference which are part of 'attribution theory'. For example, if a person behaves in the same way as everyone else – being respectful to the boss, being nice to the secretary – and if he has something to gain from such behaviour, not much can be learnt about his true attitudes towards them. We can learn his true feelings, however, (1) if he behaves in a way which deviates from the norm, or which is against his interests, such as being rude to the boss, (2) if he is consistently nice to the secretary in a variety of ways and situations, or (3) if he is nicer to some people than to others, with whom he has a similar formal relationship (Kelley, 1967).

Ingratiation and politeness are two of the main sources of error in judging interpersonal attitudes. Another is the tendency to form 'balanced' sets of attitudes and beliefs. For example, if A likes B, he will think that B likes A more than he actually does, and if A dislikes C, he will think that C dislikes A more than he really does. Of course, B will tend to like A, since such choices are reciprocated – but on average not as much as A thinks. Again, if A likes B and C, he will assume that B and C like each other, while if he likes one and not the other he will expect them not to like each other. (In the figure below, $\longrightarrow$ = 'likes'; $-\!\!\!\mid\!\!\rightarrow$ = 'does not like'.)

This perception of another's attitudes is an example of *metaperception*, that is, perceiving another's perception of oneself. As we will see later, there are certain conditions under which people become concerned about the perception of others – for example, when being interviewed for a job, or other occasions of self-presentation. Ronald Laing and his colleagues (1966)

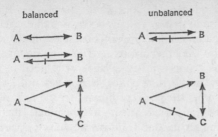

have developed a more elaborate set of measures of interpersonal attitudes. They find out how A perceives B, how A thinks B perceives A (the meta-perspective) and how A thinks B thinks A perceives B (the meta-meta-perspective). The last one is important if A dislikes or thinks ill of B, but does not want B to know this – A is then concerned with assessing how B thinks A sees B. From combining the perceptions of both parties it is possible to obtain further measures, e.g. accuracy of meta-perceptions; the various accuracy scores were found to be greater in happy compared with disturbed marriages.

INTERPRETING THE FLOW OF EVENTS

After a traffic accident, a family row, or any other social event, it is often found that people report what happened differently, or have different ideas about whose fault the accident was, who started the row, or why people acted as they did. Hastorf and Cantril (1954) studied a football game between Dartmouth and Princeton. The game became very rough and several players were injured. After the match, 36 per cent of Dartmouth students and 86 per cent of Princeton students interviewed thought that the Dartmouth team had started the rough play. This shows that interpretations can be different in important respects, and are influenced by group memberships or attitudes of perceivers. A study of British football fans by Marsh *et al.* (1978) found that they see their behaviour on the terraces as an orderly, rule-governed affair, where they have fun making threats and rude gestures at supporters of the other side, but have no intention of inflicting any bodily harm. The press and authorities, on the other hand, see football 'hooligans' as extremely violent, uncontrolled savages, who need to be kept in order by large numbers of police, wire cages and £1,000 fines. This situation has become complicated by the fact that the fans pretend to themselves and others that the official theory is true, and gain some satisfaction from the enhanced image of themselves as a frightening menace to society.

One thing we do when observing a series of social events is to divide it up into 'chunks' or 'episodes'. This can be done by showing video-tapes to judges and asking them to press a button whenever they see a boundary between two chunks; or they can sort cards describing small pieces of the action into chunks. It is found that judges agree quite well on these boundaries, though they use different scales, and find units of different sizes (Newtson, 1977). There is some evidence that people choose as units the actions leading to a particular goal (Dickman, 1963). Sometimes the chunks are quite easy to see, if there are major changes of activity or spatial position – as at a dinner party or a seminar.

We only see part of what is going on if we are taking part in an encounter ourselves, because we are busy planning our own performance, and are only looking part of the time. Repeatedly playing the video-tape of an encounter can reveal a great deal more about what was happening, especially at the level of minor non-verbal signals like head-nods, frowns, interruptions and so on. More still can be revealed by asking experts on social interaction to analyse different aspects of the encounter. However, the expert view can be greatly augmented by asking the participants how they themselves saw the events, and in particular what they were trying to do. There is some disagreement between social psychologists here. Some think that they should stick to an analysis of behaviour; some think that they should take the perceptions or 'accounts' of participants as their data, and think that the social scientists' interpretation is simply another point of view with no special validity. My view is that the social scientist should use *both* observational and interview data, and try to piece together an objective and verifiable interpretation.

The trouble with subjective interpretations is that they are often incomplete or simply wrong. One interesting source of variation in them arises from the different interpretations of an act by the performer and by an observer. The performer thinks that his behaviour was mainly due to situational factors ('I fell over because it was slippery'), while an observer is more likely to attribute it to the performer's personality ('She fell over because she's clumsy') (Jones and Nisbett, 1972). This is because the performer is attending to the environmental situation, while an observer is attending to the performer's behaviour.

We also make attributions when we have succeeded or failed in some situation where achievement is possible – it could have been due to our ability, effort, the difficulty of the task, or luck. It is found that success is over-attributed to internal factors, but that failure is *not* over-attributed to external factors. External attributions are made mainly when there is a variable pattern of success and failure (Miller and Ross, 1975).

Actors try to understand their own behaviour. Although they have some conscious access to their intentions, beliefs, and so on, this awareness is found to be incomplete. They are often unaware of the stimuli to which they are reacting, like another's gaze, or their own emotional states, or of the behaviour they emit. People are aware of the *products* of their cognitive processes, but not of the cognitive processes themselves. And when we are in action ourselves in an un-self-conscious way, we are not thinking about such processes at all (Nisbett and Wilson, 1976).

PERCEIVING AND INTERPRETING OTHER PEOPLE

We see other people quite differently from the way we see physical objects. Objects are seen as lumps of matter which are pushed or dropped according to causal laws. We see people as conscious, thinking and verbalizing, and as initiating behaviour: we are sometimes aware of them responding to social pressures, but we assume that they will act only after they have decided to do so. We also assume that they are stable and consistent. Thus, it is often assumed that if a person is intelligent he is also honest, i.e. good things go together – the so-called 'halo effect'. We also tend to think that people will behave in much the same way in different situations.

Attribution of internal causation and personality. Under certain conditions, we decide that a person acted as he did from internal causes, i.e. as a result of his intentions or personality, rather than from external causes, such as social pressure. 'Attribution theory' sets out the ways in which we decide that others are acting from internal causes:

1. When their behaviour is not in conformity with the norms or is to their disadvantage. We start making inferences about personality when a person acts unexpectedly, or deviates from conventions.

2. When a person appears to be free of social pressures. For instance, if a high-status person conforms, he is seen as freely deciding to change his mind; when a low-status person conforms, he is seen as yielding to social pressure (Thibaut and Riecken, 1955).

3. As explained in connection with interpersonal attitudes, inferences of internal dispositions are made if a person consistently behaves in a certain way, in a variety of situations, and if he behaves in a distinctive way, e.g. being nice to A but not to B.

4. Inferences are made about personality if a number of different kinds of behaviour lead to the same goal, e.g. making money, and we are likely to infer that he is motivated towards this goal (Kelley, 1967; Jones and Davis, 1966).

There are a number of common errors of attribution.

1. As explained earlier, observers tend to attribute an act to the actor's personality, while the actor attributes it more to the situation. In general, observers overestimate the importance of personality factors and underestimate situational ones. Traits

are, indeed, mainly ideas in the minds of observers, which are used to interpret others' behaviour.

2. An example of overestimating personality factors is the assumption that those involved in accidents or other misfortunes are responsible. Walster (1966) found that mishaps in which a parked car had rolled down a hill were blamed more on the (absent) driver the more damage was done.

3. An example of underestimating situational factors is the tendency to overlook our own influence on another person's behaviour. If another person is bad-tempered or competitive, this may be partly because of our own behaviour.

Categorizing other people. When we form impressions of other people's personalities, we categorize them in various ways. Since we behave somewhat differently towards males and females, old and young, and other divisions of people, it is necessary to categorize them as soon as possible.

Much may happen before two people meet at all. We shall not consider questions of previous correspondence, or telephone calls, because they are really forms of interaction. A may know a lot about B by repute, from what he has been told by other people. This can be reproduced in laboratory experiments on 'set', in which subjects are given information about one another. As we have seen, it makes a great difference to the subsequent interaction whether the other person is described as 'warm' or 'cold' for example. It also makes a difference whether the other person is known to be a friend or foe, of higher or lower status, and so on.

The actual occasion of meeting may be accidental, by introduction, or through belonging to the same group. At this point A experiences his first perception of B. An important aspect of this perception is that A will categorize B in terms of social class, race, age, intelligence or on whatever dimensions of people are most important to him, and this will activate the appropriate style of social behaviour in A.

Everyone has a number of dimensions, or sets of categories, which are most important to him, and which affect his behaviour. He may not bother about social class, but may be very concerned about whether another person is Catholic or Protest-ant (e.g. in Belfast), or how intelligent he is. One way of finding out which categories are important to a person is the 'repertory grid' devised by George Kelly (1955). The technique is as follows: the subject is asked for the names of ten to fifteen people in certain relationships, e.g. 'a friend of the same sex', 'a teacher you liked'. The names are written on cards and presented to him three at a time. The subject is asked which two of the three are most similar, and in what way the other one differs, thus eliciting one of his 'constructs'. When a number of constructs have been found, a 'grid' is made up in which all the target persons are rated on all the constructs. Statistical methods can be used to find the general dimensions which are most used by the subject.

It is found that people use three kinds of construct – roles (e.g. class, occupation), personality traits (e.g. intelligent, ex-traverted) and physical characteristics (e.g. attractiveness, height). The most commonly used personality traits are:

extraversion, sociability
agreeableness, likeability
emotional stability
intelligence
assertiveness

It is now very clear, however, that these traits are more in the mind of the beholder than in the behaviour of the target person. Different people use different traits. Women (and psycho-logists) tend to look for personality traits and social style; men on the other hand are more interested in status and achievement. People become most accurate at assessing whatever qualities concern them most – anti-semites are better at identifying Jews, for example. The categorization needs to be made, because an anti-semitic person will use quite different social techniques with Jews and Gentiles, and he wants to know which to select. Precisely the same is true of a person for whom differences of social class, or of intelligence, are of importance.

The constructs an individual uses may be extremely weird and private. Whole groups have their constructs, like *saved – not-saved*. Some people use very simple category systems, with only one or two dimensions, such as *nice – nasty*, *in the Army – not in the Army*. Others may use a considerable number of independent dimensions. A teacher might classify pupils as *intelligent – unintelligent*, *creative – uncreative*, *hard-working – lazy*, *neurotic – stable*, *socially-skilled – socially-unskilled*, etc. Those who use only a few dimensions will collapse the other possible ones, and suffer from the 'halo effect'. A more complex impression makes it possible to handle the other person in a more effective way; for example, if a teacher decided that a pupil was *intelligent*, *lazy* and *unstable*, this would enable her to select appropriate social skills.

It is found that schizophrenics do not have adequate constructs for persons and their emotional states. It has been suggested that this is a factor in their inadequate social behaviour – just as a gardener needs an adequate classification of plants and weeds, so for purposes of social behaviour we need adequate constructs for people (p. 211).

Different constructs are used in different situations. Forgas, Argyle and Ginsburg (in press) found that members of a psychology research group, for informal chat over coffee, used *extraversion* and *evaluation*. At seminars, on the other hand, they categorized each other in terms of *dominance*, *creativity* and *supportiveness*. And different traits are used to describe different groups of people: Argyle, Forgas and Ginsburg found that rather different traits are used to categorize girlfriends, children, sporting friends, professors, etc.

Stereotypes and physical cues. Impressions of others' personalities are partly based on stereotypes. If we know someone to be a *female*, *Oxford*, *psychology*, *undergraduate*, this sets off four sets of stereotyped information, based on our past experience and contact with popular culture. Katz and Braly carried out a classic study in 1933, which was repeated in 1951 and 1967, on the stereotypes of Princeton students: 84 per cent thought negroes were superstitious, 79 per cent thought Jews were shrewd, and 78 per cent thought Germans were scientifically-minded. The percentage of Princeton students holding these views has fallen a lot since 1933. (The method in these studies was not entirely satisfactory, since subjects were *invited* to express such stereo-types.) However, many people do hold stereotyped beliefs about the characteristics of Jews, old Etonians, sociology students, policemen, etc. Although psychologists usually say that it is very wicked to hold stereotypes, these often contain useful summaries of the typical attributes of different sections of the population. Stone, Gage and Leavitt (1957) found that stereotyped ratings of a number of individuals simply described as 'students' were *more* accurate than the ratings given after interviewing them. On the other hand, there is a lot more variation among, say, sociology students, than the stereotype would suggest, and it is important to be able to recognize variations from the statistical average.

Our impressions of others are partly based on inferences from their appearance. People who wear spectacles are thought to be intelligent, though Argyle and McHenry (1970) found that the effect disappears after a person has been seen in action for a few minutes. The same may be true for the other traditional findings of this type, such as:

> thick lips   – sexy
> thin lips   – conscientious
> high forehead   – intelligent
> dark or coarse skin – hostile
> and so on

There is, however, no evidence that the individuals with these kinds of face do possess the qualities in question.

Different items of information about appearance are com-bined. This has been extensively studied in person perception experiments. The main conclusion is that there is an averaging of the effects of two or more pieces of verbal information, in their implications for the target person's intelligence, etc. In the case of non-verbal materials, the process seems to be rather different, and two cues may produce a special effect in combination. Mahannah (1968) asked people to judge the personality of a girl seen wearing a blonde or brunette wig and a red or blue dress. The combination of brunette wig and red dress made her seem aggressive, masculine and self-sufficient.

Voices are decoded mainly in terms of stereotypes: a person's accent is used to allocate him to a particular social class or nationality, and stereotypes are applied accordingly. Clothes raise other problems: they are completely under voluntary control, and play an important part in self-presentation. We learn how the other person wants us to see him, which is not quite the same as how he really is (see Chapter 9).

Physical attractiveness. This is a way of classifying people which is very widely used; a person's physical attractiveness has important effects on the way he or she is treated. It can be measured very easily by asking judges to rate an individual on a five- or seven-point scale, like this:

1	2	3	4	5
not at all attractive	slightly attractive	moderately attractive	very attractive	extremely attractive

There is a high level of agreement between different judges of either sex on a person's physical attractiveness (p.a.) score. The individual, however, may not have a very accurate idea of his or her attractiveness (as seen by others); there are quite low correlations, of the order of 0·25–0·30, for p.a. as rated by self and others: some people are over-modest, others the reverse. There are individual differences in preferences which are related to the personality of the beholder; extraverted males like pictures of girls with large bosoms and few clothes. It is possible that they are more prepared to admit these preferences than introverts. There are cultural differences in preference for thin or fat women and so on.

Attractiveness in females for many people in our society today appears to be based on the following elements (Wilson and Nias, 1976):

Height: shorter than the beholder, otherwise medium: 'Miss World' winners average 5′ 8″

Physique: 36–24–35 is the ideal; each of the three components is important; fatness is a very negative feature

Face: regular features, full lips, clear skin, smiling expression
Hair and grooming: long hair; 'frizzy wig' often used in experiments to make unattractive; careful grooming of skin
Health: apparent healthiness, vivaciousness and arousal
Clothes: in current fashion
Self-esteem: people with high self-esteem get more attractive mates

It is interesting that most of these features are under voluntary control, if we include ways of increasing height, and changing real or apparent physique. To a large extent, p.a. is a style of behaviour, which can be indulged in by those who choose to do so. Sex therapy and social skills training often include suggesting improvements to appearance – which are easier to make than improvements in social behaviour.

Attractiveness in men is not as important as in women, but it has its effects. It has similar components to those for females, but height is important, and dominance is found attractive.

Experiments have shown that those who are physically attractive, of either sex, are thought to possess all kinds of other desirable attributes – they are seen as more sexually warm and responsive, sensitive, kind, interesting, strong, modest, sociable, altruistic, warm, sincere, poised and outgoing; it is thought that they are more likely to get married, would have greater marital happiness, get more prestigious jobs and be happier, but be *less* competent parents (Dion *et al.*, 1972). This is known as the 'physical attractiveness stereotype', the assumption that those who are beautiful are good; it is doubtful whether it has any foundation in fact.

Perception leads to action, and those who are seen as attractive are treated differently. The most celebrated study is the 'computer dance' at which Elaine Walster and colleagues (1966) invited 752 new students to a dance at which they were paired at random, except that the male was always taller than his partner. Ratings of attractiveness were made by the experimenters, and these proved to be the only predictor of how much each person was liked by their partner, for both sexes, but especially for females. Berscheid and colleagues (1971) found that attractiveness correlated ·61 with the number of dates in the last year for females, ·25 for males. It has been found that attractive females at an American university got better grades, and that they did it by staying behind afterwards and using their charms on the instructors (Singer, 1964). Other studies show that taller men get better jobs, and attractive girls are less likely to be found guilty in law courts (see Berscheid and Walster, 1974a).

Names and nicknames. Rom Harré (1976) has recently drawn attention to the importance of names in social behaviour. People think of themselves and each other by their names, as when asked 'Who are you?' A person's name often has clear indications of social class (Sebastian Digby-Vane-Trumpington), race (Moses Levi), or regional origins (Stuart McGregor). First names, though usually given by parents, also carry certain images – Charity, Horace, Robin, and Joan, for example. People change their names to conceal their national or racial origins ('What was your name before it was John Smith?'), or because of undesirable associations with their names (Sidebottom, etc.), or simply to give themselves a more glamorous image.

Children are given nicknames by their parents – sometimes as many as eight different ones are used in the family. They are also given nicknames by their peer group, and this signifies acceptance into a social group, and often some social role within it. Those who are not properly accepted do not have nicknames. These names may be based on personal qualities, e.g. Fatty; on particular incidents, e.g. Sneaky; or are based on the person's real name, e.g. Sherlock (Holmes). The society of childhood contains a number of traditional roles, perpetuated by school stories and comics, such as that of Piggy the fat boy, Twit, and Thinker. In these various ways a person's name and nickname contribute to impressions formed about him.

A title is a kind of appellation which is achieved – for instance, ranks in the army, Dr and Professor, Sir and Lord. The niceties of British titles, of the different kinds of Lady, are most important to those concerned, as are such German academic labels as

'Dr Dr'. In a number of countries, such as Wales, it is the custom to refer to people by their profession – e.g. 'Jones the Spy'.

The accuracy of person perception. Forming accurate impressions of others is important in all social situations, because we need to know how to handle people, how they will react. For professional interviewers and clinical psychologists, however, forming accurate impressions is their job. What is meant by 'accurate', here? It is possible to compare the judgements of interviewers or observers with the results of psychological tests. One problem here lies in separating *differential* accuracy from simply knowing the right average score for the population. Mark Cook in an unpublished study measured differential accuracy and found that judges could place target persons in nearly the right order for extraversion, after seeing a short sample of their behaviour on video-tape, but could not do the same for neuroticism – which evidently is not so easily visible.

A more basic problem is that people vary greatly in their behaviour in different situations, as will be shown in the next chapter: extraverts are not extraverted all the time. Cline and Richards (1960) showed judges films of target persons being interviewed and asked them to predict, or rather *post*dict the behaviour of these rather carefully studied target persons in a number of situations. They found that some judges were consistently better than others.

One kind of prediction of great practical importance is the prediction of success at jobs – each job involving a range of situations. We shall discuss the accuracy of personnel-selection interviewers later (p. 233f.). These results can be summarized by saying that interviewers can add a lot to other sources of information, but that their predictions are far from perfect, and that interviewers disagree a lot with each other.

The main sources of error in person perception in general are as follows:

1. Assuming a person will behave in the same way in other situations, overlooking situational causes of his observed behaviour, including the behaviour of the observer himself.

2. Trying too hard to construct a consistent picture of the other; thinking all good things go together; being unwilling to recognize that he may be intelligent *and* lazy, neurotic *and* generous.

3. Being influenced too much by first impressions, in particular by physical appearance and accent, and applying corresponding stereotypes.

4. Making positive evaluations and giving favourable ratings to people from the same town, school, social class, etc.

5. Being influenced too much by negative points, and not enough by positive features of the other.

6. Making constant errors, whereby everyone is regarded as second-rate, aggressive, or whatever.

7. Socially inadequate patients have another common problem – simply not looking enough at, paying enough attention to, or being sufficiently interested in other people.

FURTHER READING

Hastorf, A. H., Schneider, D. J., and Polefka, J., *Person Perception*, Reading, Mass.: Addison–Wesley, 1970.
Hayden, T., 'Person perception', in L. Berkowitz, *A Survey of Social Psychology*, Hillsdale, Ill.: Dryden, 1975.

CHAPTER 6

SOCIAL BEHAVIOUR AND PERSONALITY

WE want to be able to explain, and perhaps predict, the social behaviour of different people, and we would like to explain and predict what will happen when two or more different people meet.

THE INTERACTIONIST MODEL OF PERSONALITY

For many years, psychologists believed that a person's social behaviour was directly related to his personality, so that it could be predicted from tests for extraversion, dominance, and the like. It was gradually discovered that tests give extremely poor predictions of individual social behaviour (correlations usually 0·25 or less). It has also been noticed that the same person behaves totally differently in different situations, for example, a student – in a tutorial, with his girlfriend, and at a drunken party. Is he really an extravert or not?

It was realized, of course, that situations affect behaviour too – this is what psychological experiments are all about, but it was assumed that situational factors were less important than personality factors. As will be shown below, there is now extensive evidence that situational factors are at least as important as personality, if not more so. To give an example of what this means, consider three mythical people, Tom, Dick and Harry, who have different tendencies concerning lateness. If persons and situations are equally important, their typical lateness might be like this (Argyle, 1976):

minutes late for	lecture	tutorial	coffee	Person means
Tom	0	3	6	3
Dick	3	6	9	6
Harry	6	9	12	9
situation means	3	6	9	6

However, there is a further problem. The table above shows our three friends as consistently late – Tom is always earliest, Harry always latest, in each situation. However, we now know that people are not nearly as consistent as this. Tom might be keen on lectures and always arrive early, while Harry is very bored by lectures and is always late. Their average lateness might be more like this (Argyle, 1976):

minutes late for	lecture	tutorial	coffee	person means
Tom	—6	3	12	3
Dick	3	6	9	6
Harry	12	9	6	9
situation means	3	6	9	6

This is known as *interaction* between personality and situation (P × S interaction), and is reflected in low correlations between situations or tests. What has caused many psychologists to abandon the traditional trait model of personality is the realization that personality tests simply do not predict behaviour in actual situations with any accuracy; if there are low correlations between situations it follows that a test could not predict behaviour in all of them.

The traditional trait model has been replaced by the interactionist model of personality (Endler and Magnusson, 1976). This model recognizes the existence of stable, underlying features of personality, but says that these interact with the properties of particular situations to produce behaviour. This is quite different from the earlier model: it is not saying that a person has a typical or average tendency to dominance which he generalizes across situations, for example, but that he has certain drives and other aspects of personality which may or may not produce dominant behaviour on a particular occasion. Authoritarian personalities illustrate the point: an authoritarian bullies less powerful or important people and is submissive to more powerful people – there is no question of the generalization of similar behaviour.

Attempts have been made to test these two models by finding

the relative importance of persons, situations and P × S inter-action. This is done by observing, or asking for reports of, the behaviour of a number of individuals in a number of situations, and calculating how much of the variation can be explained by persons and situations. A typical study is that by Moos (1969) on the observed behaviour of mental patients.

Category	Source Persons	Settings	P × S	Within
Hand and arm movement	17·2	13·8	29·6	39·3
Foot and leg movement	27·3	13·0	31·2	28·6
Scratch, pick, rub	26·3	18·2	27·6	27·9
General movement and shifting	23·1	4·4	48·2	24·3
Nod yes	4·6	56·5	21·3	18·5
Smile	33·4	8·3	36·1	22·3
Talk	7·4	60·1	19·9	12·5
Smoke	36·5	12·2	10·2	41·1

Table 2. Percentage of variance accounted for by persons and situations (Moos, 1969). (The last column refers to variation between different occasions of observation.)

This general pattern of results has been confirmed by a series of studies of different populations, and using different variables (Bowers, 1973). The overall results are very clear: situations are at least as important as persons, and P × S interaction is more important than either. If overt, as opposed to self-reported, behaviour is studied, the weight of situational factors is greater. It is now recognized that this kind of research cannot establish whether personality or situation is more important, for various reasons (Argyle, 1976). Nevertheless, the results clearly favour the interactionist position.

In order to predict how a particular person will behave in a particular situation, we need to know something else – the equation showing how P and S interact, which is of the general form

$$B = f(P, S)$$

This states that the amount of some form of behaviour is a

mathematical function of personality and situation variables. Such equations can be given by graphs showing how behaviour is a function of person and situation. Below is an example, from a study of reactions to role conflict (see p. 173f.): notice that only people with high neurotic anxiety are affected by role conflict.

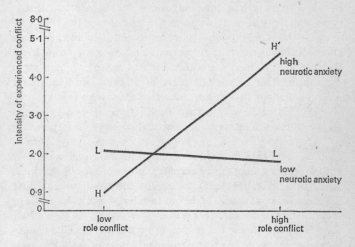

Figure 17. Effect of role conflict and neurotic anxiety on intensity of experienced conflict (Kahn *et al.*, 1964).

Notice also that experienced conflict is greater when actual role conflict is high (situation), and for people with high neurotic anxiety (personality), but is most affected by an interaction between the two (P × S).

Is it not the case that some people are more consistent across situations than others, so that there are at least some individuals for whom the trait model works? Mental patients, perhaps surprisingly, are found to be *more* consistent. Moos (1968), for example, studied twenty-two patients and ten staff in nine situations in the hospital, observing five aspects of their behaviour. The percentages of P, S and P × S variance for patients and staff are shown below:

Source	Patient	Staff
Persons	30·0	6·8
Situations	1·7	12·6
Persons × Situations	17·0	25·4

People who are high in 'internal control' (p. 123) are more resist-ant to social pressures to conform to social norms, and therefore in some ways tend to be more consistent. Patients are less affected by situations than normals, and are therefore more 'consistent'. Women are somewhat less consistent than men, thus confirming an ancient piece of folklore. And we found recently that the British are more consistent than the Japanese (Argyle, Shimoda and Little, 1978), mainly because of the elaborate rules of etiquette for particular situations in Japan.

Limitations of the interactionist model. This model has a number of limitations arising out of certain features of social behaviour. In the first place, people do not usually enter situations because psychologists put them there, but because they choose to enter them, and their choice reflects their personality. An example of choosing situations is the choice of occupation: people choose jobs where they can be creative, help others, or make money, and this reflects their pattern of interests and values (Argyle, 1972). Authoritarian students at American universities often leave to join military academies.

When a person has chosen a situation or a series of situations in this way, it also affects his personality. Runyan (1976) has shown how the stages through which a person becomes a drug addict can be traced as a series of choices of situations, each of which has implications for the next condition of the personality. For instance, at the period of regular use, the drug is readily available, most friends are drug users, and the desire for the drug is intense. Each step that is taken creates a quite new $P \times S$ equation, by changing the situation, and eventually changing the state of the personality. It is possible to anticipate such changes, or to bring them about deliberately, by commit-ting oneself to a series of situational experiences, such as going to one kind of educational establishment or another, one kind of job or another, or a course of encounter group meetings.

A second problem is that as well as choosing situations, people can change them once they are there. Some people turn every situation into a party, or try to. Informal situations, where a wide range of behaviour is permitted, can be modified, or 're-defined', quite a lot in this way; more formal situations cannot be changed much. Very often, individuals are not aware of the extent of their impact on others. They think that they are con-stantly encountering others who are bad-tempered, shy, or very friendly, for example, without realizing that they them-selves are the real cause of this behaviour (Wachtel, 1973). We will discuss below the problems of predicting the behaviour of two people in combination.

Another limitation of the interactionist model is that it can deal only with behaviour which occurs in much the same form in a range of situations – like anxiety, and amount of talk or gaze. However, we may want to predict individual differences in behaviour which is more or less unique to a situation, such as be-haviour at an auction sale, an encounter group, or in church. It is possible to use very general categories, so that both a bid at an auction and a sermon are classified as 'utterances', or 'sug-gestions', but this does not take us to the heart of the behaviour in question. I believe that each situation generates its own special class of social acts, and that for some purposes, each situation or group of situations has to be treated separately.

THE MAIN FEATURES OF PERSONS

There is no question of denying the existence of personality – everyone has a distinct biography, and relatively stable under-lying properties, some of them physiological, which generate distinctive behaviour in every situation which he enters – but they generate a very wide range of behaviour in different situ-ations. When familiar personality variables are mentioned in this section, it should be understood that they operate in con-junction with properties of situations, including the properties of others present. There are many features of persons which affect their behaviour on certain occasions, but the following have frequently been found to be important.

1. *Motivation*. Several kinds of motivation were described in Chapter 1; here we will mention the motivation to establish friendly, dominant and related kinds of relationship. If a person is high in affiliative motivation for example, he will seek out situations where it can be gratified; when he is in a suitable situation this need system will become aroused, and he will try to establish warm and intimate relationships. To simplify things, a person's motivations can be expressed in terms of the two dimensions, *friendly–hostile* and *dominant–submissive* (see p. 99).

2. *Biological core*. Research on personality has consistently yielded the two dimensions: Introversion – Extraversion, and Neuroticism (or Anxiety) – Stability. These dimensions are partly inherited, and are related to physique and to the way the brain functions (Eysenck and Eysenck, 1969). They have a general though relatively small effect on social performance. For example, extraverts talk and look more, while neurotics are more nervous and ill at ease in social encounters.

3. *Intelligence and other abilities*. Intelligent people are more likely to become leaders of groups of children or students but not of groups of delinquents or anti-school cliques. This depends on the situation, in that the individual with the greatest ability at the group task is most likely to become the leader. If the task changes, the leader may change also: for example, delinquent gangs have different leaders when playing football than when being delinquent. Intelligence fits the earlier trait model quite well, since if A is more intelligent than B, we know that A will do better at a wide range of tasks – but there is usually *something* that B can do better, through possessing special abilities.

4. *Demographic variables*. Age, sex, class and race affect behaviour in two quite different ways. In the first place, older

people really are different from younger ones in a number of measurable respects, and their social behaviour is different. The same is true of males and females, and members of different social classes – though most of these differences are learnt aspects of sub-cultures, like having different accents and attitudes. In addition, males and females, and the old and the young, occupy different positions in society, and others treat them differently.

5. *Physique and appearance* also affect social behaviour in two ways. Correlations have been found between physique and temperament – muscular individuals tend to be aggressive and extraverted, thin people to be tense and intelligent, fat people to be placid and happy (Parnell, 1958). And as we have seen, tall men and attractive girls are reacted to by others in special ways (p. 110f.).

6. *Cognitive structure.* We have seen that individuals perceive and interpret events in accordance with their system of cognitive categories; different ways of labelling and interpreting events lead to different patterns of behaviour. Attitudes, beliefs, and ideology represent larger systems of interpretation of events. They include values, and the broader goals which an individual considers worthwhile – medical, moral, aesthetic, political or religious, for example.

7. *Situation-linked features of persons.* One way of describing persons is to list the situations which they most enjoy or spend most time in. Joan is happiest in church, museums and libraries, and is clearly different from George, who prefers pubs, noisy parties and football grounds. It is also interesting to know the range of situations a person avoids or finds difficult (p. 77).

We can find out how an individual groups situations. Argyle and Little (1972) studied how a number of subjects reported their behaviour with each of twelve others, for eighteen dimensions of behaviour. The results for one person, after statistical analysis, are shown in Fig. 18.

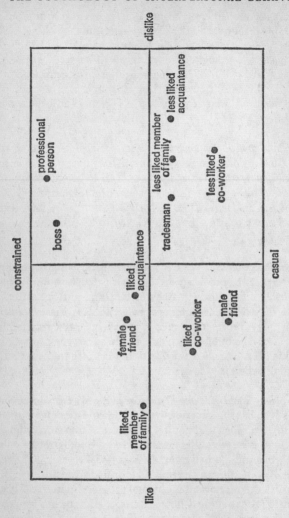

Figure 18. Social behaviour in different relationships (Argyle and Little, 1972).

It can be seen that this person, an apprentice, had five main styles of behaviour, which he used for different groups of people.

We said above that persons high in 'internal control' are more resistant to situational pressures. This dimension of personality can be measured by a questionnaire which asks how much an individual feels that he can control what happens in situations, as opposed to the effects of chance or other people. Persons high in internal control are found to be less affected by social pressures, though they are influenced by reasoned arguments; they engage in more cognitive activity, such as being alert, asking questions and trying to find out about situations. They will stick to their beliefs and values, but do not necessarily display the same social behaviour in different situations; coping successfully with a situation may require social moves which are specific to that situation. Thus mental patients are found to be *more* consistent and more externally controlled (Phares, 1976).

The seven areas of personality listed above provide a lot of information which is relevant to social behaviour, and numerous studies have shown that social performance can be predicted from them. We have said nothing about the internal 'dynamics' of persons, that is, their motivational conflicts and the ways they are resolved; these must affect social behaviour too, in ways mainly unknown. I shall discuss one area of personality dynamics in Chapter 9, in connection with the self-image.

THE ANALYSIS OF SITUATIONS

It is now clear that the situation is an important factor in the generation of social behaviour. We need to measure, classify, or otherwise analyse situations, in order to explain and predict the behaviour that occurs in them, in particular the behaviour of different personalities.

Classifying situations by behaviour. One way of classifying situations is in terms of the different kinds of behaviour that occur. For example, the main task or activity may consist of joint work, trading or negotiating, fighting, teaching, serving, self-disclosure, play, social activity, family life, or ceremonial.

Barker and Wright (1954) catalogued over 800 situations in a small town in Kansas on the basis of behaviour together with the environmental setting. But if we want to use the situation as one of the main causes of behaviour, it follows that we must describe situations in a way that does not include the behaviour itself. We also need more than a long list; we need dimensions or features of situations in general.

Physical measures of situations. Environmental psychologists sometimes assess situations in purely physical terms. It has been found, for example, that if people meet in a room at a temperature of 93·5°F, or with four square feet per person, they will like each other less than in a larger and cooler room (Griffitt and Veitch, 1971). However, the physical features of the environment work in another way, by their symbolic meaning. A room decorated in red and yellow suggests a warm emotional mood; placing some people at a greater height, as on a high table, suggests dominance; a room with a concrete floor, battered furniture and a bare light bulb suggests prison or interrogation – not love, work, social life, or committee work. In order to find out what the physical features of a situation mean to those present, we have to ask them – which takes us to:

The subjective analysis of situations. The latest approach is the use of multi-dimensional scaling, in which subjects rate the similarity of pairs of situations, as well as their scores on a number of marker scales, which are used to interpret the dimensions which are extracted. Myron Wish (1975) has found the following dimensions of situations, using this approach:

> cooperative – competitive
> friendly – hostile
> equal – unequal
> intense – superficial
> formal – informal
> social – task

There is some overlap between the dimensions – between the first two, for instance. These dimensions have been found in several studies, are obviously important, and correspond to familiar dimensions in social psychology. But they tell us only part of the story about situations. Take a particular combination – task, unequal, formal and intense: this includes a wide variety of situations which are quite different – religious confession, psychotherapy, selection interview, teaching, supervision of work, and so on. Each is quite different in terms of the goals of the participants, the behaviour that occurs, and the rules which must be followed. I would suggest that situations cannot entirely be reduced to dimensions (as in physics), but are in some ways more like the discrete discontinuous elements of chemistry, each with its own internal structure.

The analysis of situations into basic components. I want to outline a new approach to situations, which takes us further than physical measurements or subjective dimensions like friendly–hostile. It would be useful to be able to describe a situation in such a way that a newcomer to it, or a person who found it difficult to cope with, would know how to deal with it. Cricket and ice-hockey are special kinds of situations; a newcomer needs to be told certain things to understand what is going on. In order to actually play, he would need to acquire certain skills as well, and the same is true of other social situations. The basic components of situations are as follows:

1. *Elements of behaviour used.* In every game there are special moves, and in every social situation there is a particular range of social acts. This is partly because the same elements are used differently, for example giving orders on the parade ground and to a group of research workers; and it is partly because quite different kinds of behaviour are used – in church, discos, family meals, at the doctor's, and so on. This has been confirmed in several of our studies at Oxford in which we have established the repertoire of social behaviour for such situations. In addition, every situation has a characteristic repertoire of *episodes*, that is, longer periods of interaction which recur in a similar form. As we said before, the behaviour to be explained is itself a function of the situation.

2. *The motivation of participants.* Perhaps the most important feature of a situation as a cause of behaviour is the motivation of those present. The goals of different participants may be the same, e.g. making love, or different, e.g. buying and selling. Motivations may be complex: thus a salesman wants the customers to buy, but also wants them to be satisfied so that they will come again, and tell their friends. Often a whole range of motivations may be present – as at a dinner party for example. The only research methods we have for establishing this is the use of rating scales.

3. *Rules.* Two situations with exactly the same goals can have quite different rules. Buying and selling can be done by auction sale, by bargaining, as in an Arab market, or by self-selection, as in a supermarket. The social acts used are different in each case. Rules will be discussed further in the next chapter.

4. *Roles.* In most situations there are special roles which are specific to the situation, like the roles of doctor and patient, salesman and customer. The goals can be similar, but the rules may be different for those in different roles, like the chairman, secretary or treasurer of a club. There may be roles created by the situation, like those of guest and host, and also more general roles, like those of age and sex.

5. *Physical setting and equipment.* Games like football and hockey have similar goals and rules, but different equipment. The equipment makes certain social acts possible – like using the blackboard and showing slides. And the physical setting can suggest certain kinds of activity (e.g. teaching), as well as other aspects of social behaviour (e.g. formality, prestige, being up-to-date, different moods).

6. *Concepts.* In order to play cricket one must know the meaning of 'innings', 'over', 'out', and so on. In order to carry out psychotherapy one needs to know about 'resistance' and 'transference'. Probably the same is true of other social situations. As a chess player becomes more experienced, he acquires more

elaborate concepts, like 'fork', 'discovered check', and so on. Probably the same is true of social situations proper, and perhaps the kinds of concepts introduced in this book provide what is needed for many of them.

7. *Skills*. In order to actually play ice-hockey, to buy something at an auction sale, to be a committee member, or teach a lesson in school, it is necessary to master the skills involved and be able to use the repertoire of elements effectively (Argyle, 1976).

The seven components which we have listed give a fairly complete account of situations. They are not entirely independent, but form a system, so that one could be deduced from the others. These 'situations', like committees, and visiting the doctor, are not static, but are part of a continuously changing culture. On any particular occasion there has to be some agreement on the 'definition of the situation', and the precise form which it will take, or there will be chaos.

Selecting social behaviour to deal with the other. We have already seen that the same person varies his behaviour between different situations, with their different rules and conventions – parties, interviews, etc. People also vary their behaviour with the age, sex and social class of the other person, and with other role-relationships. Some people behave so differently towards men and women that they seem to undergo a personality change when moving from one kind of encounter to the other. A young man may be very relaxed with men, but terrified of women, or aggressive and competitive towards men and very amorous and at ease with women. Such differences of behaviour are learnt in the course of relations with parents, and later with male and female members of the peer group during adolescence. The effect of both sex and age are shown in a study by Block (1953). The nine members of a laboratory were asked to describe their manner of interaction with every other member, by placing a set of cards in order, with the cards best describing the interaction on top. The senior members of the department were reacted to as shown by the following cards: 'I am sarcastic to

him', 'I try to deceive him', 'I am ill at ease', and others indicating the erection of a self-protective shell in the presence of
people of higher status. On the other hand, behaviour towards
the female secretaries showed an easy 'acquaintanceship without
intimacy'. Some of the middle-ranking members were reacted
to as follows: 'I confide in him', 'I am sympathetic and warm to
him', 'I get angry at him'.

Age is a more differentiated variable than sex: some people
have different ways of behaving towards young children, older
children, teenagers, young adults, etc., with any number of fine
variations; others may use broader divisions, e.g. between those
who are older or younger than themselves.

Social class, especially in Britain, is an important dimension
for the classification of others for most people. Authoritarians in
particular treat those of greater or less status and power quite
differently – deferring to the one, and dominating the other. It
is found that salesgirls in retail stores categorize the customers
in terms of class, and feel nervous and apprehensive about the
upper-middle-class ones, because of the haughty manner they
are felt to adopt (Woodward, 1960). Social class, like age, is a
dimension which can be subdivided many times.

Social class and age each have two separate effects on the
social techniques adopted. Firstly there is the question of
whether the other person is higher or lower, secondly of how
great the social distance. There may be certain age or class
groups for which a person virtually has no social techniques at
all – he is simply unable to interact with members of them. This
can be observed for some adults in relation to children, some
upper-middle-class and working-class people to each other,
some adolescents in relation to adults, and many children in
relation to adults outside the family circle. This no doubt reflects a lack of experience with the groups in question, combined
with the discovery that the familiar social techniques are completely useless.

Different social skills are used for different personalities. One
of the main ways in which others are categorized here is *nice-
nasty*, or *warm–cold*, although, as we shall see, this is not so
much due to B's personality as to his relationship with A. The

warmth or coldness of another person can be seen from his manner, or it can be introduced experimentally in the experimental instructions, as in Kelley's experiment, in which people talked more to the supposedly 'warm' person (p. 95). If a person is seen as cold, not only is less affiliative behaviour shown towards him, but usually the whole style of behaviour is changed, in the direction of greater formality.

Introverts and extraverts need to be handled differently. Experiments with schoolchildren show that introverts respond better to praise, while extraverts respond better to blame: it may be felt that it would be unethical to use blame for extraverts on the strength of this finding, but at least it should be realized that blame is ineffective with introverts. Variation of motivation in others means that they will strive for different goals in social situations and can be rewarded in different ways. One may need a strong leader, another a submissive follower, a third needs acceptance of his self-image, and so on. For those very low in affiliative needs the usual social rewards will not be rewarding, and this will be true if the other person has no wish for affiliative relations with the performer.

Variations in anxiety, or neuroticism, mean that some people will be very ill at ease in social situations. When with them it is important to adopt social techniques which will reduce their anxiety (see p. 69). Experienced interviewers may spend a large part of an interview doing just this. Some methods of persuasion involve arousing anxiety and then suggesting ways of relieving it: for those who are anxious already this creates so much anxiety that they simply want to forget the whole affair.

Attitudes to authority and to the peer group are important. Juvenile delinquents are often very hostile to authority but behave quite differently with members of their peer group. Those in authority can only handle such boys and girls if they adopt the manner of an older member of the peer group, and make special efforts to win their confidence, such as taking them into their confidence, or granting special privileges. On the other hand, some children, and a few students, have a great reverence for authority, being strong in dependency: for them the mildest suggestion is enough to influence their behaviour.

WHO ADJUSTS TO WHOM?

What will happen when George meets Joan? George's behaviour depends on the situation, and the situation now includes Joan. However, the sample of Joan that will be present also depends on the situation, and therefore on George. We can get out of this in various ways. For example, it is found that what happens depends partly on the *relative* scores of those present. The *more* extraverted is very likely to speak first, to speak more, and to persuade the other to change his or her mind (Carment *et al.*, 1965). Other aspects of the outcome depend on the *similarity* of the two: they will like each other more if they have similar attitudes, interests and background (p. 150). They will be incompatible on the other hand if both want to dominate, or if one has strong needs for friendship and intimacy, and the other does not (Schutz, 1958). A and B size each other up in terms of their own private category systems, and select from their repertoire of social skills accordingly. It is almost certain that these two initial patterns of behaviour will not fit, and there will not be at the outset a state of equilibrium in the various senses described below. In addition it is very likely that one or both will find the other's behaviour not entirely satisfactory, in relation to his own need system. Both will be under some pressure to modify the state of affairs; they may change their own behaviour in order to synchronize better, or may attempt to change the other's behaviour. There is continual modification of behaviour until a state of equilibrium, more or less satisfactory to both parties, is arrived at. The interactors make use of reinforcement and other non-verbal signals.

To begin with a simple case, can we predict how much A and B will each talk when they meet? It is found that A's talkativeness is related, rather weakly, to his talkativeness in other similar situations; it is also *inversely* related to the normal talkativeness of B, i.e. a normally silent person talks more with silent people, a normally talkative person talks less with normally talkative people (Borgatta and Bales, 1953). Clearly people often have to shift from their average behaviour in order to accommodate to the other. But who will shift the most? There may be a 'struggle for the floor', in which they interrupt or try to shout each other down. When A does this he frustrates B; he may make B less friendly or even cause him to leave the situation. However, A can interrupt B safely under two conditions:

1. if A has sufficient power over B,
2. if A has sufficient skill to interrupt without upsetting B.

How can we predict the dominance relations between A and B? Dominance includes taking decisions, influencing the other, controlling the pattern of behaviour, as well as usually talking more. Simply measuring A's 'dominance' gives a rather poor prediction of his dominance in relation to B. A better prediction can be made from role variables: the person who is older, male rather than female, or of higher social class, is likely to be dominant (Breer, 1960) though the dominance of males seems to be diminishing. If these variables are held constant, the person with the highest score in a questionnaire measure of extraversion, intelligence and dominance, or who knows most about the task in hand, will dominate.

Let us consider a more complex prediction of both dominance and intimacy. We will take account of the motivations of A and B in the figure below. This shows that A is strong in both

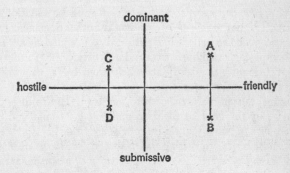

dominance and affiliative needs, and prefers to be in a warm and superior relation to others. B prefers a warm and submissive relation, so they would get on smoothly together. C and D are also in equilibrium – both are hostile, and C is slightly superior to D.

On the other hand, in the next diagram X and Y are not in equilibrium – X is friendly while Y is hostile, and both want to dominate. If Y is able to get more of his way than X, they might move to X′ Y′; if X gets more of his way than Y they might move to X″ Y″:

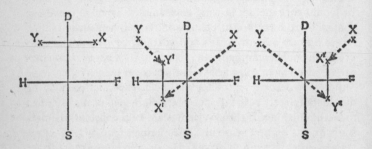

Let us take another case, where A and B play incompatible roles. For example an inexperienced interviewee thinks he has come for a pleasant chat, or to receive free vocational guidance. If one person adopts a certain role, it may force the other to adopt the complementary role that goes with it, particularly if the first person is powerful, and is in charge of the situation. If one person plays the role of interviewer the other person is more or less compelled to behave like a candidate. An interviewer can use other methods to modify a candidate's behaviour. The interviewer can modify the candidate's behaviour by (1) using non-verbal signals and reinforcements to control the candidate, (2) explaining the normal procedure, and (3) controlling the candidate by the content of his remarks, e.g. 'Could you tell me, *very briefly*, what you do in your spare time?'

It may be useful to distinguish between two levels of interaction here. There are the *alternative styles of behaviour* which A can adopt, and as we have seen people have quite a wide repertoire of such styles. At a more microscopic level are the *negotiating signals* used to communicate with B about the pattern of interaction or role-relationship to be adopted. For example an interviewer may use a verbal negotiating signal to explain the normal procedure to B. Or A may use non-verbal signals for dominance or friendship to modify B's behaviour.

When A is in charge he can use explicit, verbal negotiating signals about how he wants the other to behave. In most other situations such instructions would be unacceptable and ineffective – it is not usually possible to tell one's friends or colleagues to talk less or to be less dominating. Here non-verbal negotiating signals are normally used; they have the advantage that they are small and tentative, can be easily withdrawn, can be used to explore other possible relationships without embarrassment, and operate away from the focus of conscious attention of either party (cf. Mehrabian, 1969).

Sometimes the style of behaviour acts also as a negotiating signal. This happens if A firmly adopts a particular role, and pushes B into the complementary role ('altercasting'), as when a doctor behaves like a doctor so that the patient has to behave like a patient. Here is an example of someone *not* accepting the proffered role:

PLAYBOY: How do you get your kicks these days?

DYLAN: I hire people to look into my eyes, and then I have them kick me.

PLAYBOY: And that's the way you get your kicks?

DYLAN: No. Then I forgive them, that's where my kicks come in.

PLAYBOY: Did you ever have the standard boyhood dream of growing up to be President?

DYLAN: No. When I was a boy, Harry Truman was President. Who'd want to be Harry Truman?

PLAYBOY: Well, let's suppose that you were the President. What would you accomplish during your first thousand days?

DYLAN: Well, just for laughs so long as you insist, the first thing I'd do is probably move the White House. Instead of being in Texas it'd be in the East Side of New York, McGeorge Bundy would definitely have to change his name and General McNamara would be forced to wear a coonskin cap and shades.

[Brackman, 1967.]

How can we tell which person will have to adjust most in a

situation where the interaction styles of the two people are initially incompatible? There are a number of ways in which a person may acquire the power to control the way in which the interaction proceeds. (1) A may have formal power over B, so that he is able to deliver major rewards and punishments, as in the case of foremen or parents. (2) A may be less attracted towards the situation, and therefore less dependent on it, than B. This is the reason that performers in some situations avoid close friendships with those they have to deal with. (3) A can provide large rewards for B in that he can help B to attain some goal, whether social or otherwise. (4) If A for some reason is able to initiate the interaction, as in the case of waiters or salesmen, this gives him the chance to control the course of interaction. (5) If A is less sensitive than B to minor negative reactions from the other, or is less concerned about them, he will adjust his behaviour less. However, if he goes too far in ignoring B's responses and does not provide large enough rewards for B in compensation, B may simply withdraw.

It has been seen how everyone has a profile of motivation, so that certain drives are particularly strong, and certain goals will be sought in social situations. The more a person can succeed in establishing the pattern of behaviour which meets his needs, the more he will enjoy the situation; the more he has to move away from his preferred interaction pattern, the less he will like it. On the other hand there may be other compensatory rewards provided by a particular situation or person, in which case he will on balance still be drawn towards it or him, but in a conflictful way, generating internal tension.

FURTHER READING

Argyle, M., 'Personality and social behaviour', in Harré, R. (ed.), *Personality*, Oxford: Blackwell, 1976, pp 145–88.

Endler, N. S., and Magnusson, D. (eds.), *Interactional Psychology and Personality*, Washington: Hemisphere, 1976.

CHAPTER 7

TWO-PERSON RELATIONSHIPS

THE COORDINATION OF SOCIAL SKILLS

Two people may meet, each with his own social drives and his own social skills, but there will be no proper interaction unless the two sets of techniques mesh together in a synchronized and coordinated manner. If both talk all the time, if both shout orders or ask questions, to give three obvious cases, there cannot be said to be social interaction at all. Between such extreme cases, and a well-conducted interview or a conversation between friends, there are degrees of coordination of behaviour. Rather low on the scale for example would be conversation with a schizophrenic, with long pauses, irrelevant remarks and inappropriate emotions being expressed.

If A wants to use his favoured social skills, it is necessary for B to adopt a synchronizing set. This may involve behaving in a similar way to A, such as sharing his emotional state, or in a complementary way, such as being dominant while A is dependent. If A and B both produce their preferred skills, they will not find in general that there is a perfect fit: one or both therefore will have to charge their techniques so that there is better coordination. When they know each other well there will be excellent coordination, and getting to know a person better involves such improved coordination.

If A's and B's skills are not coordinated, neither set of techniques will be successful; in relation to affiliative needs the experience of clashing techniques is felt immediately to be particularly jarring and unpleasant. People usually attempt to correct this state of affairs at once by modifying their behaviour. If they cannot do so, as a result of having a limited repertoire, or through being unwilling to depart too far from their preferred skills, they will find the situation unrewarding, and leave it if they can. It is possible for a person to restrict his social contacts to people with whom he interacts easily. Two people may come to synchronize their social techniques by a period of gradual adjustment to one another, and may be helped by the existence of rules governing interaction, and in particular by rules of politeness and etiquette. Synchronization is necessary along a number of different dimensions for smooth and motivationally satisfying interaction to take place:

1. *Amount of speech.* In most conversations between two people, there is enough talk for nearly all of the time to be filled. If they speak more than this, there will be interruption and double-speaking; if they speak less than this, there will be periods of silence. When A has finished speaking, B should reply. The period of silence which can be tolerated before it is experienced as embarrassing depends on the situation and the general tempo of interaction. If interaction is smooth, then A speaks x per cent of the time, and B a little under (100–x) per cent of the time. As they will usually alternate, if A speaks more than B this is because his speeches are longer than B's. Details on how such-time-sharing is achieved are given on p. 70. The length and frequency of encounters is a quite different matter and, as will be seen below, is mainly a function of how rewarding each party finds them. However, this too is something on which they would have to synchronize their behaviour, as it takes two to make an encounter.

There also has to be synchronizing of the speed or tempo of interaction – the actual rate of speaking in words per second, the shortness of the interval before replying, and the rate of movements of eyes, facial expression and other parts of the body.

2. *Dominance* is partly a matter of who speaks most, partly of the degrees of deference with which A and B treat each other, of whose ideas are to be taken most seriously, and of who shall for purposes of the encounter be regarded as the more important person. If A and B both want to be the dominant member, there is incompatibility of styles – both may give orders, but none are obeyed. If A is really senior to B, but is not treated with sufficient deference, again there is disharmony: B is not

playing the necessary complementary role for A. 'If everyone is somebody, no-one is anybody'; for one person to have high status it is necessary to have enough people playing the supporting roles properly.

3. *Intimacy* we have discussed previously (p. 30) and shown to be a matter of physical closeness, eye-contact, conversation on personal topics, and so on. If A uses techniques corresponding to greater intimacy than B, A will feel that B is cold, formal, and stand-offish; B will feel that A is intrusive and over familiar. This immediate incongruity can only be overcome by the adoption of an intermediate position on the dimensions of intimacy, such as agreeing to an intermediate amount of spatial proximity and eye-contact. This will involve motivational costs to both A and B. Again, when we say that A adopts affiliative techniques, this means that he is seeking a certain pattern of response from the other. It is not enough to look B in the eye – B must look back with a friendly expression. However, the level of intimacy between two people is not fixed and may change during a single encounter, or over a series of encounters, as they come to like each other better – or vice versa.

4. *Emotional tone.* If A is elated and euphoric while B is anxious or depressed, there is incongruity. To everything that happens A and B are likely to react in quite different ways, involving incompatible reactions and remarks.

5. *Role-relations and definition of the situation.* Two people must agree on the role-relation between them. If one is to be a teacher the other must behave like a pupil, if one is to be an interviewer then the other must behave like an interviewee.

6. *Task, topic, and definition of the situation.* Two people must agree on what the encounter is for, just as two people must agree to play the same game, not different ones. They also have to agree on the different phases or episodes of the encounter (p. 147f.).

Unless two interactors can succeed in establishing these different forms of synchrony, interaction between them will be almost impossible, like a game where one person is playing croquet and the other is playing chess.

Once an equilibrium condition has been reached, can it ever be changed? It probably can, provided that this is a very gradual process, and provided that the others gain rather than lose in the satisfactions which they get from the relationship. Suppose that A talks thirty per cent of the time, B sixty-five per cent of the time, and that A wants to talk more. He can gradually increase the length of his speeches, or interrupt B, provided that what he says is sufficiently interesting, flattering, or otherwise rewarding for B. Suppose that A is dominated by B, and would like to turn the tables. He can gradually put forward stronger suggestions, and become more resistant to accepting B's, provided that the content of his suggestions is acceptable to B, or that he thinks of schemes which are to B's advantage.

INTERACTION SEQUENCES

We showed in Chapter 3 that each interactor's behaviour is like a motor skill. This analysis is very useful for situations where the person in question is in charge, like an interviewer or a psychotherapist. We shall now discuss situations where two people are both able to exercise some initiative.

First we must decide on a set of categories of social acts. The twelve categories devised by Bales (1950) are a good example. The first three and last three refer to 'socio-emotional' acts, the middle six to task behaviour. They are grouped in pairs, so that for example 8 (asks for opinion) often leads to 5 (gives opinion). Observers record interaction from behind a one-way screen, or from video-tape, on a special machine. However, as we showed in the last chapter, different social acts are used in different situations, so that different categories are needed for behaviour in the classroom, during psychotherapy, or elsewhere. Indeed, different sets of categories can be used in the same situation – there are over a hundred sets in existence for

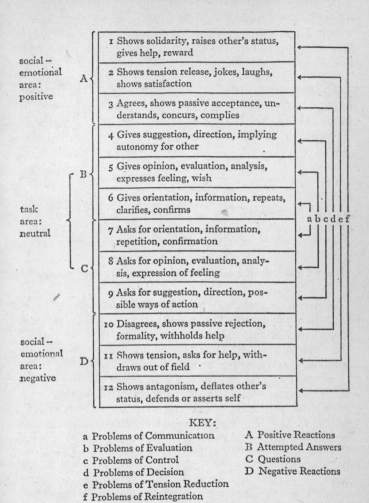

social – emotional area: positive — A

1 Shows solidarity, raises other's status, gives help, reward

2 Shows tension release, jokes, laughs, shows satisfaction

3 Agrees, shows passive acceptance, understands, concurs, complies

task area: neutral — B

4 Gives suggestion, direction, implying autonomy for other

5 Gives opinion, evaluation, analysis, expresses feeling, wish

6 Gives orientation, information, repeats, clarifies, confirms

— C

7 Asks for orientation, information, repetition, confirmation

8 Asks for opinion, evaluation, analysis, expression of feeling

9 Asks for suggestion, direction, possible ways of action

social – emotional area: negative — D

10 Disagrees, shows passive rejection, formality, withholds help

11 Shows tension, asks for help, withdraws out of field

12 Shows antagonism, deflates other's status, defends or asserts self

a b c d e f

KEY:
a Problems of Communication
b Problems of Evaluation
c Problems of Control
d Problems of Decision
e Problems of Tension Reduction
f Problems of Reintegration

A Positive Reactions
B Attempted Answers
C Questions
D Negative Reactions

Table 3. The Bales categories (Bales, 1950).

teaching alone (Simon and Boyer, 1974). Some include 'pupil initiation', or 'higher-order questions', while others do not; the only way to choose between them is to know which social acts are most important, and need to be emphasized in training, for example.

The next step is to find the sequences of social acts. This can be done by finding the probability of one kind of act leading to another, a so-called Markov chain. The basic layout is shown in Table 4.

		next act by B		
		1	2	3
last act by A	1	15	75	10
	2	20	15	65
	3	70	15	15

Table 4. Example of reactive Markov chain, with three categories.

This shows that when A produces social act type 1, this is followed in 15 per cent of cases by B using type 1, on 75 per cent of occasions he responds with type 2, and on 10 per cent of occasions with type 3. Type 1 might, for example, be asking a question, type 2 might be giving information, and type 3 giving an instruction. This is a 'reactive' sequence, showing how an act by one person leads to an act by another. It is also necessary to consider 'pro-active' sequences, where an act by A leads to another act by A: for example, a teacher comments on an answer by a child and then asks another question (Fig. 19).

There are a number of important two-step sequences, for instance:

    question→answer
    open-ended question→long answer
    smile, head-nod, etc.→smile, head-nod, etc. by other
    gives order or request→it is carried out
    is rude→is aggressive
    and so on.

In order to make the second move correctly in a two-step sequence, one needs to understand the first move. Rommetveit (1974) has shown how each utterance in a conversation takes for granted what has gone before and adds something to it. Two people must have some shared objects of attention, shared knowledge and shared concepts. Each utterance uses and adds to this shared material, as when I say, 'Professor Rommetveit did this research in Oslo.' Minsky (1975) has shown that to take part in a conversation at all, one must build up a mental picture of what the other has said; answering a question may be an example of a two-step sequence, but it can also be a very complex intellectual operation.

However, social behaviour cannot be put together from two-step sequences any more than sentences consist of pairs of words in the right order. How can longer sequences of social behaviour be discovered?

Sometimes the two-step links form repeated cycles. The

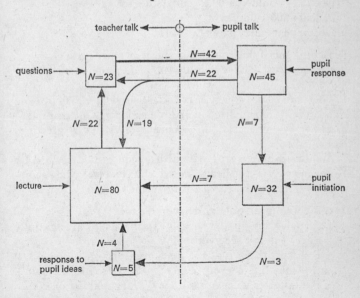

Figure 19. Cycles of interaction in the classroom (Flanders, 1970).

example in Table 4 shows such a cycle – categories 1–2–3 tend to repeat in that order. This is found in real situations. One of the most widely used sets of categories for social behaviour in the classroom is that of Flanders (1970), which has six categories for the teacher and four for the children.

A teacher might use the following different cycles:

    (a) Question(Teacher)→Answer(Pupil)
    (b) Lecture(T)→Question(T)→Answer(P)
    (c) Lecture (T)→Question (T)→Answer (P)→Question or other initiation(P)→response to P's idea(T).

A teacher might shift from one cycle to another, and part of social skill is to control such cycles.

We can link a social act to the last two moves, rather than just the last one – a 'second-order Markov chain' – for example:

Doctor: 'would you take your clothes off, please?'
Patient: takes clothes off.
Doctor: examines patient.

In fact the social skill model depends very much on such three-step sequences, with continuity of plans from move one to move three.

There are some sequences of social behaviour which become standardized, or ritualized, with little variation. One example is greeting. We described the sequence of events in greetings earlier (p. 49).

Another example is the 'remedial sequence' described by Goffman (1971) – the behaviour which takes place when someone has committed a social error of some kind:

    1. A commits error (e.g. steps on B's toe).
    2. A apologizes, gives excuse or explanation ('I'm frightfully sorry, I didn't see your foot').
    3. B accepts this ('It's O K, no damage done').
    4. A thanks B ('It's very good of you to be so nice about it').
    5. B minimizes what A has done ('Think nothing of it').

We have now described some rather different kinds of social

behaviour. It is useful to distinguish four kinds of interaction sequence, as in Figure 20.

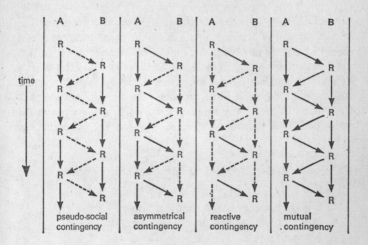

Figure 20. Classes of social interaction in terms of contingency (Jones and Gerard, 1967).

In the first kind, *pseudo-social*, the whole sequence is totally predictable, since neither interactor is really reacting to the other, except in timing. The ritualized sequences just described are like this, except that there is some variation and interaction. Formal ceremonies and acting in a play are better examples.

Reactive contingency is where each person reacts mainly to what the other person did last, as in a rambling conversation with no particular goal. This kind of sequence can be analysed as a 'first-order Markov chain'.

Asymmetrical contingency is where one person has a plan, and the other fits into it, as in teaching, interviewing, etc. The social skill model fits these situations quite well, except that it does not say anything about rules of sequence.

Mutual contingency is where each interactor has plans and exercises initiative, as in negotiation and discussion. This is the most difficult kind of sequence to analyse. We shall try to do so further by investigation of the rules of sequence, by taking account of the plans of both parties, and showing how these are integrated into a series of 'episodes'.

A successful interactor needs to be able to use the repertoire of social moves for whatever situation he is in; for example, a teacher needs to be able to ask higher-order questions. He also needs to know what leads to what, in order to control the other's behaviour, and how to set in motion various cycles of events. And he should behave in accordance with the appropriate contingencies; if he is the main performer in an asymmetrical encounter, he should be responsible for the direction of behaviour.

Rules of social interaction. Consider the following conversation:

A. No, bloody awful.
A. Well, what's been happening at home?
B. Did you have a good day at the office, dear?
B. Nothing much.
A. Hello.

It is easy to see that the interactors have not put their utterances in the right order. It follows that we have a good idea of the proper order for such remarks. David Clarke (1975) recorded and transcribed actual conversations, which were informal and apparently rambling; individual utterances were typed on cards and shuffled into random order; another group of subjects could put them back into more or less the right order – showing that we have some knowledge of the rules of sequence, even though we cannot state them very readily. The rules of grammar are like this – we follow them most of the time, and can recognize when other people make mistakes, but few of us could state the rules.

What are the rules of sequence for verbal utterances? They probably include the following:

1. An utterance by A should be responded to by B or C, without too much delay and without interruption.

2. B's response should be on the same subject, unless some explanation is given.

3. B should keep to the same social episode, e.g. interview, polite conversation, psychotherapy; or he should negotiate a change of episode.

4. People should not suddenly arrive or leave, or start a new activity, without appropriate greeting or farewell rituals.

If rule 3 was broken there would be conversations like:

A. Shall we deal with item 7 on the agenda now?
B. Have you heard the one about the Japanese rabbi?
C. The trouble is I get these terrible impulses to rape my sister.

Each of these belongs to different contexts, or to episodes in a

		possible following acts				
		1	2	3	4	5
Auctioneer	1. offers describes object			√	√	√
	2. states last bid			√	√	√
preceding act	3. closes sale	√				
Customer I	4. bids		√	√		√
Customer II	5. bids		√	√	√	

Table 5. Rules of sequence in auction sales.

developing situation; episodes will be discussed in the next section.

We have confined discussion so far to sequences of verbal utterances. Similar principles apply to social acts, consisting of non-verbal as well as verbal components, or of non-verbal elements alone. Bidding at an auction sale, for example, can be done verbally or non-verbally. The rules of sequence here are shown in Table 5. This is different from the Markov chain described earlier: here we are concerned with what is allowed, not with probabilities. We also need a three-step rule to prevent a customer bidding again after the auctioneer has stated last bid. Incidentally, there is another rule about auction sales – one should bid *more* than the last bidder, not less. Most situations have special rules of sequence–auction sales, psychoanalysis, at the pub, and so on. Auction sales are rather formal situations; informal situations could be defined as occasions where a wide range of behaviour is possible. Price and Bouffard (1974) found that the most formal situations were church services and job interviews, the least formal were being in one's own room or in a park.

Games, like cricket and tennis, have rules; unless all the players keep to the rules, there can be no game. Here the players do know the rules, but it would be very difficult for a research worker to find out what the rules are by observing the sequence of play. How can the rules of games, grammar or social behaviour be found out? Garfinkel (1963) introduced the method of experimental rule-breaking, for example, putting the noughts and crosses on the lines instead of in the spaces. We have surveyed reactions to hypothetical rule-breaking, and found that some rules are intrinsic to social situations: for example, candidates at an interview should answer rather than ask the questions, and should speak a language known to the interviewer. Rules of sequence can be studied by asking people what social moves can and cannot follow other moves, and why. Studies have been made of individuals who have been socially mobile (changing social class, changing sex) who have become forcibly aware of a new set of rules.

Rules are not true or false, like empirical laws, but describe the cultural conventions of a particular group. Some of these conventions are, however, essential to situations, as we have seen. Rules are established in social groups, and change with time: Mann (1970) has analysed the rules governing all-night football queues in Australia, e.g. how much time off is allowed.

Unskilled performers often break the rules of social behaviour, generally through ignorance of them. For example, many candidates at selection interviews try to ask the questions, or try to elicit free vocational guidance or psychotherapy (p. 237). Others have difficulties at parties through not knowing what the rules are.

To study a game or a social situation we need to find the rules. But rules are only part of the story – there is also play within the rules. To predict the course of events in a game, we need to know how hard each person is trying to win (plans), and also the skills and the strategies used by each player. There is cooperation over keeping to the rules, even in boxing and management–union bargaining, and there is often competition within the rules, whereby each person is pursuing his particular goals (Collett, 1977).

Social episodes. The stream of social behaviour can be divided up into episodes, during which a particular kind of action is taking place. The episodes of a church service or a dinner party are fairly obvious. A selection interview has four fairly clear episodes – greetings and introduction, interviewer asks questions, candidate is invited to ask questions, ending and farewell. The second part of an interview might be divided into the different areas of questioning – school career, previous jobs, etc. The division of an encounter into episodes can be made by showing a video-tape and asking observers to indicate where they think the main periods of action start and stop (see p. 102). Episodes differ in the main activity, topic of conversation, environmental setting or spatial arrangement, and so on. They also differ in characteristic sequence of events. Figure 19 showed several different cycles of classroom interaction, which would constitute different episodes. Other episodes are one-off affairs, with no repetition, such as greetings and the 'remedial sequence' described above.

How does an episode start? Sometimes it is part of a familiar sequence of events, which may be written down somewhere – like committee agendas and church services. Sometimes there is a person in charge who can decide on the next episode; a teacher, for example, can introduce the next part of a lesson by saying, 'Now we are going to start on fractions.' Sometimes an episode change can be made non-verbally, as when a hostess rises from the table, or an interviewer gathers his papers together, puts his spectacles on and starts to look businesslike. In less formal situations anyone can try to introduce a new episode, but it has to be negotiated and agreed to by the others. Someone might start serious discussion of politics at a party, but the others reject this and go back to gossip or golf.

How do episodes end? If there are repeated cycles, when do they stop? Clearly there is more to episodes than going round in circles: episodes are also goal-directed, and when the goal has been reached, the episode ends. An interviewer plans to find out a certain amount about the candidate's school career, and when that has been done moves on to the next topic. Another factor is time, and there are usually conventions about how long certain episodes should last.

There are grounds for thinking that episodes are the fundamental unit of social behaviour. Study of children's play shows that the earliest social behaviour of infants consists of repeated cycles of smiling, looking and vocalizing, in which the behaviour of infant and mother is closely coordinated (p. 27). Older children between the ages of three and five spend a lot of time in fantasy play, in which they enact such typical episodes from adult life as going to the doctor's, shopping, and getting rid of monsters (Garvey, 1974).

FRIENDSHIP AND LOVE

These are two of the most important social relationships: failure in them is a source of great distress, and so this is one of the main areas of social skills training. The conditions under which people come to like or to love one another have been the object of extensive research, and are now well understood.

Friendship

Frequency of interaction. The more two people meet, the more polarized their attitudes to one another become, but usually they like one another more. Frequent interaction can come about from living in adjacent rooms or houses, working in the same office, belonging to the same club, and so on. So interaction leads to liking, but liking leads to more interaction; in other words, a positive feedback cycle is started, which is halted by competing attractions, and the increasing difficulties of accommodation with greater intimacy – like two hedgehogs trying to keep warm. Only certain kinds of interaction lead to liking, as has been shown in research on inter-racial contacts. Two people should be of equal status, and should be members of the same group, cooperating in the pursuit of the same goals.

Reinforcement. The next general principle governing liking is the extent to which one person satisfies the needs of another. This was shown in a study by Jennings of four hundred girls in a reformatory (1950). She found that the popular girls helped and protected others, encouraged, cheered them up, made them feel accepted and wanted, controlled their own moods so as not to inflict anxiety or depression on others, were able to establish rapport quickly, won the confidence of a wide variety of other personalities, and were concerned with the feelings and needs of others. The unpopular girls on the other hand were dominating, aggressive, boastful, demanded attention, and tried to get others to do things for them. This pattern has been generally interpreted in terms of the popular girls providing rewards and minimizing costs, while the unpopular girls tried to get rewards for themselves, and incurred costs for others. It is not necessary for the other person to be the actual source of rewards: Lott and Lott (1960) found that children who were given model cars by the experimenter liked the other children in the experiment more.

Being liked is a powerful reward, so if A likes B, B will usually like A. This is particularly important for those who have a great need to be liked, such as individuals with low self-esteem.

Similarity. People like others who are similar to themselves – in certain respects. They like those with similar attitudes, beliefs and values, who have a similar regional and social class background, who have similar jobs or leisure interests – but they need not have similar personalities. Again there is a cyclical process, since similarity leads to liking, and liking leads to similarity. The effects of similarity on liking have been shown experimentally; for example, Griffitt and Veitch (1974) paid thirteen male subjects to spend ten days in a fall-out shelter, and found that those with similar opinions liked each other most by the end of the ten days. Similarity in attitudes which are important to those concerned has most effect. Steven Duck (1973) has produced evidence that similarity of cognitive constructs is important, i.e. the categories used for describing other people (p. 105f.). As far as other aspects of personality are concerned, it now seems that neither similarity nor complementarity have much effect on friendship.

Emotional state of the chooser. It doesn't only depend on what the other person, B, does. A wants to be able to talk, do things for B, and generally express his personality when with B. If B starts by being nasty and becomes nicer, A likes him more than if B had been nice all the time. Teachers used to be advised: 'Never smile before Christmas.' This so-called 'gain–loss effect' does not affect observers of the interaction, and so must be due to a change in A's emotional state (Clore *et al.*, 1975). In other experiments it has been found that having similar attitudes only worked if subjects were at a sufficiently high level of arousal (Clore and Gormly, 1974). The most dramatic cases of inter-racial attitudes being improved have occurred under conditions of high arousal, such as fighting side-by-side, and serving on ships together.

Stages of friendship. A's liking for B, and his wish to form a relationship, are first signalled non-verbally – by smiling, gaze, proximity and the rest (p. 50). He also expresses interest in the other verbally, and information is exchanged. This leads to suggestions of further meetings, which may develop into regular meetings. As they get to know and like each other more, they spend more time together, they trust one another more and discuss more intimate matters. Self-disclosure can be measured on a scale (1–5) with items like:

What are your favourite forms of erotic play and sexual lovemaking? (scale value 2·56)

What are the circumstances under which you become depressed and when your feelings are hurt? (3·51)

What are your hobbies, how do you best like to spend your spare time? (4·98)

(Jourard, 1971)

Taylor (1965) studied pairs of students who shared rooms at college. The amount of self-disclosure increased during the first nine weeks and then levelled off – but at quite different degrees of intimacy for different pairs (see Fig. 21). The main increase was at the most superficial level; there was not much increase of disclosure about intimate matters and basic values. Other studies show that intimate disclosure is increased when two people are isolated, and that if A discloses to B, B will disclose to A. Great disclosure is possible when people come to 'trust' each other more – they know that the other will not laugh at or reject the revealer, nor pass it on to others, nor use it to his own advantage (Naegele, 1958).

There is usually 'reciprocity' between friends and colleagues, that is, if A does something for B, B will later perform some equivalent act for A. Berkowitz (1968) has shown that A is more likely to help B if B has recently helped A; in another study it was found that such reciprocation was more likely if the first person had helped of his own free will. Within working groups it is common for help to be given and reciprocated between certain pairs of people. In primitive societies the exchange of gifts can be an important part of the economic system. However, as people come to know each other better, and between members of a family, they will come to help each other, and provide each other with gifts, without thought of later reciprocity – this has been described as 'altruistic' reciprocity,

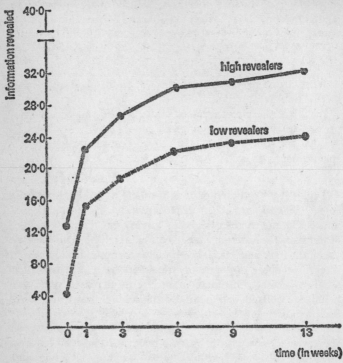

Figure 21. Amount of disclosure over time of high- and low-revealers
(Taylor, 1965).

and appears to be a characteristic part of an intimate relationship
(Sahlins, 1965).

The most common complaint of those who seek social skills
training is difficulty in making friends. Some of them say they
have never had a friend in their lives. What advice can we offer,
on the basis of research on friendship?

1. As we showed in Chapter 2, social relations are negotiated
mainly by non-verbal signals. Clients for social skills training
who cannot make friends are usually found to be very inex-
pressive, in face and voice.

2. Rewardingness is most important. The same clients usually

appear to be very unrewarding, and are not really interested in other people.

3. Frequent interaction with those of similar interests and attitudes can be found in clubs for professional or leisure activities, in political and religious groups, and so on.

Love

Loving is not the same as liking, though it includes it. Love usually involves sexual attraction, is more intense than liking, shows a rapid build-up, and later declines rather than increasing slowly; there is a great need for the other and a caring for him or her, and a high level of intimacy and disclosure. Its presence can be measured by questionnaires like Rubin's (1973) with items such as:

I would do almost anything for . . .
If I could never be with . . . I would feel miserable.

The best available theory of love is a version of the two-factor theory of emotions (p. 22f.). To be in love is the combination of a high level of arousal and labelling or interpreting it as 'being in love' as defined by the culture (Berscheid and Walster, 1974b). Several experiments show that heightened arousal of various kinds leads to love. Dutton and Aron (1974) arranged for an attractive girl to stop young men in the middle of a high and dangerously swaying suspension bridge in Vancouver; 50 per cent of them accepted her invitation to phone her to hear more about the experiment, compared with 13 per cent for those from a very low bridge. (I have been to that bridge, and noted that not everyone will go over it; perhaps those daring enough to cross the bridge are also more willing to phone strange girls.)

The nature of the love relationship varies between different cultures and historical periods; young people learn how they are supposed to feel and behave. Traditionally there are two public rituals – engagement and marriage – which publicly proclaim the stages in the relationship, and result in others treating the couple in a new way. The effect of cognitive labelling is shown in a study by Rubin (op. cit.) who found that couples who accepted the love mythology fell more rapidly in love than those who didn't. He also found that married couples had a more realistic view of love. People often try to find out, for example by writing to women's magazines, if they are 'really in love'. On the present theory there is no difference between love and infatuation, except perhaps that infatuation is what love is called when it is over.

A number of experiments have tried to find out what makes people fall in love. Physical attractiveness is most important, particularly in the early stages (p. 109f.). Parental interference tends to strengthen attraction – the 'Romeo and Juliet' effect. Playing hard to get doesn't work very well, but those who seem to be hard for others to get are found attractive. People high in internal control are less likely to fall in love. And the variables discussed for friendship also affect love – similar attitudes, being liked, and so on.

Love goes through a number of stages. As we have seen, sexual attraction is signalled by non-verbal cues – facial expression, gaze, etc. – as for friendship, but also including touch and pupil dilation. The process of falling in love is probably due to massive reinforcements, and a sudden upward surge of interaction and liking. This makes increased demands for synchronizing and mutual adjustment, and inevitably the scope for conflict and disagreement is greatly increased – while each partner is also very dependent on the other for rewards received. This has the properties of an approach–avoidance conflict and would be expected to lead to an oscillation of intimacy–withdrawal, until smoother synchronizing is attained. The periods of the engagement and honeymoon appear to be designed to help this process to happen. It is interesting that in the U.S.A. honeymoons are often found stressful, and that honeymoon couples often seek out the company of other such couples and return home earlier than planned (Rapoport and Rapoport, 1964).

ASSERTIVENESS AND SOCIAL INFLUENCE

'How to make friends and influence people' are two classical social problems, and we now come to the second. In America, social skills training has concentrated on 'assertion therapy' – how to deal with laundries who lose shirts, garages who charge too much, and, for men, girls who have some resistance to being dated. In Britain we have been less eager to train everyone in assertiveness. However, it is important in many relationships – no-one wants to have to do what the other wants all the time, and would probably abandon the relationship if they did. We have sometimes trained quiet people who had found difficulty in controlling forty children in a school classroom. Social influence is easier for the person of high power or status, but this may not be sufficient, as the last example shows.

Verbal requests usually lie at the heart of social influence: if you want someone to do something, you have to ask them. There is considerable skill in choosing the right words, the ones which will be acceptable and successful. Not 'Post this letter', but 'Would you mind posting this letter, if you are passing a pillar-box?' – or whatever is the local form of words for a polite request. Social influence is usually achieved by a combination of assertive and rewarding behaviour, and the combination generates a special style of social behaviour, as Table 6 shows.

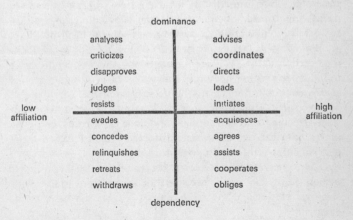

Table 6. Combinations of dominant and affiliative techniques (Gough, 1957).

It is the top right-hand corner, warm and dominant, which is most effective. One of the keys to successful leadership is consultation; it is found that people act with more enthusiasm if they have been consulted and have helped to make a decision. This principle applies to all face-to-face social influence, and means that the other person has to be persuaded and agree with what he is to do.

Non-verbal signals. Requests need to be made in a sufficiently assertive manner. We discussed these non-verbal cues earlier – talking loudly and most of the time in a confident tone of voice, interrupting others, adopting an attentive but unsmiling facial expression, and an erect posture with the head tilted back, shoulders squared and hands on hips. For most situations rather small amounts of these signals will be enough, and again these social techniques must be combined with sufficient warmth and rewardingness to keep the other in the situation. There is a clear difference between assertive and aggressive behaviour: aggressive behaviour may or may not produce the desired influence, but it also damages the relationship.

Reinforcement. It is possible to influence another's behaviour in the immediate situation by systematic rewarding of the desired behaviour immediately it takes place, and non-reward or punishment of other behaviour. Rewards based on the need for affiliation include smiling, looking, agreement, head-nodding, etc. Punishment could consist of frowning, looking away, looking bored, looking at a watch, disagreeing, etc. It may be easier to influence another person in this way if he is of higher status, so that direct influence might be inappropriate. Members of groups often conform because they want to be accepted rather than rejected. Endler (1965) found that conformity could be increased if the experimenter reinforced it, and reduced if the experimenter reinforced nonconformity.

Using the personal relationship. It is easier to influence another person if they like you – because they do not want to lose your approval or damage the relationship. This is the basis of ingratiation.

Reciprocation of favours is similar. If A does something for B first, B is more likely to do what A asks. Regan (1971) found that subjects bought twice as many raffle tickets from a confederate who had previously bought them a Coke, compared with other confederates. This kind of reciprocity or exchange of gifts plays an even more important part in African countries, where officials often have to be bribed (as we call it) before they will be helpful.

Persuasion. The design of persuasive messages has been studied most in connection with the mass media, but some of the principles apply in face-to-face situations. It is necessary to appeal to the needs, values or interests of the other in some way, and then show that what you want him to do will satisfy one of those needs: 'Come and do the washing-up while I change, then we will be able to go out to the pub earlier'; 'If you do some work during the holidays, you'll get better A levels and be more likely to get into University.' This may require some initial exploration of what the other does want, as when a salesman tries to find out the customer's needs. The objections to the behaviour being requested may be neutralized, by appealing to higher loyalties, denying that injury will result, or other ways of changing the way the act or the situation is perceived (Sykes and Matza, 1957): 'It's nothing, just a matter of taking a small present to a friend of mine in Amsterdam.' Moral exhortation on the other hand is no good if the exhorter is seen not to be behaving in this way himself (Bryan and Walbek, 1970). The very words used can create certain assumptions or ways of defining the problem – politicians may manage to make the public think primarily in terms of unemployment and the problems of social inequality, or alternatively of national prosperity and the creation of collective wealth. Similarly, face-to-face persuasion may be achieved by using the right rhetoric, making the other think in terms of your concepts.

Power. Persuasion is more effective if the source of it is regarded as an expert – on university entrance, to take the earlier example. There are other kinds of power, such as the power to reward and punish, possessed by most formal leaders. This makes influence easier, particularly if the influencer is thought to be a *legitimate* source of directions, in view of his ability, experience, or his sheer rank in a hierarchy. In the well-known experiments by Milgram (1974) it was found that 65 per cent of subjects gave what they thought were 450-volt shocks to what they thought were other subjects, who gave signs of intense suffering and apparent collapse, because the experimenter ordered them to do so as part of a learning experiment. The most likely interpretation is that subjects assumed that the experimenter was in charge and knew what he was doing, therefore it was all right to do what he said. The experiment shows the very high degree of obedience which can be commanded by a legitimate leader, with no power to reward or punish.

Bargaining and negotiating is a complex process, where each contestant tries to get the best outcome for himself. While haggling over the price of carpets in oriental bazaars is the prototype of bargaining, there is a sense in which all social encounters are like this, as was seen above. Each person wants to get the most out of the situation, in the sense that he wants to satisfy his interpersonal needs: he can't get quite what he wants because the other may leave if *his* wants are not met. The typical procedure is for each person to put forward his proposals, for example about the selling-price of a car or house, a proposed salary, or more domestic issues. There are then a series of concessions, each person matching the other's, until an agreement is reached, or there is joint problem-solving to find a solution which will make both happy. One side can do better under the following conditions: not being in a hurry to reach a decision, starting with a high 'target' (e.g. high price for the seller), having a high limit (e.g. high minimum price), and making concessions slowly. It has been found in experiments by Morley and Stephenson (1977) and others that if management–union type negotiations are conducted over the telephone, the person with objectively the strongest case wins; if it is done face-to-face, the other side may win (see p. 85). Sometimes there are strong pressures to reach *some* agreement. The two sides then try harder to reconcile their different needs, they explore a number of different solutions, and may exchange information about how much they stand to gain from each.

Persuasive strategies. By a 'strategy', I mean a planned sequence of at least two moves. These may be conscious and deliberate, as in some sales techniques, but they may also be acquired and used with little conscious awareness of what is being done. Interviewers commonly ask questions in a carefully prepared order; the more intimate ones come last, the most harmless ones first. A salesman may offer the most expensive objects first, and then produce cheaper ones, depending on the customer's reaction. This is similar to starting negotiations with exaggerated claims, with the intention of making concessions and extracting reciprocal concessions from the other party; this doesn't work if the initial demands are seen as bluffing. The foot-in-the-door technique consists of making a small request which is followed by a larger one. Freedman and Fraser (1966) found that if housewives had been asked to answer a few questions earlier, 53 per cent agreed to allow a survey team into their houses for two hours, compared with 22 per cent who had not been asked those questions.

FURTHER READING

Argyle, M., *Social Interaction*, London: Methuen, 1969.
Clore, G. L., 'Interpersonal attraction: an overview', in J. W. Thibaut, J. T. Spence and R. C. Carson (eds.), *Contemporary Topics in Social Psychology*, Morristown, N.J.: General Learning Press, 1976.
Goffman, E., *Relations in Public*, London: Allen Lane The Penguin Press, 1971.

CHAPTER 8

GROUPS, ORGANIZATION AND CULTURE

IN the previous chapters, problems of social interaction have been simplified by concentrating on encounters between two people. In this chapter, social situations involving more than two people will be considered. First, interaction may take place between members of small social groups with three, four, or more members. Second, there may be differences of power, status or role in social organizations. Third, people are steeped in a cultural and social class background, which prescribes the verbal and non-verbal means of communication, as well as the rules governing behaviour in different situations.

MEMBERSHIP OF SMALL SOCIAL GROUPS

We have seen that most animals live in groups; many human activities are also carried out in groups between three and fifteen in size. There are several rather different kinds of small group – families, work-teams, committees, groups of friends, social clubs, etc. Some processes of social interaction are similar in all kinds of group – all form norms and have leaders; on the other hand there are distinctive forms of social behaviour in each kind of group. Much research on small groups has taken the form of laboratory experiments – these have the advantage of being able to test hypotheses rigorously – but they tend to omit important features of real-life groups, and are stripped down to those elements of group life which the experimenter knows about already.

People may form or join a group primarily to carry out a task, play a game or pursue some leisure activity, or because they like the other people, and want to interact with them. All groups have these two sides to them – task and sociable motivations and activities, though the balance varies. People often join a group for economic or other non-social reasons in the first place; they then become involved in group activities, find these satisfying, and become attached to the group. A group of friends may want to enjoy each other's company, but they have to do something, i.e. a task must be devised.

The social behaviour in groups can be divided up as follows:

	TASK	SOCIABLE
VERBAL	Information and discussion related to the task.	Gossip and chat, jokes and games, discussion of personal problems.
NON-VERBAL	Task performance, help, NV comments on performance, NV signals conveying information.	Communicating interpersonal attitudes, emotions, self-presentation.

Group Formation. Different kinds of group come together in different ways – friendship groups through mutual attraction, leisure groups through shared interests, work-groups are brought together under a leader, and so on. Observers of groups report that they usually go through a number of developmental stages:

1. *Forming* – anxiety, dependence on leader (if any), members find out about the task, rules and nature of the situation.

2. *Rebellion* – conflict between individuals and sub-groups, rebellion against leader, resistance to rules and demands of task.

3. *Norming* – development of stable group structure, with social norms, conflicts are resolved, cohesiveness develops.

4. *Cooperation* – interpersonal problems are solved, the group turn to constructive solution of problems, energy is directed to the task (Tuckman, 1965).

As in dyads (groups of two), it may take some time before a group is able to arrive at a pattern of interaction which is more or less acceptable to all; there may be some alternation between concern with the task and concern with interpersonal problems. As with dyads there are some groups of individuals for whom there is no stable pattern of interaction.

Schutz (1958) set up experimental groups whose members were incompatible in that more than one was high in dominance – thus creating a struggle for dominance and an initial failure of meshing. These groups were found to be very ineffective in the performance of cooperative tasks. There may be failure of meshing in another way. Haythorn (1956) created groups of four, where one member was designated the leader, and where different combinations of authoritarian and non-authoritarian leaders and followers were compared. The groups ran most smoothly, with least conflict between leader and followers, when both leader and followers were authoritarian, or where both were non-authoritarian. In each case leader and followers were using social styles which fitted in a complementary way.

Once equilibrium has been established, the group may persist in this condition for some time, though changes in membership and changing external conditions will affect it. A 'cohesive' group is one in which the members are attracted to each other or to the task, and are therefore attracted towards the group. Cohesiveness can be measured by the proportion of sociometric choices which are made to members of that group, or by the frequency with which the word 'we' is used as opposed to 'I'. A group will become cohesive under the following conditions: frequent interaction; similar attitudes, interests and background; rewarding experiences in the group; a leader who can preserve harmony; absence of aggressive, schizoid or otherwise disturbing personalities; a task which requires cooperative, complementary behaviour for its completion (Lott and Lott, 1965).

Groups of two are of special interest since they provide the simplest instances of social interaction, and because more complex cases are explicable in terms of the principles which work here. However, dyads are unique in a number of ways – they are less stable and there is more danger of interaction collapsing, there are more signs of tension, but there is less expression of agreement and disagreement (Thomas and Fink, 1963).

Groups of three also have certain unique features. The addition of a third member to a dyad, even as an observer, changes the situation entirely. Each of the original participants now has to consider how his behaviour will be seen by the new member – and his behaviour will be affected differently if this is (1) an attractive girl; (2) his mother; (3) his tutor, etc. The phenomena of 'impression management' are discussed further in Chapter 9. If the new member takes part in interaction, the situation is changed further. A and B may have worked out their dominance relationships and the proportion of the time each will speak. C now has to be fitted into this hierarchy – he may dominate both, be intermediate, or be dominated by both.

In groups of three there are various kinds of internal competition and jockeying for position. With three males there is usually a straight battle for dominance, and the weakest becomes excluded. If there are two males and one female, the males will compete for the attention of the female. Females behave rather differently: if there are three females and one begins to get left out, the others will work hard to keep her in (Robson, 1966). If there is one powerful and dominating member of a triad, the others may form a coalition in which they combine together against him. The collaboration of the weak against the strong is observed in small group experiments and in real life: it has been summarized by the proposition 'in weakness there is strength'.

As group size increases from four to ten or more, the character of interaction changes. It is less easy to participate, both because others want to take the floor and because of greater audience anxiety; it is less easy to influence what the others will do; there is greater discrepancy between the amount of interaction of different members – in large groups the majority scarcely speak at all; the variety of personality and talent present is greater, and there is greater differentiation of styles of behaviour; discussion is less inhibited and there is ready expression of disagreement; if the group has work to do, there is a greater tendency to create rules and arrange for division of labour. Most people seem to prefer to belong to a fairly small group of five or six – they can talk nearly as much as they want to and exert influence over the others; at the same time there is sufficient variety of personalities and talents among those present for tackling common tasks or for purely social purposes (Thomas and Fink, 1963).

Norms. All small social groups develop 'norms', i.e. shared patterns of perceiving and thinking, shared kinds of communication, interaction and appearance, common attitudes and beliefs, and shared ways of doing whatever the group does. Members will have something in common from the beginning, and there is also convergence towards shared norms, particularly on the part of individual deviates. Such norms will govern the styles of social behaviour which are approved and admired. Anyone who fails to conform is placed under pressure to do so, and if he does not is rejected. Numerous experiments show that a deviate becomes the object of considerable attention, and of efforts to persuade him to change his behaviour. This is particularly likely to happen when his deviation is on some matter which is important to the group, which may affect the success of the group, or which challenges deeply-held beliefs. Deviates may conform to avoid being rejected by the group, or because they regard the group's views as a valuable source of information. The other group members might be more expert, while consistent behaviour on the part of the group may be taken to indicate the operation of some unknown rule; the latter may explain why subjects in conformity experiments are prepared to go along with the group when it gives, unanimously, an apparently wrong answer. It is important that people should deviate from time to time in a constructive way and lead the group to adopt a better solution to its problems in response to a changing external situation.

It is now known that there are several different kinds of norm

1. Norms about the task, e.g. the method, rate and standard of work in work teams. Deviation affects group goals and hence individual rewards.

2. Norms regulating interaction in the group, which make the

behaviour of others predictable, prevent conflicts, and ensure fair distribution of rewards.

3. Norms about attitudes and beliefs; the opinions of group experts are accepted and beliefs are checked against those of the group rather than against reality, which may be more difficult.

4. Norms about clothes, hair or other aspects of appearance, which project the identity of an individual, and thus may bring the group into disrepute.

Characteristic interaction sequences take place in connection with norms. A member may deviate because he does not like a norm, or is conforming to another group, or has thought of a better way of doing things. His deviation is greeted with surprise, non-verbal signals of disapproval, verbal attempts at influence and finally by rejection and exclusion from the group. An interesting exception to this is for persons of high informal status, in virtue of their contributions to the group; Hollander (1958) has suggested that they earn 'idiosyncrasy credit' and the group gives them permission to deviate – their deviation is seen as a possibly new line of action rather than as a failure to attain the approved standard. However, innovation in science and politics often comes from defiant, uncompromising minorities, rather than from diplomatic, conciliatory individuals who have earned their idiosyncrasy credit.

A persistent minority, even of two, may be able to change the norms. One deviate can be seen as an eccentric failure, but two deviates are taken more seriously. A second person simply disagreeing with the group casts doubt on the correctness of group norms. By their consistent behaviour, confidence and appearance of certainty, a minority can demonstrate the existence of a viable alternative to the majority point of view. An individual member of a committee may sway the committee if he can obtain social support from another member, preferably someone who is of high standing in the group, or who is an expert on the subject in question (Moscovici, 1976).

Hierarchies and roles. All groups of animals and men form hierarchies and there are advantages in having leaders who are able to direct task activities and prevent conflict in the group. During the early meetings of the group there is a struggle for status amongst those individuals strong in dominance motivation, as with groups of two and three. When the order has settled down, a characteristic pattern of interaction is found. The low status members at the bottom of this hierarchy talk little, they address the senior members politely and deferentially, and little notice is taken of what they have to say. A person's position in the hierarchy is primarily a function of how useful he has been in the past; thus the hierarchy is maintained in equilibrium – people are allowed to talk and are listened to if their contributions are expected to be useful. Position in the hierarchy bears little relation to personality traits, but is connected with ability at the group task. The group uses techniques of reward and punishment to maintain this system: a person who talks too much is punished, while high-status members who feel sleepy are stimulated to speak. When people with different positions in the hierarchy interact, the pattern of relationship between them is part of the total scheme of group organization (Bales, 1953).

As well as differing in power or influence, members may also differ in status; individuals may be esteemed and admired because of their past glories independently of their present power.

In addition to having different degrees of status and influence, group members adopt styles of behaviour which are differentiated in other ways. Slater (1955) first noted this effect and found that in discussion groups there was usually a popular person, or 'socio-emotional' leader, and a task leader. It is interesting that the same person did not do both these things – reflecting contrasting types of motivation among the members. Each kind of group has a characteristic set of roles which are available, though the roles of task and socio-emotional leader may occur in every kind of group. A role of 'leader of the opposition' is often found in juries, work-groups and T-groups. These roles appear for various reasons – because there are jobs to be done in groups (task leader), because groups have certain common structures (leader of the opposition), because members with different personalities want to behave differently (socio-emotional leader), and because members want to present themselves as unique individuals (joker, scapegoat).

The effect of the group on behaviour. Simply being in the presence of others increases the level of physiological arousal and general activity and causes one to emit familiar, well-learnt responses (Zajonc, 1965). This is true for ants and rats as well, but for humans the effects are only produced by others who are evaluating or judging in some way – the presence of blindfolded people does not increase arousal (Cottrell *et al.*, 1968). In some group situations, individuals behave without the usual restraints, engage in aggressive or other anti-social behaviour, and cannot remember clearly who did what. This is known as 'de-individuation', and occurs in lynch mobs, and in experiments in which subjects are made anonymous by wearing masks and white coats (Zimbardo, 1969). Groups can provide social support: people who are frightened, adolescents who can't get on with their families, and those who don't know what to think or believe, are greatly helped and comforted by belonging to close-knit social groups.

Groups are better than individuals at several kinds of activity. They are better at physical tasks because these often need more than one person, and because individuals can specialize in different parts of the job. Groups are better at decision-taking, because different skills and knowledge can be combined, and because members can both stimulate and criticize one another. Group decision-taking has the added advantage that those concerned become committed to carrying the decisions out.

Inter-group relations. The growth of positive feelings towards other members of the group is often accompanied by negative feelings to members of other groups. Sherif and colleagues (1961) divided eleven- to twelve-year-old boys at a summer camp into two groups. It was found that competitive sports, and an occasion when one group frustrated the other, led to a dangerous level of hostility. Peace was restored by getting the groups to work together for shared goals, such as restoring the (deliberately) interrupted water supply. Hostility to the out-group can arise without any conflict of interest, as experiments by Tajfel (1970) have shown; subjects gave preferential treatment to others who were believed to belong to the same 'group' defined vaguely in terms of similar aesthetic interests, and they were keen to give more to in-group than out-group members. It has been suggested that belonging to a group enhances feelings of self-esteem, but only if the group is believed to be superior to other groups. A group can be seen as superior to others in terms of its own values and norms – compared with which other groups fall short. The 'selfish gene' theory of evolution suggests that there is an innate tendency to favour one's own family in order to promote the continuation of one's own genes; this extends in a weakened form to members of groups, those of the same social class, nationality, and so on (Dawkins, 1976a).

Different kinds of group. So far we have been concerned with the properties of groups in general; we shall now look at some of the special features of particular kinds of group – families, work-groups and groups of friends.

Families differ from many other kinds of group in having a distinctive role-structure of father, mother, sons and daughters. In every culture there is a culturally prescribed relationship between husband and wife with some differentiation of the roles, and between mother–son, older–younger daughter, etc. There is variation between families, as a result of the personalities and abilities of the members. Family life takes place in the home and centres round eating, sleeping, child-rearing, other domestic jobs, and leisure. The activities of the different members have to be coordinated within the space and with the facilities available. They share the same financial fortunes and position in society. Interaction inside the family has a special quality of great informality – there is almost no self-presentation, and little restraint of affection or aggression. In other kinds of groups the members do not usually take their clothes off, laugh uproariously, cry, attack or kiss each other, or crawl all over each other, as family members do. The links between family members also have a unique quality: the parents are tied together by a long history of love and life together, they see their children as part of themselves, while the children are very dependent on them; the death of a close relation is a deeply distressing experience from which people may never fully recover (Gorer, 1965). Family links entail long-lasting bonds of concern and mutual obligation, and do not depend on common interests or values in the way that friendships do (Adams, 1967).

Groups of friends are different in many ways; they have no formal structure and no task, but consist of people of similar age, background, values and interests, who come together primarily for affiliative purposes. Members also obtain social support, advice and help with common problems. For young people between fifteen and twenty-five the peer group is of great importance; it gives them a social milieu, where they can be independent of the home, meet the opposite sex, and develop new social skills and an ego-identity (Muuss, 1962). Friendship groups have no 'task' in the usual sense, but they devise activities which generate the desired forms of social interaction – eating and drinking, dancing, playing games, and just talking. The character of the interaction varies between different cultures and age-groups, but usually has a warm and relaxed character. On the other hand self-presentation is important; members want to be accepted and thought well of; they dress up, and clothes are important in this setting.

The sociometric structure is important, who likes whom, who is in and who is out. Acceptance depends on conforming to the group norms and realizing the group values, as well as being kind and helpful. The hierarchical structure is not important, though informal leaders appear from time to time to deal with particular jobs, and there are several opinion leaders whose advice is taken on clothes, books, politics, etc. The group norms are important and distinguish the group from other groups; the in-group who conform are greatly valued, the out-group who do not conform are not.

In *work-groups* the task is the primary reason for the group's existence. The task affects the relations between people. A may inspect B's work, may be B's assistant, may cooperate with B in a joint task or may be next to him in an assembly line – a distinctive kind of relationship is likely to result in each case. Work-groups meet in a complex environmental setting and sub-culture, which limits and defines social behaviour. They are also part of a social organization, and have a leader and other kinds of role-differentiation. However, work groups have a life of their own which affects what happens and how much work is done. If cohesiveness is very low there will be little cooperation and output will fall – in addition there will be a lot of absenteeism and labour turnover. The group may have a different pattern of communication, incentives, leadership, or division of work from that officially laid down, because it suits the members better. In addition to their work behaviour work-groups engage in purely sociable behaviour such as jokes, games and gossip. The social relations formed involve only part of the personality and mem-bers may know little of one another's life outside. However an important part of the personality is involved, in that livelihood, career and identity depend on work, and there can be consider-able intensity of feeling over both cooperative and competitive relationships. There can be relaxed intimacy over the purely sociable activities at work, but physical violence may be used against those who deviate from work norms.

We now have a fairly clear idea how work-groups should be designed to ensure maximum productivity and maximum job satisfaction. They should be fairly small – not more than fifteen members; cohesiveness should be high; they should work as a cooperative team for shared rewards; status differences should be small; and there should be the optimum style of supervision (see p.249f.), with participation in decision-taking (Argyle, 1972).

SOCIAL ORGANIZATIONS

A great deal of social behaviour takes place against a background of social organization – in schools, industry, hospitals, and else-where. 'Social organization' means the existence of a series of ranks, positions or offices – such as teacher, foreman, hospital sister, etc. – which persist regardless of particular occupants. Behaviour in organizations is to a considerable extent *pre-*

programmed, having been worked out by previous members. The roles interlock, doctor–nurse, patient–nurse, and so on.

The growth of organization. As groups become bigger and their tasks more complex, a formal structure gradually develops, with a leadership hierarchy and divisions of function. Social organization is an essential part of modern life, because it would be impossible to coordinate the activities of the numbers of people involved in large-scale enterprises without extensive division of labour and a hierarchy of leadership. As a small workshop expands to become a factory, or when a guerrilla band becomes an army, the paraphernalia of social organization become necessary. To manufacture motor cars, for example, thousands of different parts must be made by a large number of different people and fitted together. This requires a great deal of planning and coordination. Social organization is essential, but the precise forms which we have are not necessarily the best, and are in fact found to be dissatisfying by many who serve in them.

Organizations have developed slowly. Industrial organizations as we know them today for example are derived from the first small factories established during the industrial revolution, by trial and error methods. Factories have developed both in response to changing technology and to changing ideas about organization – classical organization theory and the human relations movement in particular.

There are several different kinds of social organization. Etzioni (1961) distinguished between

coercive, e.g. prisons and mental hospitals; people do what they are told because they have to, through fear of punishment, and are unable to leave

utilitarian, e.g. industry; members work in exchange for rewards

moral, e.g. churches, hospitals, universities; members are committed to the values and goals of the organization

The senior members have quite different kinds of power in the three cases – by punishment, reward, or appeal to shared goals, respectively.

Organizations differ in the jobs they do – compare hospitals, universities, and factories. They differ in the content of the roles in them – compare hospital sisters, professors, and managers – and in the social distance between them. They differ in the 'organizational climate', i.e. the general pattern of relationships between members, and particularly the styles of supervision which are used. The climates of different firms and different universities are also different.

Behaviour in organizations differs from that in small social groups in a number of ways. Interaction patterns are not so much a product of particular groups of personalities, but are part of the organizational structure. People come to occupy positions of influence or leadership not through the spontaneous choice of their subordinates, but because they are placed there by higher authority.

Not all doctors or nurses behave in exactly the same way – there are variations due to personality and past experience. However, deviation from official practices goes a lot further than this. It has long been known that industrial workers engage in a wide range of unofficial practices, including ingenious forms of scrounging and time-wasting, in order to make life tolerable. The same has been reported of life in the army and in mental hospitals. Elizabeth Rosser has recently studied the underworld of English schools. She found that the pupils have their own ideas of what should happen; they have their own 'rules' for teachers: if a teacher breaks these rules – for example, by being unfair, too strict or boring – she is punished. What appears to be uncontrollable chaos from the point of view of the authorities turns out to be the operation of another set of rules (Marsh, Rosser and Harré, 1978).

Positions and Roles. Organizations consist of a set of related positions, whose occupants play interlocking roles. A role is the pattern of behaviour shared by most occupants of a position, and which comes to be expected of them. In a hospital, for example, there are obvious differences between the behaviour of patients, doctors, nurses, visitors, etc. Roles include a variety of aspects of behaviour – the work done, ways of interacting with other members of the organization (e.g. doctor–patient, doctor–nurse), attitudes and beliefs, and clothes worn.

The pressures to conform to a role can be very strong. Zimbardo (1973) paid a number of normal, middle-class student volunteers to play the roles of prison guards and prisoners, assigned arbitrarily, with appropriate uniforms, in an imitation prison. Many of the guards became brutal, sadistic and tyrannical, and many of the prisoners became servile, selfish and hostile, and suffered from hysterical crying and severe depression. The experiment had to be stopped after six days and nights.

Why do people conform so strongly to roles? There are various pressures to conform to the role, and someone who deviates too far will be regarded as eccentric, mad, or not a 'proper' prison guard, doctor, etc. Roles are *interlocking*, so that if the doctors and nurses play their roles, the patients have no choice but to play the patient role. The role may be the best way of doing a job; teachers have a loud, clear and didactic voice – adopting this role may save a lot of trial and error. Only certain kinds of people want to become, or are able to become, bishops or barmen, for example, so that a certain type of person is found in the job. Newcomers learn the role by imitating senior members, and may be given special practice at role-playing during training courses.

Many members of organizations experience *role conflict*, which can take various forms. A person may be under conflicting pressures from different groups of people in the organization. For example, different demands may be made on foremen by managers and by workers, female students may be expected to be hard-working and intellectual by their teachers but not by the male students. In this case there may be withdrawal from those exerting the pressure. There may also be ambiguity about what the role is, when jobs are not clearly defined, as can happen with new roles. There can be conflict between role and personality; for example, an authoritarian personality in a democratic organization. And a person may find himself playing two incompatible roles, e.g., a military chaplain, or a teacher whose own child is in the school. Role conflict leads to anxiety, withdrawal, illness and inefficiency, and to attempts to resolve the role conflict (Kahn *et al.*, 1964).

Interaction in organizations. Social organization introduces a totally new element which has not so far been considered. To predict how A and B will behave towards one another it may be much more useful to know their positions in the organization than to know about their personalities or preferred styles of interaction. In the extreme cases of church services and drill parades the whole course of interaction can be 'predicted' by knowing the formal procedure. Even a person's popularity may be more a function of his position than of his personality – it depends whether he has a rewarding role like awarding bonuses and giving out free buns, or has a punitive role.

It is impossible to understand why the members of an organization interact as they do without knowing their organization chart. There have been many studies of the communication between the members of industrial management hierarchies, like that shown in Fig. 22 (reviewed in Argyle, 1972). The main findings are as follows:

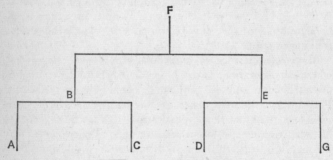

Figure 22. Organization chart.

A and B. Relations with the immediate superior are often rather strained and formal. A may ask B for help, information or advice; A may have to report progress – which may be delayed and distorted if the news is bad; A may want to make suggestions or complaints – which B may not be very eager to hear. B may give orders or advice, expert information or comments on A's performance.

A and C. Relations with immediate colleagues can vary from close cooperation in a team, through carefully reciprocated helpfulness, to cut-throat competition.

A and D. Lateral relations with equal status people outside the group are often more friendly and relaxed; they are useful in enabling rapid information-flow and help to occur, and are the basis of the 'grapevine'; friendship choices are often in A–D relationships.

A and E. Relations with those of different status, but outside the line of command, are easier than direct superior–subordinate links and can act like an A–D relationship.

A and F. It is difficult for F to communicate with persons two or more steps below him in the hierarchy. If he goes through B, four encounters have to take place before some delayed and distorted feedback reaches him; if B is left out he will be upset; if notices or other mass media are used there is no feedback.

Since behaviour varies with the rank or position of the other, it is important to be able to categorize people; many organizations have uniforms, and members of others can usually be placed by more subtle aspects of their appearance. When an outsider enters an organization, even for a short visit, there is great pressure to find out his 'equivalent rank' so that everyone shall know exactly how to treat him. In many primitive societies the main principle of social organization is not rank but family relationship; a potential mother-in-law is avoided, an uncle is played jokes on, and so forth. It is reported of one savage tribe which operated such a classificatory kinship system that if it could not be discovered how a visitor was related to everyone he was eaten – because people did not know how to behave towards him. In Western society, when people of different social status meet, at conferences, office parties and the like, there is a characteristic type of interaction:

note the keen interest, the total absorption of the lesser members
. . . the greater member is looking past the ear of the lesser, scanning the throng for an acquaintance whose status is greater than
his own from whom enhancement may be drawn [Brown, 1965].

Permanent relationships in the organization have a similar
quality. Less important people are much concerned about what
their superiors think of them; their superiors, however, are more
concerned with what *their* superiors are thinking.

Nearly all organizations have a hierarchical structure and this
seems to be necessary to provide the necessary administration
and coordination. However there are a number of difficulties
about hierarchies. As we showed above, there are difficulties of
communication up and down hierarchies; these become more
acute when there are many levels in the hierarchy or if relationships are authoritarian. It is often found that those in the lowest
ranks are discontented, alienated and inefficient. There are
several ways of changing organizations to minimize these effects.

1. The style of leadership can be changed so that it is more
democratic, leaders delegate more, and encourage participation
in decisions (cf. p. 249f.).

2. The number of levels can be reduced by increasing the span
of control and decentralizing the organization into smaller units.

3. Formal arrangements can be made for consultation of all
levels as in 'industrial democracy' and student representation
(Argyle, 1972).

Another aspect of social organization is the work-flow system.
Workers may, for example, be on an assembly line, which
means that they interact only with their neighbours, but are
dependent on the whole group for their pay. They may be in a
group under a foreman on individual piece-work, or may be
isolated at control points in an automated system. These
arrangements have definite effects on the relations between
people – it may make them love or hate each other – depending
on whether they are helping or hindering one another; it may
make communications easy or impossible. The Tavistock Institute of Human Relations has shown that it is possible to devise
improved social arrangements, with exactly the same tech-

nology. For example, Trist and colleagues (1963) found that the Longwall method of coalmining could be employed with greater productivity and less absenteeism if the three main jobs were done on all of the three shifts; previously the jobs of cutting, filling and stonework were done by different shifts, who never met, resulting in a lack of cooperation.

CULTURE

Social interaction takes place within a cultural setting. By the culture of a group of people is meant their whole way of life – their language, ways of perceiving, categorizing and thinking about the world, forms of non-verbal communication and social interaction, rules and conventions about behaviour, moral values and ideals, technology and material culture, art, science, literature and history. All these aspects of culture affect social behaviour, directly or indirectly.

Human infants are born with basic biological needs and a certain amount of intrinsic equipment. However, human beings have greater powers of learning than animals, as well as a longer period of dependence on their parents, so that different solutions to life's problems can be learnt. As a result of the development of language humans can communicate their solutions to these problems to one another, and there is continuous modification of the cultural store.

There is a culture that is shared by the inhabitants of Great Britain, and there are sub-cultures for particular geographical areas, social classes and organizations, and even for particular small social groups. Several aspects of culture affect the processes of interaction, notably the conventions governing social behaviour, moral rules about interpersonal behaviour, verbal and non-verbal means of communication, and other social techniques.

Language. This is one of the most obvious differences between cultures. However, when a new language has been learnt there are still problems about the use of language. In several cultures there is polite usage – where words are used to please rather than inform; Collett and O'Shea (1976) found that many people in Persia would give directions when asked the way to a non-existent hotel. Americans often give instructions or orders as if they are questions – 'Would you like to . . .?' Cultures vary in the use of exaggeration: 'If an Arab says what he means without the expected exaggeration, other Arabs may still think that he means the opposite' (Shouby, 1951). Thus an Arab will continue to pursue a girl who does not rebuff him vigorously enough, and will assume a visitor really wants more to eat unless he refuses three times. English upper-middle-class speech includes considerable understatement; a person who fails to follow this convention is regarded as boastful. There are differences in the range of personal pronouns available: we have only 'you', the French have 'tu' and 'vous'; in Sri Lanka there are about twenty alternatives communicating degrees of intimacy and deference.

The language also carries the categories of thought which are important in a culture. For example, the colours of the rainbow are divided up differently in different cultures; Zuni Indians have difficulty in recognizing an orange stimulus shown them previously, because they have no word for orange. The Eskimos have three words for snow, where we would need several words to describe each variety (Brown and Lenneberg, 1954). Special styles of social behaviour are labelled, such as *machismo* (Mexico – flamboyant bravery), *chutzpah* (Yiddish – outrageous cheek). When a concept or distinction is important in a culture, this becomes reflected in the language, which in turn helps people to deal with situations common in the culture, and in the production of relevant behaviour. Old concepts and words disappear and are replaced by new ones: a long time ago, an uncle of mine advised me about tipping – 'a half-crown is a gentleman's coin'; both concepts have since disappeared.

Non-verbal communication. The non-verbal accompaniments of speech vary in different cultures. For example, Italians make a great deal of use of gestures with speech, and have a large vocabulary of meaningful gestures. Arabs and others touch a lot during conversation. Tone of voice is very important for Arabs too, since their words tend to be ambiguous and stereotyped. Japanese speech includes a number of sounds like hissing, which means deference, and the word 'Hai', which means understanding.

As we saw in Chapter 2, there are cultural differences in the use and meaning of non-verbal signals for interpersonal attitudes and emotions.

Facial expression. Much the same facial expressions are used in all cultures, but there are different rules about when they can be used; for example, the Japanese rarely show sadness or other negative emotions, and may smile or giggle instead. *Bodily Contact* is used more in some countries and takes very diverse forms – various kinds of embracing, stroking, buffeting, or kissing to greet people, various kinds of hand-holding or leg-entwining during encounters. *Distance.* Arabs and others stand much closer than Europeans or Americans, and at a more directly facing angle. *Gaze.* In the 'contact' cultures where people touch and stand closer, they also look more. *Gesture* shows the greatest cultural diversity, since there are almost no innate gestures. The same gesture may have a quite different meaning in different cultures. Sticking out the tongue means an apology in parts of China, the evil eye in parts of India, deference in Tibet, a rude sign in England, and simply means 'No' in the Marquesas.

Other aspects of social interaction. Greetings have similar components in most cultures – touching, mutual gaze, bowing, head-nods, smiling. The Indians and Japanese do not touch, and a variety of exotic greetings are found in primitive societies – smelling cheeks and rubbing noses, taking off some or all clothes, kissing beards, and so on (Argyle, 1975). *Establishing rapport.* Americans are able to establish a certain, rather superficial contact very quickly, whereas the British are experienced as more 'stand-offish', 'closed', or simply difficult to get to know. This may be due to differences in affiliative motivation, or to differences in the social techniques which are acquired. *Self-presentation* occurs in all cultures. However, in Britain there is a taboo on direct, verbal self-presentation, and it must be done less directly (p. 200); in India and Japan it is quite normal to speak highly of oneself. In most of the East, 'face' is of great importance and must not be lost. *Etiquette*. All cultures have their rules and expectations; when these are elaborate and rigid they are referred to as 'etiquette'. In Western countries, it is only in old-fashioned upper-class circles that these rules are made into explicit codes of etiquette. In the Far East, especially in Japan, formal etiquette is more widely followed, but this only applies to certain traditional social situations, and not apparently to getting on buses and trains. There has been a tendency to move away from formality in America: according to Riesman and his colleagues (1960) there is a cult of the informal or 'familial' style of behaviour; when people speak, they do not 'perform', they do not have 'presence'.

Rules and Conventions. The pattern of conventions varies sharply between different cultures and sub-cultures, and certain types of encounter may be unique to a particular culture. Visitors to the U.S.A. may have to learn what happens at a pyjama party, a bull session, a picnic, a baby shower, and may have to learn the elaborate rules which surround dating. According to Barker and Wright (1954) there are over 800 such situations for which the rules would have to be learnt, to engage in everyday life in a small American town, or any other town.

Goffman (1963) has shown how these rules penetrate to the key processes of social interaction, and govern for example the detailed sequences of eye movements and other bodily movements. Kissing one's wife goodbye is done quite differently at a bus-stop and at an air terminal, for example. Such rules are usually unverbalized, and we are only dimly aware of them until someone breaks them; this is disturbing, and may lead to anger, consternation or embarrassment because the regular, predictable flow of social events is disrupted. In some social situations it is necessary to teach clients some new rules – as with members of T-groups and encounter groups, or patients undergoing psychotherapy. It seems to be usual to create the impression that there *is* a stable tradition, which the newcomer hasn't heard about. A peculiarity of research in psychology is that subjects are placed in very unusual situations – but even here there has come to be a tradition, governing how long it shall take, how much subjects are paid, how much they are told, and so on.

Ideals and moral values. Cultures vary in the moral rules about sex, drugs, and other matters. In modern societies there are great variations between different groups of people in the extent to which different moral values and ideals are accepted. They are taught by parents, teachers, clergymen, politicians, and others, and are learnt by children brought up in the culture. Values and ideals function as restraints which control and inhibit certain spontaneous patterns of behaviour. While aggressive and sexual behaviour are among the main targets of these controls, the whole style and strategy of social behaviour may also be affected.

Telling the truth is valued in most cultures, but the truth is often not told. In our own culture it is also thought important not to hurt people's feelings, and in some cultures there is a great desire to please the hearer.

Moral codes may be learnt as simple sets of rules – 'It is wrong to tell a lie', or as rather high-level principles such as 'Do unto others as you would they do unto you'. They may be expressed as attitudes which should be adopted – 'Love your neighbour'. Most moral codes in fact recommend behaviour which is more affiliative, less dominating, and less aggressive than social behaviour often is. Moral codes prescribe the conditions when another person should be helped. Experiments have shown that in the British and American middle classes there is a norm that a person should help those who depend on him or need his help; in many other social groups help is given only on a reciprocal basis, or to members of the same family or tribe (Berkowitz and Friedman, 1967). Morals may take the form of ideals to be followed, and cultures can be distinguished by the heroes which they admire most. In many cases the hero has a well-defined style of social behaviour – for example, the nineteenth-century English gentleman and the cowboy of 1880 vintage. There are rewards for behaving in accordance with such ideals. The grosser failures are punished by legal sanctions, the less gross by general public disapproval. The higher levels of moral attainment are rewarded by social approval, sometimes by social mobility, or by hopes of better prospects in the next life. These styles of social behaviour spread like social movements, from a few leaders, by means of the mass media or other channels of influence. In recent years the spread of the hippie lifestyle from California, of student unrest, of concern with ecology, are examples of this rapid diffusion.

Culture and personality. People may behave differently in two cultures because of differences of personality. Much of what is sometimes described as 'national character' can be looked at simply as differences in social techniques and in norms of behaviour. When Latin Americans stand closer than North Americans, it does not follow that their desire for intimacy is greater; it may just be that they have learnt different social rules. On the other hand, if the people from some cultural group are consistently aggressive, affiliative, or dominating in several ways, we *could* say that their norms are different; but it may be more useful to say that their level of motivation is different, and to regard this as a feature of their 'national character'. A difficulty with this notion is that there are great variations in personality *within* a given culture, and the overall difference between two cultures may be hard to detect; on the other hand, there may be much more homogeneity in social rules: whatever else is said about the national character of the French, there is no disputing that they speak French.

It is very difficult to establish that there are differences in national character; this really requires extensive social surveys using personality measures that are valid in several countries. There have been a number of smaller-scale studies, showing for example that Germans and Arabs tend to be authoritarian, that Americans and Australians are extraverted, that Norwegians conform more than the French, and so on.

Social class. In every society there are distinctive relationships between men and women, the old and the young, and different sections of societies. Most societies, and all modern industrial ones, are stratified into social classes. These are groups of people who regard members of the other groups as inferior or superior, and where each group has a common culture. The higher groups have more money and property, and are more powerful. Members of each social class mix freely and can form intimate relationships with other members, but are much less likely to do so with people from other classes. Class is really a continuous variable, and boundaries are hard to define, though groupings and barriers appear from time to time. A development in the British class system during the 1950s was the emergence of an upper working class, whose members shared much of the material culture of the middle class, but did not mix socially with that class or have the same pattern of social behaviour (Goldthorpe *et al.*, 1969). Social class is shared by families, and depends mainly on the husband's occupation, income and education, and on the size and location of the home. Class systems vary in different countries. While class is mainly a function of occupation and education in Britain, it depends almost entirely on money in the U.S.A. The social distance between classes, i.e. the difficulties of communication and interaction and the difficulty of moving from one class to another, are greatest in caste and feudal societies, and very low in the U.S.A.; Britain is intermediate in this respect.

Classes have different cultures, so what was said about different cultures applies here too. Instead of individual languages there are different accents, and in Britain this is of course one of the main clues to class.

There are also class differences in the way language is used. Bernstein (1959) suggested that working-class people used a 'restricted code', consisting of short and simple sentences, often uncompleted, with a lot of slang and idiom, many personal pronouns, and rhetorical questions of the type 'didn't I?' The middle-class 'elaborated code' is more impersonal, more complex and more grammatical. Bernstein suggests that the restricted code is suited to maintaining relationships in face-to-face groups, while the elaborated code is better for decision-taking and administration. Labov (1964) has found that working-class Americans are able to speak in a wide range of accents on different occasions, though they normally use the working-class one. Similar considerations probably apply to linguistic codes.

As far as other aspects of behaviour are concerned, it seems likely that, in Britain, working-class people make social contact more readily, are less distant and formal, but are more aggress-ive and make less use of complex strategies and techniques than middle-class people.

When people from different social classes meet, the kinds of problem arise that are discussed below in connection with people from different cultures. The results are the same – there is mis-understanding and mutual rejection. There is the additional problem that social classes are ranked in a social prestige hier-archy, so that people react to those from other social classes as superiors and inferiors. For many people the social class of others is as important as sex and age, and is recognized fairly easily from their speech and clothes – or from their social be-haviour. This leads to the adoption of the appropriate style of social behaviour – which may also be culturally prescribed. Such encounters are often a source of discomfort and tension to both parties, the more so the greater the difference in class, and the more feudal the society. People who are found formal, dull or remote by outsiders can be genial, gay and relaxed when with members of their own group.

On the other hand, there may be perfectly easy relationships between members of different social classes when they are in some established role-relationship. The Bertie Wooster–Jeeves relationship is a case in point. It is in public places, on purely social occasions, and between strangers that inter-class difficul-ties appear. Mary Sissons arranged for an actor to stop eighty people in Paddington Station, and ask them the way to Hyde Park. For half of them he was dressed and behaved as if upper-middle-class, for half he appeared to be working-class. The interviews were filmed and tape-recorded, and the social class of the respondents was obtained by subsequent interview. It was found that the middle-class/middle-class encounters went most smoothly compared with the other three combinations of social class; there was instant rapport, the encounters lasted longer, respondents smiled more, and there was a definite ending (Sissons, 1971).

Social mobility upwards is widely desired, and in industrialized societies is very common, but it has its drawbacks. Like the immigrant, the mobile person has to learn a new language, a new set of conventions and values, and has to unlearn the ones he had before. Unless he does so he will not be accepted by the new group.

Intercultural encounters. When people from two different cultures meet, there is infinite scope for misunderstanding and confusion. This may be a matter of misinterpreting the other's communications, verbal or non-verbal. There is the Englishman who depreciates his own abilities in what turns out to be a highly misleading way; there is the Arab who starves at a banquet because he is only offered the dishes once; there is the African who puts his hand on a Western knee. There may be difficulties in setting up a stable pattern of interaction – Americans and Europeans have been seen retreating backwards or gyrating in circles at international conferences, pursued by Latin Americans trying to establish their habitual degree of proximity (Hall, 1955). Westerners are perplexed by Japanese who giggle when hearing or delivering bad news. American businessmen find it difficult to adjust to the more hierarchical pattern of relationships in their overseas branches, where subordinates do not speak their mind to their superiors.

The result of these cross-cultural misunderstandings is likely to be that each person rejects the other as one who has failed to conform to the standards of civilized society, and looks on him as impossible to get on with. There are several solutions to this problem: one is to find out the cultural patterns of the other, and either conform oneself, or at least use them to interpret the other's behaviour properly. The difficulty here is that many of these patterns of behaviour are very subtle, and it takes a long familiarity with the culture to know them all. Another approach is to be far more flexible and tolerant when dealing with people from other cultures, and to make a real effort to understand and to control one's reactions to the unusual aspects of their behaviour. Several research groups have been engaged in developing methods of training people to function effectively in alien cultures.

One approach has been to collect critical incidents of when members of culture A have got into difficulties in culture B, and to teach members of A how to deal with these situations. The Arab Culture Assimilator developed at the University of Illinois consists of fifty-five problem episodes for trainees to solve, which are intended to teach them about such matters as the role of women, dealing with subordinates, entertaining guests, and the importance of religion. It has been found that this kind of training produces some improvement in interaction with Arabs and Thais (Fiedler *et al.*, 1971). Another approach has been used by Peter Collett at Oxford. Englishmen were taught the interaction styles known to be used by Arabs – standing closer, touching, etc. These trainees got on better with Arabs and were liked better than untrained subjects (Collett, 1971).

The immigrant to another country is faced with the problems of learning the new language, rules and values. At first he is inclined to reject the new ways – and to be rejected himself for not conforming to them. Immigrants often keep to the company of others from the same country until they are thoroughly assimilated. It was found a few years ago that British immigrants to Australia had very little informal contact with Australians for the first two or three years, and disliked their 'excessive familiarity' in personal relations, such as the use of Christian names after only brief acquaintance (Richardson, 1961).

FURTHER READING

Argyle, M., *The Social Psychology of Work*, Harmondsworth: Penguin Books, 1972.

Goffman, E., *Behavior in Public Places*, Glencoe, Ill.: Free Press, 1963.

Shaw, M. E., *Group Dynamics: The Psychology of Small Group Behavior*, New York: McGraw-Hill, 1971.

CHAPTER 9

SELF-IMAGE AND SELF-ESTEEM

WE showed in Chapter 5 how people categorize each other in order to know how to behave towards them. When a person is constantly categorized and treated in a particular way, he acquires a *self-image*. Depending on how far others treat him with approval and respect he will acquire some degree of *self-esteem*.

It was postulated in Chapter 1 that people have a need for a distinct and consistent self-image and a need for self-esteem. This may result in attempts to elicit responses from others which provide confirmation of these images and attitudes towards the self. The self-image is one of the central and stable features of personality, and a person cannot be fully understood unless the contents and structure of his self-image are known.

THE DIMENSIONS OF SELF AND THEIR MEASUREMENT

The self-image, or 'ego-identity', refers to how a person consciously perceives himself. The central core usually consists of his name, his bodily feelings, body-image, sex, and age. For a man the job will also be central – unless he is suffering from job alienation. For a woman her family and her husband's job may also be central. The core will contain other qualities that may be particularly salient, such as social class, religion, particular achievements of note, or anything that makes a person different from others.

One method of finding the contents of a person's self-image is the Twenty Statements Test: subjects are asked to give twenty answers to the question 'Who am I?'. The first part of the answers are usually roles – sex, social class, job, etc., and the rest consist of personality traits or evaluations – happy, good, intelligent, etc. (Kuhn and McPartland, 1954). A person may play a number of different roles; he may be a lecturer, a father, and a member of various committees and clubs. He plays these roles in a characteristic style; the way he sees himself in these roles is a part of his ego-identity. He may perceive himself vaguely or clearly. The more he has discussed his personal problems with others the more clearly he is likely to see himself. During psychotherapy, the therapist may provide the concepts which the patient can use to talk about himself. Some aspects of the self-image are more important to a person than others: it is more upsetting if these are challenged.

Another method of assessing the self-image is by seven-point scales such as the 'Semantic Differential'; subjects are asked to describe 'the kind of person I actually am' along a series of seven-point scales such as:

```
cold      – – – – – – – – warm
attractive – – – – – – – – unattractive
stupid    – – – – – – – – clever
strong    – – – – – – – – weak
kind      – – – – – – – – cruel (Osgood et al., 1957)
```

The answers are affected by the tendency to give a favourable impression, although that does not necessarily matter since it is useful to know how favourably a person views himself.

The body image is an important part of the self-image, especially for girls and young women. Males are most pleased with their bodies when they are large – females are most pleased when their bodies are small, but with large busts (Jourard and Secord, 1955). This, at any rate, was the situation in the U.S.A. in the 1950s; the most desired male and female physiques vary quite a lot between cultures and historical periods.

How far does a person's self-image correspond with the way he is seen by others? As will be seen, people present a somewhat improved, idealized and censored version of themselves for public inspection, and may come to believe it themselves. On the other hand, reality in the form of others' reactions prevents the self-image from getting too far out of line. It is no good thinking you are the King of France if no one else shares this view. However, some people succeed in insulating themselves from the views of others so that they are simply unaware of how they are regarded.

The ego-ideal is the kind of person one would most like to be; it is a personal goal to be striven for, and it may also be the image that is presented to others. It may be based on particular individuals who are taken as admired models, and who may be parents, teachers, film stars, or characters from literature. It may consist of a fusion of desired characteristics drawn from various sources. The ego-ideal may be remote and unattainable, or it may be just a little better than the self-image in certain respects. The gap between the two can be assessed by means of the measures described already. The Semantic Differential can be filled in to describe 'the kind of person I actually am', and 'the kind of person I would most like to be'. The average discrepancy between scale scores is then worked out thus:

$$\begin{array}{cc} \text{(ego-ideal)} & \text{(self)} \\ \text{X} & \text{X} \end{array}$$

attractive – – – – – – – unattractive

A number of studies have found that neurotics have greater self/ego-ideal conflict than normals, and that the discrepancy gets smaller during psychotherapy – though this is mainly because of changes in self-ratings. However there are some groups of people, by no means well-adjusted, who show very little conflict – because they perceive themselves so inaccurately (Wylie, 1961).

When there is much conflict, it contributes to low self-esteem. It may also lead to efforts to attain the ego-ideal: when there is actually movement in this direction there is said to be 'self-realization'. There may be efforts to actually change the personality, i.e., some aspects of behaviour, in some way; or there may be efforts to persuade others to categorize one differently, by better self-presentation. A curious feature of the ideal self is that a person who attains it does not necessarily rest on his laurels enjoying the self-esteem, but may revise his goals upwards – like a high-jumper who moves the bar upwards a notch.

This development of the ideal self is part of the growth of personality. Existentialist writers maintain that people are continually revising and re-creating their personalities, in much the same way that writers create characters. Carl Backman has suggested that changes in the self-image are first tried out on friends; if successful, the new component is adopted more permanently.

Self-esteem is the extent to which a person approves of and accepts himself, and regards himself as praiseworthy, either absolutely or in comparison with others. Like ego-identity, self-esteem has a stable core, together with a series of peripheral esteems based on different role-relationships, and it varies quite a lot between situations (Gergen and Morse, 1967). One complication about self-esteem is that some people develop an exaggerated self-regard in compensation for basic feelings of inferiority. In these cases it is difficult to decide whether they 'really' have high or low self-esteem – it would depend on whether this is measured by direct or indirect measures. A measure of self-esteem can be obtained from self/ego-ideal discrepancies, but a better measure is the direct rating of self on evaluative scales (e.g., good–bad). Rosenberg (1965) constructed an attitude scale for measuring self-esteem that was found to agree well with free self-descriptions, and in the case of hospital patients with ratings by nurses.

Dimensions of the self. A child may admire saints and soldiers, poets and financiers, but eventually he has to decide which is the direction in which he really wants to go. The degree of integration or diffusion of ego-identity is an important aspect of personality. At one extreme are the completely dedicated, single-minded fanatics, at the other are those adolescents who do not yet know 'who they are or where they are going'. The more integrated the self-image, the more consistent a person's behaviour will be: one effect of the self-image on behaviour is the suppression of behaviour that is out of line. This 'consistency' may take various forms, depending on whether the self-image is based on the attributes of some person, on a set of ethical or ideological rules of conduct, or on an occupational or social-class role.

Another aspect of the self-image is the extent to which a person sees himself as unique and different from others. The child in the family, a soldier in the army, a member of a crowd – they may simply see themselves as members of a group, not differing notably from the others. Most adolescents try to separate themselves from the corporate family identity by joining a group outside the family; this is still a shared identity, but it gives them a new status in society. Or they can engage in eccentric, deviant or delinquent behaviour to show their separate identity. Adolescent drug-takers, isolated old people, and others feel apart from other people and do not share the common goals and norms of the surrounding society. Probably the normal condition is a combination of unique and shared elements, such as taking a role in a group where all members share common ways of behaviour, but recognize and accept the individual contributions and idiosyncrasies of each person (Ziller, 1964).

THE ORIGINS OF THE SELF

The reactions of others. The main origin of self-image and self-esteem is probably the reactions of others – we come to see ourselves as others categorize us. This has been called the theory of the 'looking-glass self' – to see ourselves we look to see how we are reflected in the reactions of others. There is experimental evidence that others' reactions affect self-ratings. In one experiment subjects were asked to read poems; some were evaluated favourably, others unfavourably, by a supposed speech expert; self-ratings on ability to read poems and on related scales shifted accordingly (Videbeck, 1960). If parents tell a child he is clever, or treat him as if he is untrustworthy, these attributes may become part of the ego-identity. The whole pattern of reactions is important here, the spoken and the unspoken.

Adults and teachers do not hesitate to give full descriptive feedback to children, but amongst older people there is something of a taboo on such direct verbal feedback, especially in its negative aspects. It is reported that those who go on leadership training courses ask to be told point-blank how others perceive them (Bennis *et al.*, 1964), and it has been suggested that it would be helpful to provide people with rather more of such information than is currently regarded as polite. On the other hand, it can be very traumatic to find this out, and it should be done with tact, or indirectly by subtle hints, and non-verbal reactions. The effect is greater when the critic is regarded as an expert or if his opinion is valued for some other reason. Parents are a most important source of both self-image and self-esteem for children: those who are rejected come to reject themselves and have low self-esteem in later life.

Comparison with others. Self-perception may include concepts such as 'tall' or 'clever'; however, these only have meaning in comparison with the height or cleverness of others. An important source of the self-image is the comparison of oneself with brothers, sisters, friends, or others who are constantly present and are sufficiently similar to invite comparison. If other families in the neighbourhood are wealthier, a child will regard himself as 'poor'; if his brothers and sisters are cleverer, he will see himself as not clever, and so on. It is possible to change a child's self-image completely, and quite rapidly, by sending him to a different school, where the other children are, for example, more athletic, or of a lower social class. People compare their abilities or fortunes with others who are similar: a tennis-player does not compare himself either with Wimbledon champions or with hopeless beginners, manual workers do not compare their wages with those of the managing director or of Indian peasants. Subjects in experiments are most interested to know about those who are slightly better than themselves (Latané, 1966), as if they were trying to do better by small instalments. In a study of a large number of adolescents in New York State, Rosenberg (1965) found that those with the highest self-esteem tended to be of higher social class, to have done better at school, and to have been leaders in clubs – all of which could be bases for favourable comparisons of self and others.

Roles played. Medical students come to see themselves as 'doctors' during their training – 31 per cent in the first year, 83 per cent in the fourth year; most medical students see themselves as doctors when dealing with patients (Merton *et al.*, 1957). The third source of the self-image is simply the roles a person has played in the past, or is playing in the present. Adults often see themselves primarily in terms of the job they do, although roles of particular importance or excitement in their past may be even more salient. Roles provide an easy solution to the problem of ego-identity – there is a clear public identity to adopt. There are individual differences in role performance, and a person may come to see himself as an *intelligent* juvenile delinquent, i.e. as combining a role and a trait. Goffman (1956) suggested that in order to perform a role effectively, the newcomer has to put on a mask to act the part; however when he has acted the part for long enough and others have accepted the performance this becomes a real part of his personality and is no longer a mask.

Identification with models. Children identify with a succession of people – parents, teachers and other models, i.e. they admire these models and want to be like them. The ego-ideal is mainly based on a fusion of these models. However, it has been found in a number of experiments that identification also modifies the self-image, i.e. people feel that they *already* resemble the model. A very important part of the self is mainly acquired through identification – the sex-role. If a child has plenty of contact and a warm relationship with the same sex parent it will come to behave in a male (or female) way, and feel male (or female) accordingly (Mussen and Distler, 1964).

The adolescent identity crisis. Children play at roles, adolescents experiment with them. During student life it is possible to try out a number of roles and identities without commitment, such as being an actor, journalist, or revolutionary. However, pressures to commit oneself build up, and somewhere between the ages of sixteen and twenty-four there is often an identity crisis when a young person is forced to make up his mind which of all these bits and pieces of identity to hang on to, and which to suppress (Erikson, 1956). The basis of this is partly the need to choose one job rather than another, a marital partner, a political and religious outlook, and a lifestyle. In addition, the development of greater powers of abstract thought probably makes it more important than before to be *consistently* vegetarian, radical, intellectual or whatever it may be. At this stage the choice is helped by the existence of alternative models to identify with, and of a number of 'social types' in the community. These models are different in different communities and social classes. To have formed an ego-identity is to have 'a feeling of being at home in one's body, a sense of knowing where one is going, and an inner assurance of anticipated recognition from those who count' (Erikson, *op. cit.*).

The course of identity-formation does not always run smoothly, and a number of intermediate and temporarily unsuccessful states of the identity are commonly found in young people. (1) A conflict between two or more alternative identities which cannot be reconciled, such as wishing to be both a clergyman and a whisky-distiller: if the two cannot be combined (e.g. making sacramental wine, or being a Benedictine monk), one is usually chosen and the other relegated to week-ends or holidays. (2) A state of 'moratorium' in which decisions about identity are postponed. After going to university (which itself provides such a moratorium) some students travel to remote and exotic lands to 'find out who they are'. (3) Forming a prestigeful identity, which cannot really be sustained, and requires continual confirmation from others. (4) There are various pathological conditions – forming a totally unrealistic identity as in paranoia, and forming no identity at all as in schizophrenia. (5) The most recent form of failure in identity formation is that of the well-adjusted dropout – who does absolutely nothing and is quite happy with it.

The need for self-esteem. We have seen that there are forces in the personality to achieve a *unified* identity, and that this is controlled by outside forces to keep it *realistic*. There is a third force – to produce a *favourable* self-image, which provides sufficient self-esteem. We have seen that self-ratings are usually somewhat more generous than ratings given by others. However, the self-image depends on the reactions of others; this is why such a lot of effort is put into self-presentation, the manipulation of others' perceptions. What happens if others' evaluations are *more* favourable than self-evaluation? Experiments show that such evaluations are neither believed nor remembered (showing the effect of consistency), but the positive evaluator is liked (showing the effect of the need for esteem). (Shrauger, 1975.)

The need for self-esteem is limited by reality: otherwise behaviour becomes absurd and preposterous, and there is continual lack of confirmation by others. This happens in the case of paranoia (p. 212f.). In fact people differ widely in their feelings of esteem, from conceit to inferiority. Both extremes usually reflect failure to perceive accurately the present responses of others, and can be regarded as failures of adjustment. A mythical psychotherapist is said to have told a patient who suffered from feelings of inferiority, 'But you really *are* inferior.' The real reason that people feel inferior is usually that they have been unduly rejected by their parents, or have chosen too elevated a comparison group.

It is quite possible to select prestigeful items out of the long list of self-attributes and roles once played, and such items often become a favourite item of conversation. However, the total self-esteem is greatly affected by the ego-ideal. Thus self-esteem depends jointly on a person's position on a series of evaluative dimensions, and upon the value placed on each of these dimensions. Values depend on the group, so self-esteem depends on whether the group values a person's attributes – but a group will have been joined because it does value them.

CONDITIONS UNDER WHICH THE SELF IS ACTIVATED

The self is not at work all the time: people are not continually trying to discover, sustain or present a self-image. For example, when at home rather than at work, in the audience rather than on the stage, the self-system is not very active.

Most people feel self-conscious when appearing in front of an audience, and some people feel very anxious. It has been found that these effects are greater when the audience is large, and fails to give positive responses. The performer is the centre of attention for a number of people and his performance will be assessed, so that there is the danger that he will receive disapproving reactions, and self-esteem may be damaged.

When someone addresses any kind of audience it is no good his speaking in the informal 'familial' style – he won't be heard properly: it is inevitable that he must put on some kind of 'performance'. Once he does so he is accepting a certain definition of the situation and presenting a certain face: he is someone who is able to perform before this audience and is worth attending to. It is this implicit claim which creates the risk of loss of face. We shall discuss later the social skills of dealing with audiences, including how stage fright can be reduced (p. 258f.).

There are many social situations where other people can be regarded as a kind of audience and where one's performances may be assessed. Argyle and Williams (1969) asked subjects 'To what extent did you feel mainly the observer or the observed?' after they had been in different situations (see Fig. 23). It was found that they felt more observed (1) when being interviewed, rather than interviewing (2) when with an older person (3) when a female with males. Individuals differ in the extent to which they see themselves as observers of others or being observed by others. It is found that some people consistently see themselves as observed, particularly males who are insecure and dependent. It is interesting to find that females feel observed, especially by males. Females tend to wear more colourful and interesting clothes and to take more trouble about their appearance. On the other hand, males more commonly try to put on a performance in the field of physical prowess.

The self can be activated in other ways. Duval and Wicklund (1972) called this 'objective self-awareness' – the awareness of oneself as an object, as seen from outside. They produced this state simply by placing people in front of mirrors. An indi-

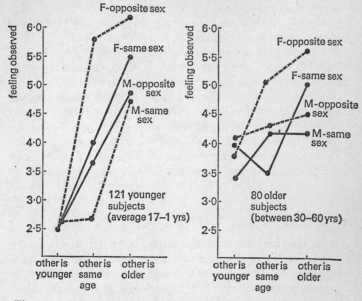

Figure 23. Effect of age and sex of the other on feeling observed (Argyle and Williams, 1969).

vidual will be more self-conscious if he or she is different from everyone else present, for example, by wearing different clothes or by being the only female or the only black present. Conversely 'de-individuation' can be brought about by dressing everyone up in white lab coats or other uniforms; this produces a loss of individual responsibility, and people even forget who said what (see p. 167). Self-awareness is produced by 'penetration' of territory or privacy – being discovered with too few clothes on, or when one has not been able to arrange one's appearance, or when awkward private facts are disclosed.

There are individual differences in self-consciousness. Some people suffer from *audience anxiety*, that is feel nervous when appearing in public or being the centre of attention. Another variable is *exhibitionism*, which is the desire to appear in public and be seen. It is found that these two dimensions are independent, so that some people both desire to be seen and are made anxious by it; such people are found to make a large number of speech errors when speaking in public (Paivio, 1965).

Those who have low self-esteem are shy, easily embarrassed, eager to be approved of, and are easily influenced by social pressures; they are clearly taking the observed role. Insecure people, i.e. those who have not formed a stable self-image, are very sensitive to the reactions of others, since they are still seeking information which will affect their self-image. Those who have achieved an integrated identity are no longer so bothered about the reactions of others, and are not upset if others mistake their identity, or react negatively to them (Marcia, 1966).

THE EFFECTS OF THE SELF-IMAGE ON BEHAVIOUR

What happens when the self is activated, by audiences, mirrors, or in other ways? In the first place there is a heightened level of physiological arousal, which results in greater effort, greater productivity if some task is being performed, as well as disruption of that performance if arousal is too great. Secondly, attention is directed towards the self rather than to others, and the self is seen as from outside. Duval and Wicklund suggest that this makes people aware of the discrepancies between self and ideal self, and self-image and the perception by others. They found that subjects who had been made aware of such discrepancies and were placed in front of a mirror, left the mirror as soon as they could; in other experiments it was found that subjects gave lower self-ratings when in front of a mirror. When people are in social situations, what they are concerned about is the reactions of others, and this can be controlled by appropriate self-presentation (Wicklund, 1975).

The motivation for self-presentation. People want to project a self-image for several reasons. To begin with, for interaction to occur at all it is necessary for the participants to be able to categorize one another – they need guidance on how to respond to each other. It was shown before that different styles of behaviour are used depending on the social class, occupation, nationality, etc. of the other. If it is not clear where a person falls on such dimensions, or if the important things about him are concealed, people do not know how to interact with him, and will be very perplexed. It is essential that all interactors should present themselves clearly in *some* way. It is necessary to arrive at a working agreement about the identities of those present.

An individual may be concerned about his face for professional purposes. Butlers, Lord Mayors, and film stars, as well as teachers, psychotherapists, and salesmen, all need to project a certain image of professional competence. There is a good reason for this: clients are more likely to respond in the desired way if they have confidence in the expertise of the practitioner. There is widespread evidence that pupils learn more if they think their teachers are good, and that patients in psychotherapy recover faster if they believe that the therapist can cure them. Another reason a person may need confirmation of his self-image or self-esteem is that he may be 'insecure' – i.e. be in constant need of reassurance from others that he is what he hopes he is. If the self-image has not been firmly established in the past, more time has to be spent looking in the mirror of others' reactions in the present. Adolescents, who have only just formed a tentative self-image, are particularly sensitive to the reactions of others, and are 'insecure' in this sense. People who have changed their social class, their job, or their nationality are often in a similar position.

Goffman (1956) observed that undertakers, salesmen, waiters, and other professional and service workers engage in a lot of deception and impression manipulation, which is often in their client's interests. The stage is set in the 'front regions' of premises, and may involve collusion between team-members; members of the public are kept out of the back regions, which are dirtier and less impressive, and where behaviour is more vulgar and informal. Goffman maintains that a similar degree of deception occurs in many other non-professional situations, such as a family receiving guests.

How do people project an identity? The easiest way would be

simply to tell other people how nice, important or clever we are. It is fairly obvious why this doesn't work – everyone would like to make such claims, but are they true? Jones *et al.* (1963) instructed army cadets to try to make themselves attractive to another cadet. When the other was of lower status subjects were very modest, when the other was of higher status they drew attention to their own assets in unimportant areas.

Verbal self-presentation appears to be acceptable provided that it is very indirect; if such messages are too direct they can easily become ridiculous, as in 'name-dropping'. Stephen Potter has given a satirical account of indirect ways of claiming a prestigeful identity in his book *One-Upmanship* (1952). For example:

LAYMAN: Thank you, Doctor. I was coming home rather late last night from the House of Commons ...

M.D.–MAN: Thank you ... now if you'll just let me put these ... hair brushes and things off the bed for you ... that's right ...

LAYMAN: I was coming home rather late. Army Act, really ...

M.D.–MAN: Now just undo the top button of your shirt or whatever it is you're wearing ...

LAYMAN: I say I was coming ...

M.D.–MAN: Now if you've got some hot water – really hot – and a clean towel.

LAYMAN: Yes, just outside. The Postmaster-General ...

M.D.–MAN: Open your mouth, please.

Self-presentation is done most efficiently by non-verbal communication. Non-verbal signals like clothes, hair, voice, and general style of behaviour, have more impact than words. Sometimes these non-verbal signals are actually part of what is symbolized – like upper-class speech or football-fan clothes. Sometimes they symbolize aspects of the self which cannot be easily displayed in the course of interaction, like being honest, or intelligent.

The main non-verbal signals here are clothes. Social class is easily signalled and recognized in this way. Accents are equally effective, and professional people may impress their clients by their offices and cars. Clothes can also send information about personality. Gibbins (1969) found that English grammar-school girls were agreed as to what kind of girl would wear various kinds of clothes, whether she would be promiscuous, go to church, drink, etc; the clothes they themselves preferred had images which resembled both their actual self and their ideal self.

Hair is used in a similar way. In many times and places long hair has been worn by male outcasts, intellectuals, dropouts and ascetics; having it cut represents re-entering society or living under a disciplined regime, like monks and soldiers do. On the other hand, some rebellious groups wear very short hair (e.g. skinheads), and long hair for males has sometimes been socially acceptable. Perhaps hair has no constant meaning at all, but is simply an important area for expressing opposition to prevailing norms.

Clothes, hair and other aspects of appearance differ from other non-verbal signals in that there are changes in fashion. The explanation is probably that élite fashions are copied by those of lower social status, so the higher-status groups have to adopt newer fashions to show that they are different. This doctrine was confirmed in an American survey by Hurlock (1929) in which 40 per cent of women and 20 per cent of men admitted that they would follow a fashion in order to appear equal to those of higher status, and about 50 per cent said they changed their styles when their social inferiors adopted them.

Deception and concealment. Another feature of self-presentation is concealment: people are careful not to reveal aspects of themselves which are likely to lead to disapproval. Jourard (1964) surveyed large numbers of students, using a questionnaire asking how much they had revealed about themselves to other people. This varied greatly with content: more was revealed about opinions and attitudes than about sexual behaviour or money for instance. People will reveal more to people who they can trust not to reject them – to their mothers, close friends, people who are similar to themselves, and (we may add) to psychiatrists and clergymen. Another case of concealment is the cautious, ritualized and conventional behaviour which people display on first meeting strangers. Disclosure is a risk, as there is a danger of the other person disapproving. There is extensive evidence that self-disclosure is reciprocated – a principle which is used by some psychotherapists and interviewers. People who disclose more are liked – provided that what they disclose is acceptable (Chaikin and Derlega, 1976).

As we saw above, Goffman (1956) believes that social behaviour involves a lot of deliberate deception, in that impressions are created for others. Jourard and others have argued that behaviour *ought* to be authentic.

I shall not discuss the moral issue here but shall list the main forms of deception, and consider their consequences. (1) The self presented is partly bogus, and nearer the ideal self than the actual self. We shall see below that this can lead to embarrassment if the deception is unmasked. On the other hand it is part of the process of moving towards the ideal self – being accepted as a somewhat different kind of person; people can help each other to move towards their ideal self and there will be consistency pressures to bring behaviour outside the interaction situation into line. (2) Discreditable episodes or features of the self are concealed. In any group of people who know each other well, there is collaboration in the process of forgetting unfortunate events. Similarly, if someone has a low opinion of a colleague it is probable that the most constructive line of action involves some concealment of these opinions. (3) Some people are 'stigmatized', in that they would be socially rejected if the truth were known – homosexuals, ex-convicts, mental patients, members of disreputable professions. They conceal these facts from outsiders, but can often recognize one another. (4) Deception by undertakers and waiters is not so much about the self as about other features of the professional performance. Sometimes this is to the performer's advantage – as for salesmen and waiters, sometimes it is to the client's advantage – as for undertakers and doctors.

Embarrassment. Embarrassment is a form of social anxiety which is suddenly precipitated by events during interaction; the victim loses poise, blushes, stutters, fumbles, sweats, avoids eye-contact, and in more severe cases flees from the situation and (mainly in the Far East) commits suicide. Embarrassment is contagious, it spreads rapidly to the others present. Once a person has lost control this makes the situation worse, as he is now ashamed also of his lack of poise. He is temporarily incapable of interacting.

Goffman (1955) offered a theory of embarrassment: people commonly present a self which is partly bogus; if this image is discredited in the course of interaction, embarrassment ensues. For example, a person's job, qualifications, or social origins may turn out to be less impressive than had been suggested. This theory can be checked against the 1,000 instances of embarrassment collected by Gross and Stone (1964). About a third of these cases involved discrediting of self-presentation, but the rest could not really be classified in this way, and two other sources of embarrassment need to be considered.

A second source of embarrassment is 'rule-breaking'. Garfinkel (1963) has carried out some intriguing 'demonstrations' in which investigators behaved in their own homes like lodgers, treated other customers in shops as salesmen, or flagrantly broke the rules of games – such as by moving the opponent's pieces. This produced embarrassment, consternation and anger. Rule-breaking may involve mistaking the role of others, disagreeing over the nature of the situation, breaking the basic rules of interaction or simply offending against arbitrary cultural conventions. Rule-breaking causes consternation because it is unexpected, it breaks the smooth flow of interaction, and because others may not know how to deal with it.

Accidents are a third source of embarrassment – tripping over the carpet, uncontrollable mirth or drunkenness, forgetting someone's name, social gaffes like talking about an apparently harmless matter which unexpectedly upsets someone, e.g. about his college when he has just been sent down, or his grandmother who has just died. Gross and Stone report an extraordinary case of a man at a banquet who got the tablecloth caught in his trouser zip-fastener, and pulled everything off the table when he rose to speak. Such episodes are more embarrassing at formal occasions since one is to some extent putting on a performance and implicitly making claims of competence.

Can embarrassment be avoided? Some people are able to remain poised when embarrassing incidents occur; they 'keep their cool' and prevent the situation from disintegrating. Adolescents often tease and insult one another, perhaps as a kind of training in dealing with embarrassment. Some of the possible causes of embarrassment can be avoided by presenting a face which cannot be invalidated, and it is less likely to happen to those who are not dependent on external confirmation of their self-image and self-esteem. Breakdown of interaction may still occur, however, as a result of accidental errors, as in social gaffes. Rules of etiquette and skills of tact help to avoid such breakdowns. An example of etiquette is the rule not to send invitations too long before the event, because it is difficult to refuse them. An example of tact is knocking on doors or coughing when a couple may be making love on the other side of it. Embarrassment can perhaps be controlled by understanding its causes. There is really no need to be disturbed by accidents committed in good faith and without hostile intention – it is more useful to put things right.

When a person is embarrassed, the others present usually want to prevent the collapse of social interaction, and will help in various ways. To begin with, they will try to prevent loss of face by being tactful in the ways described. They may pretend that nothing has happened, make excuses for the offender – he was only joking, was off form etc., or in some other way 'rescue the situation'. Finally, if face is irrevocably lost they may help the injured party to rehabilitate himself in the group in a new guise (Goffman, 1955; Gross and Stone, 1964).

Disconfirmation of self-image. When A's face has been disbelieved or discredited there are various strategies open to him. One is simply to ignore what has happened or to laugh it off as unimportant. It would be expected from the analysis given in earlier chapters that a person who had failed to project an image would try alternative ways of doing so. If he is rattled he may fall back on less subtle techniques of the kind 'Look here, young man, I've written more books about this subject than you've read', 'Do you realize that I . . .', etc. This may succeed in modifying the other's perceptions, but it will almost certainly cause embarrassment and make the speaker look ridiculous.

What very often happens is that A forms a lower opinion of a person or group that does not treat him properly, and he goes off to present himself to someone else. It has been found that sales-girls in shops preserve their image of competence in the face of customers whom they can't please by categorizing them as 'nasty', or in some similar way (Lombard, 1955). If a low opinion is formed of B, it doesn't matter whether B confirms the girl's self-image of competence or not. A number of experiments show that people withdraw from groups who do not react to them in the desired way, and that they prefer the company and friendship of those who confirm their self-image (Secord and Backman, 1974).

Sometimes a person is still keen to belong to a group even though it does not accept his self-image or does not treat him with enough respect. When it is mainly esteem which has been withheld by the group, it is possible to alter behaviour in a way that will produce the desired response from others. It is found that insecure people are more affected by social influences and pressures of all kinds. In small social groups, for example, one of the main causes of conformity is the avoidance of being re-jected, as deviates tend to be. Those who conform most are those who feel inferior, lack self-confidence, and are dependent on others (Krech, Crutchfield and Ballachey, 1962). People may embark on all kinds of self-improvement, either apparent or real, in response to negative reactions from others, including the modification of styles of interaction as in operant verbal conditioning.

The remaining responses can really be regarded as 'defence mechanisms', whose main object is the avoidance of anxiety, while no realistic adjustment of self-image or behaviour is in-volved. One of these is self-deception in its various forms. A person may distort the reactions of others in a favourable direc-tion, or simply not perceive them at all. The extreme of this is psychotic withdrawal from the difficulties of interpersonal relations into a private world of fantasies which cannot be disturbed by outside events.

FURTHER READING

Gergen, K. J., *The Concept of Self*, New York: Holt, Rinehart and Winston, 1971.

Goffman, E., *The Presentation of Self in Everyday Life*, Edinburgh University Press, 1956.

Wicklund, R. A., 'Objective self awareness', *Advances in Experimental Social Psychology*, 1975, pp. 233–75.

CHAPTER 10

SOCIAL BEHAVIOUR AND MENTAL DISORDER

THIS topic is of importance for two reasons. We can learn a lot about normal social performance by studying the ways in which it goes wrong; each kind of failure in social performance shows us a feature of normal social behaviour which has to be managed properly. Secondly the study of the social behaviour of mental patients may throw light on the nature of mental disorders and have implications for new forms of treatment. In fact it has already done so: social skills training for mental patients is one of the main practical applications of the research described in this book.

We shall not attempt in this chapter to give a complete or balanced account of mental disorders, and shall only be concerned with the *social* behaviour of mental patients. Freud maintained that mental disorders were primarily disturbances of the sexual instinct. Sullivan suggested that they were disturbances of social behaviour. In fact the social behaviour of patients is inadequate in a variety of ways. There are at least two views about how the failure of social behaviour may be related to the other aspects of disorders. One theory is that failure to learn the right social skills in childhood results in later social rejection and failure to cope with life events; this in turn causes anxiety, depression or other symptoms. According to the other theory, genetic and physiological processes are primary, resulting successively in personality disturbance, disturbed social performance, rejection, and an exacerbation of the condition.

There is evidence from twin studies that mental disorders are partly inherited, and this is particularly true of the psychoses, such as schizophrenia, rather than of the neuroses; this would lend support to the second theory. On the other hand the psychoses are affected by childhood experiences, are often precipitated by rejection or other social stresses, and some of the main symptoms are in the sphere of social performance, so that the first process may also be operating, and this is even more likely with the neuroses. Following either theory, it would be valuable to retrain patients in social skills, and according to the first this would be the most useful treatment.

SOCIAL BEHAVIOUR OBSERVED IN THE MAIN MENTAL DISORDERS

In this section a descriptive account will be given of the social behaviour which is observed in the main types of mental disorder. Some of this is commonly reported by clinicians, and can be seen in any mental hospital. The more subtle aspects require the use of some of the research methods described earlier – such as the analysis of voice quality, direction of gaze, synchronizing of speech, person perception, and so on.

The categories into which patients are classified vary between countries and historical periods; American psychiatrists label five times as many patients 'schizophrenic' as British psychiatrists (Cooper *et al.*, 1972). I shall use the current British classification.

Schizophrenia includes a wide variety of patients, but the basic syndrome consists of withdrawal from social relationships, disturbance of thought and speech, a failure of persistent, goal-directed behaviour, and a flat and apathetic emotional state. The disturbance of social behaviour is only one of their symptoms, but it is one of the most characteristic ones and it is a principal reason for their inability to deal with everyday life. They simply cannot communicate properly, or take part in ordinary social encounters. They are of great interest to social psychologists, since the failure of social behaviour is more basic than for other patients – there is no meeting of minds, no collaboration to send and receive messages. Many schizophrenics engage in very little social behaviour; they remain isolated and detached from other people, and are engaged with private fantasies and daydreams. When they are in a group or interview situation they appear not to be attending to the situation at all, and may make irrelevant remarks, giving a clue to the fantasies with which they are preoccupied.

Considering first the details of social performance, schizophrenics look odd and untidy, and do not wear their clothes well; they adopt unsuitable proximities – either too near or too far; they orient themselves away from other people – often against a wall; postures and gestures may be weird – they symbolize private fantasies and may not be intended to communicate anything; facial expression is blank, though there can be grimaces; there is very little speech, and this is rambling and incoherent, is not synchronized with the speech of others, and is often on totally irrelevant topics. Schizophrenics are often found to avert gaze; however, Rutter has found that there is no gaze aversion if they are talking about impersonal topics (p. 91).

Turning to more general patterns of social behaviour, there is no cooperation or formation of social groups; schizophrenics do not form relationships with one another, though they may be on the receiving end of relationships with hospital staff; they are made anxious by social situations, are upset by criticism, and do not like being supervised; they are very unresponsive to nonverbal signals, though to some extent they can receive verbal messages such as simple instructions. There is evidence that schizophrenics avoid people more than other stimuli; Ederyn Williams (1974), working at Oxford, found in a test situation that schizophrenics spent more time looking at a TV film about fish than attending to a second person in the room.

The causes of schizophrenia are not yet known, nor is there any known cure, although tranquillizing drugs suppress the symptoms while they are being taken. Since about 0·8 per cent of the world's population suffer from schizophrenia, this is an extremely pressing scientific and social problem. One possibility is that the primary cause is biochemical – it may be due to some substance in the brain, like mescaline or LSD, which produces symptoms similar to schizophrenia. This has been likened to the effects of spraying a computer with water; however, the quest for this substance has so far been unsuccessful. Twin studies show that schizophrenia is partly inherited, but it need not be transmitted biochemically, any more than intelligence is. It is worth exploring hypotheses about possible social origins of schizophrenia. Schizophrenics are found to come from families which are disturbed in certain characteristic ways, such as having dominant and rejecting mothers and various kinds of failure of communication – e.g. one person's remarks are not acknowledged by another, members of the family fail to come to an agreement but then act as if they had, together with a lot of conflict and hostility (Jacob, 1975). Schizophrenia is often triggered by stressful life events, such as death, ill-health, or other disasters in the family, or sudden disturbances to the patient's way of life, during the three weeks before onset (Brown *et al.*, 1973).

There are several very interesting lines of thought and research which between them provide a possible social psychological explanation of most features of schizophrenia. We shall describe three of the main approaches briefly.

1. *Failures of non-verbal communication.* It has been suggested that the failure to communicate properly is due to verbal signals being accompanied by meta-signals (usually non-verbal) which deny the original message, or deny that anything sensible was said, or which create a paradoxical communication, as in 'I am a liar' – a so-called 'double-bind'. It is suggested that schizophrenics behave in this way in order to escape from intolerable social situations. Clinical studies have suggested that the parents of schizophrenics use such paradoxical communication, as in 'Why don't you love me?' (said crossly), and it is argued that the behaviour is learnt (Watzlawick *et al.*, 1967). The evidence for this general theory is weak, though it has been found that schizophrenics report that their parents used double-binds (Berger, 1965).

An alternative formulation in this area might be to assert that schizophrenics simply have a deficiency in the perception and emission of non-verbal signals. There is clear evidence that this is so. A number of studies have shown that they are less responsive to non-verbal cues than are normal people. Such a deficit could be partly genetic, partly due to faulty socialization. It would lead to a failure of synchronizing, feedback and all other aspects of social interaction controlled by non-verbal signals.

2. *Failures of thought processes needed for social behaviour*. The two main symptoms of schizophrenia are thought disturbance and failure of social behaviour; are they related? It has been found that schizophrenics find it more difficult to rank photographs of people consistently than to rank photographs of physical objects, and that they make no inferences from one dimension to another (Bannister and Salmon, 1966). Later studies have shown that *inconsistency* is the basic problem – a schizophrenic might rate A as more intelligent than B, B more than C, and C more than A (Haynes and Phillips, 1973). Other studies have found that schizophrenics use very few concepts relating to personality or emotions when describing other people, and that this deficit correlates highly with social withdrawal, and to a lesser extent with emotional flattening; they refer to clothes or physical features of the person or background instead. It looks as if schizophrenics may have a specific cognitive deficiency – of not being able to conceptualize persons or emotions – though it is not known what the cause is.

I would like to put forward another idea. Schizophrenic social behaviour fails in the most basic way – the sequence of social events is wrong in a way otherwise found only in experiments on rule-breaking. Depressives, alcoholics, criminals and the rest can at least get the basic sequences of social behaviour right. To do so requires the cognitive ability to grasp the nature of the situation, and what other people are trying to do, to be able to cooperate in such basic sequences as question–answer, greetings, and the rest (see p. 144f.).

If these or other theories are correct, it follows that forms of treatment might be devised aimed at correcting the particular cognitive deficits described.

3. *Persistent rule-breaking*. It has been suggested by some sociologists that the only common feature of the diverse symptoms produced by schizophrenics is rule-breaking. This could be because they come from weird families which broke rules, or

because they found that some advantage came from breaking rules. It has been found that schizophrenics report much worse symptoms if they are interviewed to see if they should be discharged, than if interviewed to see if they should be placed in a closed ward (Braginsky *et al.*, 1969). It seems that they want to stay in hospital, but on an open ward, and can manipulate their symptoms in order to bring this about. It is found that schizophrenics adjust to the hospital in diverse ways, including avoiding the staff and making full use of the leisure facilities. Braginsky *et al.* found that while 82 per cent of patients knew where the bowling alley was, and 80 per cent the swimming pool, only 36 per cent knew where the psychologist's office was, and 26 per cent the name of the psychologist. These, of course, were American schizophrenics, and the theory may best fit those social misfits and failures who have found life outside stressful and frustrating, and seek a pleasant refuge which is undemanding and comfortable, and requires little work and contact with other people. They are, however, quite different from hippies, who drop out in groups, and are perfectly able to take part in social interaction.

Paranoid reactions consist of delusions, about self and others. Where there is personality disintegration but with strongly held delusions this is called paranoid schizophrenia. Where the personality is more intact it is called paranoia. Paranoid reactions are commonest in the middle-aged and elderly, while other kinds of schizophrenia occur in the young. Paranoids, it is found, are secretive and seclusive, do not trust people or confide in them, but are generally able to communicate and get into rapport better than schizophrenics. They are always found to be suffering from thought disturbance – but this disturbance is invariably focused on relations with other people. Paranoids feel that they are being plotted against, spied upon, or otherwise victimized, and that this is the explanation of their other failures. They may believe that their behaviour is being controlled from a distance, by TV, laser beams or whatever is the latest technology, by the Brazilian railways or the secret police. Their perception of the world is disturbed in that they think that the behaviour of others is oriented primarily towards themselves. They may also have delusions of grandeur, believing that they have some important mission, message, or discovery.

While perfectly capable of normal interaction, they are extremely sensitive to minor slights, insults and rejections, and are quite unable to receive or profit by feedback from others concerning their ideas or self-image. At the first hint of negative feedback, their defences become rigid, and other people are blamed instead. Paranoids often cause annoyance by their touchy, hostile, arrogant and dominating behaviour, in which they constantly want to demonstrate their superiority. They think that there is a conspiracy against them, and that people are talking about them behind their back; as they become gradually excluded from the community this belief becomes true (Lemmert, 1962). Their chief social motivation seems to be a desire for praise and recognition, and a bolstering of their grandiose but precarious self-image.

Paranoia can be regarded as mainly a disturbance of the self-image, made possible by the tendency to form false beliefs, in order to reduce anxiety. For example, a child may explain his failure in an examination by saying that the teacher was not fair; if the parents support this view they are encouraging paranoid thinking. This is more likely to happen to children who are isolated from the healthy ridicule of the peer group. Paranoia is precipitated by social stresses such as failure, competition, or loss of a supporting social relationship.

Manic and depressive states are mainly disturbances of mood, but there are also characteristic styles of social behaviour. Some patients are manic or depressive at different times, and some alternate between the two: this shows that the two states are probably closely related. Manics are euphoric, self-confident and full of energy; depressives are overwhelmed by feelings of misery, guilt and inadequacy, and are lacking in motivation.

Manics wear smart, striking but rather loud clothes, look extremely well and very pleased with themselves, are smiling and alert, and have a loud confident voice of robust, resonant quality. They talk incessantly, and tend to monopolize the conversation with their hilarious jokes and outrageous stories, but are easily distractable and move rapidly from topic to topic. Their excitement and jollity are infectious, and they are good at being the life and soul of the party. Manics have a self-confidence and self-esteem for which there is no adequate basis, and they will not take criticism from others. They enjoy making speeches, and writing letters to important people. On the other hand they are quite good at handling people. This, together with their energy and self-confidence, often leads to a successful career in one of the more colourful occupations such as politics or show business. Their chief failings in social competence are an inability to perceive themselves accurately, and in annoying others by their dominance and unsuitable jokes. Their delusional self-importance, their constant talking, and a tendency to bizarre behaviour may lead to their becoming a public nuisance.

Depressives are drab and sombre in appearance, they look miserable, have a drooping posture, and their voices are flat, low-pitched and monotonous. They keep to themselves and, if engaged in conversation, will give brief replies, without initiating anything. They have little energy and will sit and brood by themselves. They have a lower opinion of themselves than is warranted, and are obsessed with feelings of failure and guilt, and may contemplate suicide; they are completely lacking in self-confidence. Their self-image is as inaccurate as is that of manics.

Manic and depressive conditions are partly genetic. They are also affected by childhood experience – death of a parent before the child is five, families where there is a lot of pressure to be respectable and successful, and competition between siblings. The conditions are brought on by specifically social events – the breaking of an important social bond by bereavement, divorce or leaving an organization. Depression in particular is brought on by social isolation. Seligman (1975) has suggested an interpretation of depression in terms of 'learned helplessness'. Dogs that had experience of uncontrollable electric shocks made little attempt in a later situation to escape from shocks – they had been trained to give up. Human beings are more complicated, however: at first, when they are faced by a situation of loss of control, they engage in vigorous positive efforts to gain control, known as 'reactance'; it is only if the loss of control continues that learned helplessness sets in (Wortman and Brehm, 1975).

However, there are some patients who experience both manic and depressive phases. They presumably cannot be accounted for in this kind of way, and other processes, biochemical or psychological, must be involved.

Neurosis – general. Neuroticism is a matter of degree, and everyone experiences anxiety sometimes, and is upset by some degree of stress. However, between five and eight per cent of the population are unduly anxious, can stand very little stress, have reduced energy, function below their true capacity, have headaches or other aches and pains, can't sleep, and find other people difficult to deal with. People with anxiety neurosis may have a general 'free-floating' anxiety about nothing in particular, phobias for height, travel or other situations, and obsessions, such as a concern with dirt and cleanliness. If they suffer from social anxiety, they can be seen to be in a state of tension in social situations, from their strained faces, trembling hands, and tense postures. Such people talk very fast, nervously, and rather indistinctly, and they tend to speak first at an encounter. However their utterances are short, they make many speech errors, and may lose control of the quality of their speech. They may be competent at social interaction, and are often very sensitive to the responses of others, but they may get into difficulties as a result of their other symptoms. An obsessional who is worried about the smell of bad breath, and a person with a phobia of closed or open spaces, will have difficulties in taking part in many encounters. Like other neurotics, people with anxiety neurosis tend to be self-centred and demanding, more concerned with their own needs and problems than with those of others. In addition, anxiety neurotics are tense, irritable and easily upset, they are often found annoying and unrewarding by others, and so can become gradually isolated.

Neurotics may engage in queer, destructive social techniques, whose effect is highly disturbing. The motivation may be aggression, or relief of inner tensions in complex ways, as described by Berne (1966). For example, a fraudulent contract may be offered, as in 'Rapo': a female leads a male on until he makes an advance, whereupon she indignantly rejects him. In 'Why don't you – Yes, but' someone appears to be seeking advice about some problem; whatever solution is offered he is able to point out the obvious objections to it. In 'Alcoholic' a person may seek a relationship in which another is forced into playing the role of the moral persecutor and the sympathizing rescuer. In these and many other cases the neurotic game-player is able to obtain the peculiar social relationship he wants, often at another's expense.

Neuroticism is partly inherited, partly the result of overstrict and over-intense upbringing. Failure of social competence is the main trouble for some neurotics. Bryant *et al.* (1976) studied the social behaviour of out-patients diagnosed as neurotic. It was found that of 92 patients studied, 27 per cent were judged to be socially inadequate, 46 per cent of the males (mostly unmarried) and 16 per cent of the females; 21 per cent were thought to be suitable for social skills training. This is a minority of the whole population of neurotics, though one which is of particular interest to social psychologists. In this study, the socially inadequate were significantly less extraverted, sociable, dominant and confident, and they reported more difficulty in social situations. They appeared colder, less assertive, less happy, less controlling, less rewarding and more anxious than the socially adequate group. They were also significantly more likely to have had in adolescence a history of solitariness and difficulty in making friends, and of unsuccessful attempts at 'dating'. In terms of elements of behaviour, they tended towards the 'inactive' or unassertive side, being on the whole rather silent, showing little interest in others, speaking very briefly and in a slow and rather monotonous voice, rarely handing over the conversation, sitting very still and rigid, and with a dull, fixed expression.

Hysteria is a form of neurotic breakdown which is more common among extraverts, whereas anxiety neurosis is more common among introverts (Eysenck, 1957). There are also hysterical personalities among normal people, who share some of the same behaviour. Hysteria consists mainly of apparent bodily complaints, which are based on blockages at higher levels of the central nervous system. These include motor blockages (paralyses), sensory blockages (anaesthesias), and failures of memory. The characteristic social behaviour of hysterics also has a quality of role-playing: they over-dramatize themselves, exaggerate their emotional states, and pretend to be more interesting and exciting than they really are. They are very anxious for their self-image to be reinforced, and very sensitive to feedback concerning it. They like to be the centre of attention, need to be admired, and are often successful as actresses, politicians and public speakers. They are competent interactors, more active than normal people, but not so active as manics.

Hysterical breakdown may involve a sudden change of identity, as in the case of the impostor who adopts some high-status role, in which he half believes, partly for the material rewards which may be gained, partly for the admiration. Helene Deutsch (1955) describes the cases of a number of people of this type, one of whom made a rapid transition from juvenile delinquent to 'country gentleman'. Slightly different is the hysterical 'fugue' in which a person escapes from some intolerable life situation by adopting a quite different identity and completely forgetting his former life.

Hysterics are often females, who have been over-protected by their mothers. One theory is that they have been rewarded for minor illnesses, both by avoiding events and by receiving extra maternal care, so that feeling ill becomes the automatic reaction to stress. This can be regarded as a special kind of non-verbal communication, used when verbal utterances have failed. The message may be a demand for attention, love, sympathy or help, or it may signal guilt and self-punishment. The hysteric uses these signals to control people in the same way that she was able to control her mother (Szasz, 1961).

Delinquents and psychopaths. Of particular interest here are the so-called 'pseudo-social' delinquents. These are not abnormal in any clinical sense, and are quite different from the impulsive and affectionless psychopaths. They reject adults and others in authority, but behave perfectly well to members of their group or gang, and indeed may be loyally devoted to it. Their most interesting feature for present purposes is the total barrier which exists between them and adults – a one-sided barrier in that it is extremely difficult for adults to establish a relationship with them. Various techniques have been suggested for use in institutions, such as the use of young adults who can be seen as suitable models, and who work hard to establish rapport.

Groups of football hooligans, drug addicts, violent revolutionaries, and others are similar. The behaviour of these and other delinquent groups can partly be explained in terms of learning to be members of an alternative social world, with its own rules, values and beliefs, which gives gratifications which cannot be obtained in the outside world. They are labelled by the outside world as 'football hooligans', for example, and this label becomes part of their self-image, helping to separate them from society, in a process of 'deviance amplification'. There appears to be a failure of social behaviour in dealing with 'straight' society. Sarason and Ganzer (1971), however, have had some success in training delinquents to go for job interviews, for example.

Psychopaths are a very interesting group from the present point of view, since they show none of the usual symptoms of neurosis (e.g. anxiety) or of psychosis (e.g. disturbances of thought or mood), but are disturbed primarily in the social sphere. The main symptoms are impulsiveness, unrestrained aggression or sexuality, lack of conscience, and lack of sympathy, affection or consideration for others. Examples are aggressive young males, and nymphomaniac young females. While they appear to have no interest in affiliative relations with people, they often join groups and organizations and become a very disturbing influence. When a psychopath is a member of a small group there is little hope of the group being cohesive or cooperative. It is as if they are sensitive to sources of conflict or tension, either in individuals or between different group members, and succeed in making things worse. In other ways their perception of social events is probably defective. McDavid and Schroder (1957) found that one hundred juvenile criminals and delinquents were poor at discriminating social responses of approval and disapproval, as presented in a series of situational descriptions.

Psychopaths sometimes behave with charm and spontaneity. They are thus able to manipulate other people to their own ends – but their relations with others are always a means to ends and never ends in themselves. Psychopaths are rather like some salesmen – they want to interact with people so that they can get their bonus, but have no further interest in the people concerned. Whereas salesmen usually satisfy their affiliative needs in other encounters, psychopaths behave like this in all encounters. They cannot form relationships of friendship, love, or permanent attachment with other people. They are not concerned about the welfare or sufferings of others, are basically indifferent to them, and quite lacking in remorse for their own past acts: it is as if they are unable to understand how other people are feeling.

There is some genetic basis, to psychopathy at any rate. More important is a childhood history of lack of love, ill-treatment, neglect, lack of discipline, and lack of a stable home, combined with certain social conditions – social and economic deprivation, juvenile gangs in the area, and absence of satisfying work opportunities.

TYPES OF BREAKDOWN OF SOCIAL PERFORMANCE IN MENTAL DISORDER

Our immediate interest in this chapter is finding out the different ways in which social behaviour may break down, since this will throw light on the mechanisms of social skill. Study of breakdown of social behaviour in mental patients may be of practical importance too. If mental disorders are either caused or exacerbated by a failure of social performance, this information may be valuable in suggesting methods of prevention and cure.

It is a matter of extreme urgency at the present time to discover more effective ways of treating mental patients, so these ideas are worth pursuing.

Failures of social competence can be of a number of different types, as has been seen in the last section. These will be classified and related to different parts of the social-skill mechanism. These forms of failure occur in extreme forms in mental patients, but they are widely found in 'normal' members of the community.

Rewardingness. Nearly all mental patients are very unrewarding to be with, which leads to their isolation, and makes life difficult for hospital staff. Different kinds of patient are unrewarding in different ways – schizophrenics have been described as 'socially bankrupt' since they are so unresponsive; depressives are depressing, neurotics are preoccupied with themselves, and psychopaths are only interested in other people as means to ends.

Taking the role of the other. Many mental patients are unable to take the role of the other. In general they are found to be ego-centric, and to talk about themselves more than other people do (Meldman, 1967); this is very marked in hysterics. They are often totally unable to see anyone else's point of view, as in schizophrenia and psychopathy; or they are mistaken about the reactions of others, as in paranoia and to a lesser extent in anxiety neurosis.

Perception of other people is inaccurate for many patients. Schizophrenics are very unreceptive to non-verbal signals and are not able to interpret the behaviour of others in terms of emotions or other psychological constructs. Paranoids fail to receive messages which contain any criticism of themselves. They are thus unable to modify their behaviour or their self-image. Patients with anxiety neurosis on the other hand are *too* sensitive to signs of criticism or displeasure on the part of others.

Disturbances of social motivation. Manics, as well as being high in dominance, are aroused too much, depressives too little, and that is the central feature of these conditions. In anxiety neurosis there is over-arousal, combined with expectation of punishment, rejection, or disaster; in social situations such patients are anxious since they constantly anticipate rejection. In other disorders a particular social drive may be unusually weak. For psychopaths a lack of affiliative motivation appears to be a central part of the disorder, and can be traced to the absence in early childhood of those relations with the mother that are necessary for the development of affiliative behaviour.

Social skills. Schizophrenics are grossly deficient in social skills. Many neurotics, and many socially isolated people, have inadequate social skills of some kind. They may be unable to deal with everyday encounters without great awkwardness; they may have difficulty in sustaining an ordinary conversation; they may be unable to deal with whole groups of people – the opposite sex, older persons, different social classes, dominant people, etc. Other groups, such as paranoids and psychopaths, are able to get into rapport and synchronize their interactions smoothly, but do not form long-term relationships with others, because interaction with them is not rewarding to others, or demands the acceptance of ridiculous ideas.

Self-presentation. There are disturbances of self-image in most disorders. Hysterics are perpetually trying to get others to accept their own over-dramatized self-image. This is seen most clearly in impostors and pretenders who half-believe in the parts they are playing. It can be regarded as a case of high self-esteem combined with insecurity. Paranoids are rather different: they are in no doubt about their self-image, but they are annoyed that other people will not accept it. Both hysterics and paranoids emphasize the unique aspects of their self-image, whereas many adolescents and pseudo-social delinquents have an identity which is shared with other members of the group.

THE EFFECTS OF TREATMENT ON SOCIAL BEHAVIOUR

We must distinguish at this point between the neuroses, such as anxiety and hysteria, and the psychoses, such as schizophrenia and the manic and depressive states. The neuroses have traditionally been treated by psychotherapy, though the recovery rate is very slow, not much faster than the spontaneous rate of recovery for untreated patients. The psychoses have traditionally been treated by physical methods, though the value of psychological and social techniques is being increasingly recognized. The present position is that schizophrenics can be temporarily improved by means of drugs, but that they deteriorate as soon as they stop taking the drug: some success is claimed for social therapy while the patients are sedated.

The outlook for depressives is rather better, since electroconvulsive therapy and anti-depressant drugs are often successful. For both the neuroses and the psychoses there is an urgent need to find better methods of treatment. If the breakdown of social performance is an important element for any of these conditions it is important to know how far it is affected by existing methods of treatment. We may also be able to deduce something about the pattern of causation by seeing whether the social behaviour or the other symptoms are affected first.

Individual psychotherapy. Many patients who enter psychotherapy suffer from interpersonal difficulties, either about specific problems at work or in the home, or more general social difficulties. Some come to the therapist since they have no one else to talk to; he provides a kind of friendship, but may be able to use it to teach them how to get on with other people (Lennard and Bernstein, 1960). Although therapists vary in what they do, certain procedures are common to all (see p. 245f.).

Some psychotherapists believe that interpersonal problems lie at the root of mental disorder, and they direct their therapy towards the patient's social behaviour and relationships. For example Berne (1966) analysed his patients' behaviour in terms of the game-like techniques which they are using (see p. 216), and whether they were using child, adult or parent roles. Rogers (1942) directed his treatment primarily towards the self-system of his patients, to bring about greater self-acceptance, less conflict between self and ideal self, and more commitment to persistent courses of action.

There has been a lot of disagreement over whether psychotherapy actually cures people any faster than they would recover spontaneously – up to 70 per cent recover after two years without treatment. However a number of carefully controlled studies show that there is more improvement both in social behaviour and in other respects, though it is very slow and many therapeutic sessions may be required (p. 246f.).

In *group therapy* the treatment is more directly concerned with the patients' social behaviour, and the situation is more like real life. In the version devised by Bion (1948–51), and practised at the Tavistock Clinic in London, the therapist comments on the social behaviour of people in the group, and makes little reference to other aspects of their behaviour. This is rather similar to T-group training (p. 274f.), which has been influenced by group therapy. In other kinds of group therapy, which are more like psychotherapy in public, it is hoped that patients will profit from belonging to a friendly and supporting group, will learn to get on with a variety of people as met in the group, and will be able to try out new social techniques in this safe environment, as well as being able to understand their own problems better when they are manifested in others, and feeling less guilty after finding that others are just as bad. Group therapy seems to be most effective with those who are isolated, shy and withdrawn. It became popular partly because psychiatrists thought that they were getting better results than with individual treatment, partly because of shortage of psychiatrists.

Behaviour therapy consists of a number of training techniques based on learning theory. Early successes were obtained in the treatment of certain rather specific, and non-social symptoms. Bed-wetting can be cured by Mowrer's machine which rudely awakens the bed-wetter with a loud bell. Alcoholism and other attachments can be stopped by aversion training, in which the patient receives electric shocks or is made sick following exposure to the forbidden stimulus. The most widely used form of behaviour therapy is 'desensitization' for phobias: the patient is lightly hypnotized, relaxes deeply, and imagines the least frightening of a hierarchy of fearful stimuli, such as heights, flying or spiders, relaxes again, and imagines the next stimulus in the hierarchy. A recent development is 'flooding', in which the patient confronts the most frightening stimulus either in reality or imagination for twenty minutes or so. These methods are very successful with specific phobias, and it is claimed that more general personality disturbance can be helped by dealing with central areas of anxiety. For discussion of the numerous follow-up studies see Kazdin and Wilcoxon (1976).

Behaviour therapy has been applied, with some success, to disturbances of social behaviour in three ways. (1) Social anxieties, for example about public speaking, can be cured by desensitization, and recovery is faster than under psychotherapy (Paul, 1966). (2) Social anxiety and general social inadequacy can be helped by arousing incompatible response patterns, such as dominance and aggression. This is the theoretical basis of assertion therapy (Wolpe, 1958). (3) The social behaviour of psychotic patients can be improved by regimes under which they are reinforced by tokens (later exchangeable for food or cigarettes), for cooperation or other specified forms of behaviour (Ayllon and Azrin, 1968).

It is recognized by some behaviour therapists that further training in social behaviour may be needed. For example, homosexuals may need to be taught how to deal with women as well as not to feel attracted towards men. We now turn to such methods of training.

Social skills training for neurotic patients (*SST*). For the last few years, the author and his colleagues have been treating neurotic patients who have difficulties with social situations (Trower, Bryant and Argyle, 1978). These methods are discussed in the next chapter p. 269f.

Areas of social behaviour which have been taught include: conducting an informal conversation; taking an interest in and finding out about another person; making a date; taking part in a group decision; and speaking in public. It seems probable that after training a patient approaches social situations in a more rewarding and constructive manner, and thus elicits quite different reactions from other people. A number of our patients have improved markedly, not only in social performance, but in other aspects of their behaviour as well, including apparently 'physiological' symptoms such as anorexia (not eating) and amenorrhœa (stoppage of periods).

Follow-up studies have found that SST is somewhat better than other forms of therapy, both for improving social behaviour and for other aspects of the mental health of socially inadequate neurotics.

Similar methods have been developed for psychotic patients in the U.S.A. by Goldstein (1973) and others, partly in the hope that working-class patients would benefit from these less verbal techniques.

Therapeutic community treatment. The previous methods described are mainly applicable to neurotic patients. Schizophrenics and other psychotic patients are usually treated in hospitals, and the therapeutic community is a way of organizing mental hospitals. Mental hospitals have come under severe criticism in recent years: it has been argued that they treat patients as if they were irresponsible and naughty children, and force them into the role of lunatics. It was found by Wing (1967) that the longer patients are inside, the more 'institutionalized' they become – i.e. they get adjusted to their dependent position in the hospital, and lose all contact with the outside world. Szasz (1961) has argued that mental hospitals actually make people worse, by classifying harmless eccentrics as lunatics and teaching them the appropriate role behaviour.

In hospitals organized as therapeutic communities efforts are made to train patients in more desirable social skills. The staff are trained to treat the patients less autocratically and to conduct group therapy on the wards. The patients do manual work for regular hours each day and are paid for it. Patients are given various other jobs and responsibilities such as helping to run clubs, and social contacts with other patients are encouraged, as are trips outside the hospital. In these ways patients are given practice in various aspects of social behaviour and relationships.

Experiments have been made with new kinds of therapeutic community, in which small groups of patients are made less dependent on the staff, take more responsibility for themselves, and work in the community. Fairweather and colleagues (1969) compared the effects of a 'small-group ward' and a traditional ward in a mental hospital. In the first, small groups were made responsible for getting jobs done, recommending patients for increased privileges, and other matters. Behaviour on the ward was greatly improved, patients left hospital sooner, more were employed later, and they spent more time with friends.

Other studies have found that such milieu therapy alone is not very effective: the best outcomes for schizophrenics and other severely disturbed patients are obtained with a combination of a therapeutic milieu, tranquillizing drugs and individual or group therapy (May, 1968).

CONCLUSIONS

There is some disturbance of social performance in nearly all mental patients, both neurotic and psychotic. In other words some of the symptoms are in the sphere of social behaviour, and for certain patients these are the main or only symptoms. The causes of mental disorders are partly in the social sphere – peculiar childhood experiences and more recent social stresses. Other causes are clearly non-social – the effects of inheritance and of internal states, such as those produced by drugs.

The evidence is not clear as to when the failure of social behaviour is primary or secondary. If we can speculate, it looks as if the disturbance of social behaviour may be primary for the neuroses. In other cases it is not so clear what the sequence of causation may be. In the case of schizophrenia, for example, it looks as if the failure of social performance may be the result of more basic genetic factors – affecting non-verbal signalling or cognitive processes, or both, and that this leads to withdrawal and hospitalization.

Since other forms of treatment for pervasive neurosis and for schizophrenia are so ineffective, it is worth trying out various kinds of social treatment. Social skills training for neurotics with interpersonal difficulties seems very promising; for schizophrenia there have been a number of interesting experiments with different kinds of therapeutic communities such as the token economy and the self-governing commune.

Some kinds of treatment seem to be directed mainly at the social performance of patients, as in therapeutic community treatment and some kinds of psychotherapy. Schizophrenics benefit from therapeutic community treatment, and it may be that training in social skill can be therapeutic even when the skill breakdown is not primary.

FURTHER READING

Carson, R. C., *Interaction Concepts of Personality*, London: Allen and Unwin, 1970.

Orford, J., *The Social Psychology of Mental Disorder*, Harmondsworth: Penguin Books, 1976.

Trower, P., Bryant, B., and Argyle, M., *Social Skills and Mental Health*, London: Methuen, 1978.

CHAPTER II

SOME PROFESSIONAL SOCIAL SKILLS

SOCIAL behaviour has been looked at as a skilled performance which is used to elicit certain desired responses from other people. This approach can be used to give an account of professional social skills; in each of these the performer carries out a task which consists mainly of handling other people in order to get them to react in certain ways. The criteria for success at such professional tasks were discussed earlier (p. 75f.), and are clearer in some cases (such as selling) than in others (such as teaching). For some of these tasks there has been a good deal of research into which social techniques, or which kinds of people, are most effective. It is found that there are fairly large individual differences – for example, a ratio of five to one in average takings is not uncommon among salesgirls in the same department, and there are similar variations between the absenteeism and labour turnover rates under different supervisors.

Some social skills for which there is a substantial body of research have been selected for discussion here. Others which might have been included are the skills of the barrister, the negotiator, the social worker, as well as the more female skills of the nurse, air hostess, and receptionist. However, the skills discussed are relevant to some of these – barristers use the skills of public speaking, and social workers use therapeutic skills, for example. The social skills of everyday life have been covered to some extent in previous chapters. The professional skills which are described below involve rather special techniques which are not necessarily acquired as a result of everyday experience. They also require a certain amount of knowledge – teachers need to know their subject as well as how to teach; this side of social skills will not be considered here.

We shall start with five skills in which one person is handled at a time:

Selling
Selection interview
Survey interview
Personnel interview
Psychotherapy and counselling

Then we shall discuss four skills involving social groups:

Supervision of work-groups
Committee chairmanship
Teaching
Public speaking

In this chapter we shall draw on what empirical research is available to show which ways of handling these situations are most successful. In the case of some skills, like teaching and supervision of work-groups, there is extensive evidence of this kind.

DEALING WITH INDIVIDUALS

Selling

Selling is done all over the world, though in very different ways at different times and places: compare the endless bargaining with vendors in the markets of the Middle East, the mechanical rigidity of encyclopedia salesmen, the high pressure methods once common in the U.S.A., and the passive role of supermarket attendants. In this section we will concentrate on a type of selling which is common in Britain today – selling in department stores.

The aim of selling is in the first place to sell as much as possible. In department stores this is opposed by other goals: for example, to satisfy the customer (C) so that she will come again, and to sell C clothes that suit her, and therefore help the reputation of the shop. High-pressure selling has declined because it annoys customers, and because in any case they are liable to return the goods, and then go somewhere else. Salesmen (Ss) may fail in two main ways. Firstly their rate of sales may be very low. It is common to find that some Ss are selling twenty to forty per cent of what others in the same department are selling: this is an excellent example of the effects of different degrees of social skill shown in objective and quantitative terms. Secondly, Ss may achieve a high rate of sales, but by high-pressure methods which annoy Cs and ultimately lower the total sales of the shop.

Ss in department stores are often paid a bonus related to the amount they sell. This tempts them to use more persuasive methods and to go for the more prosperous-looking Cs; it also causes conflicts between the sales staff. A better scheme is probably to pay a group bonus that is shared between members of a department or counter, though this is inconvenient to administer and many shops manage without a bonus at all. The Ss in a department are supervised by the buyer for that department. The relation between C and S is rather delicate: S has no power over C, who is at liberty to wander round the shop having a look. If S is to control or influence C at all it must be by subtle means. On the other hand S does possess knowledge that C does not have – about what is available, what it will do, how much it costs. Ostensibly C has power over S, and may indeed treat S as a kind of servant; this is particularly true of some upper-middle-class Cs, and is much resented by Ss.

Many books have been written on salesmanship. Most of them suggest a definite sequence of steps in making a sale. According to studies of department stores by myself and Mary Lydall, what actually happens is usually not what the books describe at all. Most sales do not involve a complex sequence of steps: persuasion by S is rare, and Cs spend a lot of time looking by themselves at the goods on display. Some of the briefer sales encounters which we have observed include the following: C selects stockings from the stand, hands them to S, who takes the money and wraps them; C asks for a particular object, naming make, size, price, etc.; C looks through dresses on the rack, selects those she is interested in, and S shows C to a changing room where she tries them on and decides which to have. What happens is totally different in different departments in the same store: in some C can help herself, in others she has to be served;

the physical setting and the way items are displayed greatly affect the social behaviour that occurs. In the cheap millinery department, for example, C simply helps herself; in the expensive millinery very few hats are on show and C has to approach S at the outset.

We will now try to give an account of the complete possible sequence of events involved in a sale.

1. Categorization of C by S. Before contact is made, S often categorizes C. This is sometimes in terms of how much money C is likely to spend, or what style of clothes C is wearing – which is a useful guide to her tastes. It has been found in some shops however that Ss categorize Cs in terms of a kind of local mythology – 'peppery colonels', 'elderly frustrated females', etc. (Woodward, 1960). Such categories reflect hostility to groups of Cs who are arrogant and rude and don't buy anything, but may not be a very useful guide to how C should be approached.

2. Establishing contact with C. C may ask for help, ask specific questions, ask to see particular objects, or stand expectantly at the counter. If C is wandering about or looking at goods on display, S may approach her, but this requires skill and judgement about whether C is ready to be helped. Rather than risk 'No' to the question 'Can I help you, madam?', some Ss may draw C into conversation about the goods, demonstrate them, ask if C would like to see the goods not on display, or say that something C has tried on looks nice on her.

3. S finds out C's needs. C may approach S directly, or may respond to S's opening by saying, 'I would like to buy a tie', though she may at this point specify her needs in greater detail, 'I would like something fairly bright'. S should listen carefully to whatever C has to say, and try to understand what C is really after. Often C's wishes are vague, and S now needs to find out which of a thousand possible ties C would be most interested in. S needs to ask questions, to narrow down the field of choice. The strategies which can be used are similar to those in 'Twenty Questions' (except that direct questions can be asked, e.g. 'Which colour would you prefer?'). However C may be thinking in terms of all manner of private classification schemes, as in-

dicated by describing ties as 'bright', 'blue', 'terylene', 'with-it', etc. and S must attune herself rapidly to C's conceptual structure. In addition to which C may not know what she wants until she sees it. S should try to find out something about C's motivations – what needs the object is to satisfy, when it will be used, and so on.

4. S shows C a variety of items, if necessary demonstrating them or letting C try them on. There are several different strategies here. In the matter of price, for example, some Ss show the middle-range item first, others show the most expensive. In either it is important to make use of feedback: C's reaction is studied to see what should be shown next. Similarly a clearer idea of C's needs can be obtained by studying her reactions to the objects shown. Again it is important to show the right number of objects: if too many are shown C feels confused and can't decide, if too few C feels coerced. C's ideas may be clarified by seeing the objects, she may be attracted by what is shown, or may not have known before that certain things were available. The way S handles the goods can convey a message: in some shops the more expensive goods are handled more reverently.

5. S gives information and advice. C may ask questions about the goods at this stage, or raise objections. The experienced S will know the answers to the questions, the replies to criticisms, and can point to particular advantages of each object. If S has found out C's needs, she can point out how various objects would meet her needs. If S really believes in the goods, and wants to help C, this will be a quite genuine argument.

6. Clinching the sale. This can be done in a variety of ways, different ones probably being suitable for different Cs. Some Cs can be left to decide for themselves, others can be persuaded that a particular object would be the best one for them; for others it can be assumed that they have decided already – 'Will you take it now, or shall we deliver it, Madam?'

7. After the sale S can increase C's feelings of satisfaction by providing further information about the object chosen and discussing after-sales service. She attends to payment and delivery, and suggests further related purchases to C.

It is necessary for S to be able to adapt to C's style of inter-action, and to be able to handle different Cs differently. This will affect whether C should be approached or not, whether C should be offered advice and information or not, and what kind of goods should be offered – in terms of price and style. Special tech-niques are needed with awkward customers – they may be handed over to another, preferably older, S or they may be left with a large assortment of goods to choose for themselves.

S will be more persuasive if she really knows the goods, and projects an image of competence. C will be more likely to at-tend to S if S is friendly and easy to get on with. Observational studies by myself and Mary Lydall found that high-selling salesgirls established good rapport and had a smoother pattern of interaction than others. Chapple and Donald (1947) gave the standard interview to 154 Ss. The best Ss were very active and talked a lot, but were flexible and could adjust well to different styles of interaction. Those who oversold and had goods re-turned were dominant and made a lot of interruptions. The Ss in different departments had rather different styles: in open-floor situations they had long silences, while on counters they had very short silences – there is less information to receive here and Cs can be handled faster.

The selection interview

Millions of interviews take place each year to assess the suit-ability of applicants for jobs. The main purpose is to find out information from the candidate (C), from which the interviewer (Int) can predict how well C would do in the job. In addition Int may provide C with information about the organization, im-prove its public image, and persuade C to take the job – here the situation becomes one of bargaining or negotiation. In fact this often happens at the end of the interviews after one C has been offered the job.

Although interviewing is universally used as at least a part of selection schemes, there has been some criticism of its validity by psychologists. Part of the problem is that Int has other in-formation about C – biographical, examination and test results, etc. – from which it is possible to make a prediction without any interview at all. However the results of a number of studies show that the predictions made following the interview are better than those made from background data alone (Ulrich and Trumbo, 1965). It has also been found that some Ints are very much better than others – and that some are unable to predict job success better than chance; we shall discuss later which kinds of Int are best. Further it has been found that certain areas of information can be assessed more accurately by interview than others. C's style of interpersonal behaviour, and his likelihood of adjusting to the social aspects of the job situation is one such area; another is C's motivation to work, which can probably be more accurately assessed by interview than in any other way.

There are certain conventions about selection interviews. It is usually expected that these should last between 10–40 minutes, with longer interviews for more important jobs, that Int will ask most of the questions and take notes, though C will be able to ask questions later, and that it is a formal occasion where Int and C will face each other across a desk, though this convention is changing in favour of a 90° orientation with a low coffee table or no table at all. If any of these rules is broken some explanation should be given to C.

The assessment interview can be given by one Int, or by a whole panel of them. As will be seen, one of the major problems with this kind of interview is overcoming the anxiety of C, especially with young or inexperienced Cs. This is far worse with a board interview: Cs have been known to collapse physically, and this method gives an advantage to the most self-confident and self-assured Cs – who may not be the best-equipped in other ways. It is far easier to establish a good relationship and to get C talking freely in a one-to-one interview. It is nevertheless valuable for C to be interviewed by several Ints with different personalities and different points of view and areas of expertise, so it is probably best for C to have a series of individual interviews.

Some of the social techniques which have been found useful by experienced interviewers will now be described. It is unfortunate that it cannot be claimed that there is any more rigorous research backing for these. First, Int will greet C and try to put him in the right frame of mind for the interview. Int should treat C as a guest or friend, establish an 'atmosphere of timeless calm', and give C his undivided attention. The room should be quiet, there should be no interruptions, and the status difference between Int and C should be minimized by the seating arrangements. Cs are usually anxious, and steps must be taken to reduce this anxiety. This can be done by a period of a few minutes' relaxed small talk, and by attempts to improve rapport by discovering common friends or interests, or by asking C questions about interesting or successful things he is known to have done recently. The more anxious C is, the longer this period should be. C should now be told what is expected of him in the situation – that he will be asked questions covering certain topics, and will be expected to do most of the talking. Int then uses techniques which will increase C's amount of speech – open-ended questions, agreement and encouragement, and the use of silence (see p. 68). Int should listen carefully to the emotional undertones and implications of C's speech, and respond in a way that shows he understands, accepts, and sympathizes. However he should not take the role of C to the extent of trying to get C the job – because there are other Cs to be considered; Int should remain somewhat detached while at the same time being genuinely sympathetic. While Int's role is to carry out selection rather than vocational guidance, he may give some vocational advice if it is asked for. The interview should be a rewarding experience for C, and he should feel that he has been properly and fairly assessed.

The selection interview has four main phases. (1) Welcome, in which the procedure is explained, C is put at ease, and encouraged to talk freely. (2) Gathering information, in which Int goes over C's record, with the aid of the dossier, and tries to assess C on a number of traits. (3) Supplying information, in which C is invited to ask any questions he may have. (4) Conclusion, in which it is explained what happens next. There may also be a phase of negotiation (in which C is offered the job) for which the interviewer requires further social skills.

Int should have a definite list of topics to be covered in a certain order: research shows that the interview is more effective when it has a definite plan such as going through the biographical record. These topics will often include C's family and home background, his education at school and later, his past jobs and present employment, his interests and leisure activities, his attitudes and beliefs, his health and adjustment.

There are special skills in asking questions. Each topic is usually introduced with an open-ended question, followed by a series of follow-up questions. Int's question should be responsive to what C has just said, so that there is a proper dialogue, or flow of conversation. The questions on a given topic can be designed to obtain information about different aspects of C's abilities or personality. For example, leisure activities can be pursued to find out about social skills, creativity or emotional stability. Some areas need carefully-phrased questions to elicit relevant answers; for example, *judgement* can be assessed from questions about C's opinions about complex and controversial social issues with which he is acquainted. Int will have some ideas about C from biographical and other data, which he may have in front of him – in fact the more such data he can have before the interview the better. He can then test various hypotheses about C, e.g. that C is lazy, neurotic, and so on. It is found that much more notice is taken by Ints of adverse information, and the interview can be regarded to some extent as a search for such information. This is partly justified by C's use of the complementary strategy, i.e. of covering up his weak points. Nevertheless it is useful for Ints to be on the look-out for strong points in Cs as well.

It is important for Int to be able to extract negative information, and he may need to find out for example why C left a certain job so quickly, or why he was sent down from college. The putting of such questions requires considerable skill. It is partly a matter of careful phrasing of the question; for example the latter question could be put 'I gather you had some difficulties with the college authorities – could you tell me about that?' Such questions need to be delivered in a friendly, perhaps slightly humorous manner, and C's face should be saved afterwards by a sympathetic comment.

Int should try to assess a number of abilities and personality traits that are thought to be most relevant to the job. Here are some of the dimensions which are commonly assessed at selection interviews:

Intelligence
Judgement
Creativity
Social skills
Attitudes to authority
Stability
Self-image
Achievement motivation

Each of these dimensions can be assessed from the answers to suitable questions. For example, attitudes to authority can be assessed by asking questions about past relationships with others of higher or lower status, and attitudes towards traditionally respected groups and institutions, and towards commonly despised social groups. In each area several different questions should be asked, in order to sample the dimension in question.

The behaviour of a C during interview cannot be regarded as a typical sample of his performance from which a prediction can be made; Int should concentrate on eliciting verbal reports of behaviour in situations resembling the future work situation, from which predictions can be made. Thus an estimate of a C's creativity can be obtained by asking him to describe situations in which he might have displayed originality.

Part of the skill of interviewing consists of being able to deal with awkward Cs. General experience suggests that there are a number of types of awkward C that are most commonly encountered:

Talks too much
Talks too little
Very nervous
Bombastic
Wrong role (e.g. seeks vocational guidance, or tries to ask all the questions)
Over-smooth presentation

Unrewarding
Not interested in job
Neurotic
Different class or culture

There are special ways of dealing with each of these problems. For example, the C who talks too much can be dealt with by (1) asking more closed questions, (2) using less reinforcement, or (3) indicating that a short answer is wanted.

Research into the accuracy of the selection interview shows that there are considerable differences between Ints. The most accurate Ints are those who are similar to the Cs in age and social background, intelligent and well-adjusted, not easily shocked, quiet, serious, introverted, unexcitable, and giving an impression of sincerity and sympathy. The reason for the first is probably that Int can communicate better with C, and interpret his answers better – an older Int might dismiss a C because of the length of his hair, while a younger one would be more tolerant of such changes in fashion. Introverted Ints make less of an impact on the social situation, and therefore will have a smaller effect on C's behaviour during the interview. There are a number of common sources of error in selection interviews and these were described earlier under person perception (p. 112f.). Perhaps the main point is that Int should treat his impressions of C as hypotheses to be investigated, by questions about his past experiences.

What social skills should be used by C to make Int more likely to give him the job? It has been found that C is more likely to be accepted when Int does most of the talking (Anderson, 1960), and when the interview flows smoothly, with few disagreements being expressed (Sydiaha, 1961). Ints seem to prefer Cs who are well-washed and quietly dressed, who are politely attentive, submissive, and keen, and they are likely to reject Cs who are rude, over-dominant, not interested, or irritating in other ways. There seems to be a definite 'role of the candidate' – he is expected to be nicely behaved and submissive – although he may not be expected to be quite like this if he gets the job. There are certain subtleties about being a good C – it is necessary for C to draw attention to his good qualities while remaining modest and submissive. He may need to show what a decisive and forceful person he is – but without using these powers on the selection board.

The social survey interview

The aims of the survey interviewer (Int) are to obtain accurate replies from the respondent (R) about his opinions, attitudes, behaviour, or whatever the survey happens to be about. The most common kinds of failure are that Int will be unable to persuade R to take part in the survey at all, or will not create enough motivation for him to answer all the questions properly, or that R will give biased or inaccurate replies for one of a variety of reasons. In fact the reliability of survey interviews is not very high: in a number of studies the same Rs have been asked the same questions again after a short interval; it was found that about eighty per cent gave the same answers if the same Int was used, and about sixty per cent did if a different Int was used (Hyman *et al.*, 1955).

The relationship between Int and R is that Int asks R to take part in the survey as a favour, since R gets nothing material out of it. This suggests the first main problem of the survey interviewer – that of establishing contact with and motivating R. Int is typically of rather higher social class and more education than R, which leads to problems of communication. Rs are generally unused to the interview situation and often give the wrong kind of answer, which is a further problem for Int. It is found that R's willingness to cooperate and the content of his answers both vary with the role of Int. If Int appears to be connected with Income Tax, for example, Rs will be unwilling to talk about their income, and will distort their replies. Industrial workers will give different answers to representatives of management or of the unions; the most accurate replies would probably be given to an independent investigator from outside, and the author usually wears a 'neutral suit' for such interviewing. This is a good example of the importance of a social-skill performer establishing the right identity from the outset. It is becoming increasingly easy to handle this situation as people become more familiar with the role, and the survey interview becomes an accepted type of social situation. The expectations concerning it are that Int will ask a number of personal questions, that R will do most of the talking, and that the whole thing will last not longer than five to fifteen minutes. When psychological research interviews or motivation research interviews are given, R has to be taught a new tradition.

Male and female Ints are liable to be given different answers on certain topics; so are Ints from different racial or social-class groups. The best results are obtained when Int is similar to R in these respects. This helps to avoid another source of error – Ints may have stereotyped expectations about how a person like R will reply, and this may affect the way he asks the questions or records the answers. It is interesting but curious that social survey agencies report greatest satisfaction with Ints who are married women in their thirties, who are educated and intelligent, but who are introverted and low in social adjustment (Hyman, op. cit.).

We now come to the social skills used by the survey interviewer. Firstly he must establish contact with R and persuade him to take part. If rapport is not established, R will refuse to take part; some Ints have a high rate of failure of this kind, and it leads to error in the results. By rapport is meant a smooth pattern of interaction in which both feel comfortable, and there are few pauses and interruptions, together with some degree of mutual trust and acceptance. When good rapport is established it is probable that the answers obtained are more accurate. The first few seconds are all-important: probably a friendly smile, eye-contact, and a pleasant appearance and tone of voice are part of it. Int should treat the other as an equal and eliminate social barriers. He should show a keen and sympathetic interest, listen carefully, be accepting and uncritical of what is said, and indicate that there is plenty of time. For different purposes different degrees of rapport may be needed: to ask intimate questions about income or sex requires more rapport than asking questions about interests or attitudes. Some research workers favour the 'interpersonal' style of interviewing, in which Int makes positive and sympathetic responses, establishes a warm relationship and ensures that R enjoys the interview; others prefer the 'professional' style in which Int is more detached, is formal and polite, and is most concerned with the accuracy of replies (Gordon, 1976). If R refuses to answer, a skilled interviewer may leave the topic in question, returning to it later when more confidence has been established. Int explains who he is, what organization is doing the survey, how R was chosen, what the survey is about, and that R's replies will be confidential and anonymous. There are two general methods of motivating R. One is to interest him in the survey, suggesting that it may accomplish results that R would like. The other is to make the interview satisfying in itself by the provision of a friendly and sympathetic listener to R's opinions. It is usually recommended that Int should not pretend to be a 'friend' of R, since this would lead to R distorting his replies to please Int; rather Int should be helpful and sympathetic towards R's point of view, while remaining somewhat detached and retaining the 'stranger value' of a person who will not be seen again. It is essential that Int should indicate, by the wording and tone of his questions, that he accepts and supports R, as opposed to rejecting him.

It is important that Int should communicate clearly with R, and this may be difficult because of their different backgrounds. Each question should be clear, unambiguous, and concerned with a single idea. The questions should be appropriate to the level of sophistication of R. If R simply lacks the necessary words or concepts, explanation or examples may be necessary. It is sometimes the practice to alter the wording of questions for use with cultural minority groups so as to make them of 'equivalent meaning'.

There are two main types of question which are used in surveys. One is the closed question in which R is invited to choose between 'yes', 'no', and 'don't know', or between some other series of alternatives. The other is the open-ended question in which R is invited to talk freely about his behaviour, opinions, or experiences in some area. In most surveys both kinds of question are used, though the proportions vary considerably:

public opinion polls use more closed questions, research surveys make more use of open-ended ones. Open-ended questions are useful if R's attitudes are being explored in detail, if he has not formulated his views, or if it is not known what the main alternative answers will be.

Skill is involved in phrasing the questions so as to get un-biased results. It is most important that questions should not be leading questions, or in any way invite the answer 'yes'. For this reason 'yes–no' questions should be avoided, and other alternatives offered instead. It is important that one answer should not seem to be more socially desirable than another; if alternative choices are offered, each should appear equally re-spectable. Int should conceal his own views from R, and should not argue with him, no matter how absurd the views he puts forward. Particular skill is needed with potentially embarrassing issues, such as income or sexual behaviour. Int should adopt a relaxed matter-of-fact manner, or he can present R with a list of alternatives to check. He can explain to R that he is not con-cerned with assessing R, and that all answers are equally accept-able, perhaps indicating that a wide range of different answers is commonly obtained. A number of special methods are used in motivation research interviews to get at genuine feelings. R is more likely to be cooperative if he sees how each question is relevant to the main purpose of the interview, and it may be useful to explain the point of certain questions.

When open-ended questions are used, a series of follow-up questions is needed, and this provides an excellent example of reactions to feedback. When Int has asked an open-ended question on some topic, R will often give a reply that is in-adequate in one way or another:

1. R partly misunderstands the question and talks about the wrong things: Int can then repeat and clarify the question, stressing what is wanted.

2. R doesn't produce enough information: Int can ask him to 'tell me more about this'.

3. R is confused about the issue: Int invites him to talk the topic out to clarify his ideas.

4. R deals only with certain aspects of the problem: Int can ask

more specifically about the areas omitted. Sometimes a series of increasingly direct questions is used in a 'funnel' structure (Kahn and Cannell, 1957).

A definite sequence of topic areas is also adopted. The easiest and least threatening are taken first, and more difficult ones later, when more confidence has been established. There should also be some sequence of topics so that the interview makes sense to R. Care is taken with the very first questions, and also with the last, so that the interview can end on a pleasant note.

Finally Int should listen very carefully to what R has to say. He should not be concerned about whether what R says is true or false, but should see it as the expression of his attitudes and of his way of looking at the world: this is what the interview is trying to find out.

The personnel interview

This kind of interview is really part of the supervision of work groups. It includes dealing with an employee whose behaviour has been unsatisfactory, as well as the inspection and evaluation of work. In other settings it includes rather similar interviews between tutors and students, and between parents and adolescent children. This is a very difficult kind of interview to do: it is feared and resented by the interviewees, and is often funked by those who ought to carry it out. Research on supervision has suggested a totally new approach to it, which can make it a pleasanter and more effective occasion. What is recommended is something like the strategy that follows.

1. The supervisor (S) finds out as much as he can about the performance and relevant circumstances of the client (C). He also decides on a strategy, what goals he will try to achieve, and what kinds of persuasion he will use. This strategy is provisional, since new facts may come to light during the interview.

2. S establishes rapport with C, who may be very nervous about the interview. This will be easier if S maintains good day-to-day contacts with C. They may chat briefly about common interests, so that status barriers are reduced, and C is ready to talk freely.

3. It may be necessary for S to explain that there is a problem – C has been persistently late so that production has fallen, C has been getting very low marks, etc. This should be done by stating objective facts, not by passing judgement, and should be done in a manner that is pleasant rather than cross.

4. S now invites C to say what he thinks about the situation, what he thinks the reason for it is. This may involve a certain amount of probing for fuller information, if C is reluctant to open up. S is sympathetic, and shows that he wants to understand C's position. S may ask C whether he thinks the situation is satisfactory; in an appraisal interview he can ask C to evaluate his own performance. C may produce new information, which explains the cause of the trouble, and suggests how it can be tackled; the interview could then end at this point.

5. Failing this, there now follows a period of joint problem-solving, in which C and S try between them to work out a solution to the problem. This may involve action on S's side as well as on C's – such as giving C a different job, or making some other change in the situation. It may involve a trial period after which S and C will meet again to review the situation. The interview may end at this point.

6. If the problem cannot be solved in this way, and some change of behaviour on C's part is indicated, which C is unwilling to make, further steps may be necessary. The first of these is persuasion. S may be able to point out that C will not reach his own goals by his present line of action – as with a student who will fail his exams if he doesn't work harder. Such social influence is a subtle skill in itself, and depends on being able to appeal realistically to the right needs in a particular individual. The interview may end here.

7. If this fails, and if further interviews become necessary, sterner means of influence may have to be resorted to. Most Ss are in a position to control material sanctions, such as bonuses, promotions, and finally dismissal. S will not usually want to sack C – what he wants is to keep him but make him behave differently. The possible use of such sanctions should first be mentioned reluctantly as a rather remote possibility – for example by the quite objective statement, 'There are several other people

who would like this job', or, 'I may have to tell the people who pay your grant about your progress'.

8. The interview should end with a review of what has been agreed, the constructive steps that have been decided upon, when S and C will meet again to discuss progress, and so on. The meeting should end on as friendly a note as possible.

Psychotherapy and counselling

These terms will be used fairly broadly to include any situation in which one person tries to solve another's psychological problems by means of conversation. There are many different techniques of psychotherapy, but some of the main varieties can be indicated briefly:

1. Freudian psychoanalysis: patients recall dreams and early childhood events; the psychoanalyst interprets the patient's condition in terms of psychoanalytic theory. The full treatment involves about three sessions a week up to a total of three to six hundred, though many fail to complete the course.

2. Rogers' non-directive therapy: here the therapist (T) helps the patient (P) to understand his emotional reactions by verbally labelling or 'reflecting' what has been expressed, and by giving non-directive encouragement for further revelations. Treatment requires thirty to fifty sessions.

3. Counselling and brief psychotherapy: this consists of discussion about P's here-and-now problems, and what can be done about them. T may use one of a variety of psychological theories or an 'eclectic' combination of them; the number of sessions is typically five to ten. This is the most widely practised kind of psychotherapy – it is given by National Health Service psychiatrists in England, by numerous American non-medical psychotherapists and counsellors, and of course by even more numerous clergymen, general practitioners and sympathetic friends.

4. Existentialist psychotherapy is a recent development of some interest because it introduces a new theoretical outlook. Emphasis is placed on P's subjective experiences, and he is seen as growing through experiences of crisis: he is helped by T to

245

integrate his ego-identity and relate it to his ultimate values. When it is practised by medical psychiatrists, this form of psychotherapy is combined with the use of other methods such as drugs.

The goals of psychotherapy vary somewhat according to the theories held by T. They usually include: the removal of feelings of psychological distress or discomfort, such as anxiety and depression; improving P's functioning in work and interpersonal relations; the removal of other symptoms of mental disorder. The relation between P and T is that P comes voluntarily because he wants to be cured (unless sent by the legal authorities); traditionally P pays a fee, though this is not true in the National Health Service; T has power and prestige based on his medical or other professional standing, his psychological expertise, and often his social class. Since P can terminate treatment whenever he wishes, T has no formal power over him, but P may come to see T as the means to the much-desired goal of recovery.

The recovery rate for neurotic patients is something like 66–70 per cent in two years, while some get worse. However, neurotic patients also recover 'spontaneously', i.e. without any formal treatment. There is considerable controversy as to what the rate of spontaneous recovery is. One view is that the neurotic condition simply waxes and wanes in response to external stresses, so that patients may appear to get either better or worse while being treated (Subotnik, 1972). There have been a number of studies comparing recovery rates of Ps receiving psychotherapy with those of control groups of similar Ps who had no treatment. In a number of such studies the treated patients did better than those in the control group (Bergin and Garfield, 1971). In comparison with behaviour therapy it is usually found that patients under psychotherapy recover more slowly – though a wider range of patients can be treated by psychotherapy. Furthermore it has been found that some Ts have higher success rates than others, as do certain types of P – so it is evident that under the right conditions psychotherapy can do some good. A lot of therapy is with more than one person – husband and wife, or parents and an adolescent child –

and here there is no alternative form of treatment. It is clear that some Ts actually make some Ps worse, and that there are considerable variations in social skill here. We will discuss later which Ts are the best, but first we will describe some of the social techniques which are widely used in psychotherapy. The following techniques are common to all forms of treatment.

(1) T expresses a warm, accepting and uncritical attitude of interested concern towards P, and creates a strong interpersonal relationship; it is a kind of ideal friendship, in which T participates emotionally, though it is restricted to the therapeutic hour. (2) P is encouraged to talk about his anxieties, conflicts and other bottled-up emotions; the cathartic expression of these feelings, and sharing them with another person who does not react critically, helps to relieve them, and enables P to think about painful problems. (3) T tries to explore P's subjective world of feeling and thinking, tries to understand P's point of view, and to open up communication with him. (4) T tries to give P insight into why he reacts as he does, and thus to change him. This is done by the verbal labelling of P's behaviour; psychoanalysts and others will offer a theoretical interpretation as well, e.g. obsessional hand-washing may be explained as the symbolic cleansing of guilt. (5) T helps P to make plans and positive decisions; he is encouraged to try out new ways of dealing with people and situations; he is asked to make positive efforts, to become committed, rather than be indifferent and passive (Sundberg and Tyler, 1962). Different therapists place different emphasis on these common elements, and they vary particularly in their handling of number (4), bringing about emotional or cognitive changes. Much psychotherapy is given in groups, and it is possible that group therapy is beneficial for patients with interpersonal problems; the procedure is described on p. 223. Lastly, T must terminate the treatment, at the end of each session and at the end of the series. This is anticipated by previous remarks; T summarizes what has been accomplished and refers to possible future meetings.

We have condensed into a short space what has been described in a large number of books and to which entire journals are devoted. However a number of recent studies have suggested that the detailed techniques used by T are less important than T's personality and more general social skills. Fiedler (1953) found that the most successful Ts of a number he studied had very similar styles of social behaviour, but that success was unrelated to the techniques of psychotherapy they were using. What is more important is T's general style of social behaviour, and the kind of relationship he can establish. Recovery rate is fastest for Ts who are warm, permissive, are interested in and like P, and are able to empathize with him (Truax and Mitchell, 1971). In several studies it has been found that briefly-trained students and non-graduate housewives have been as successful as highly-trained therapists. It has been argued by Schofield (1964) that everyone experiences unhappiness and distress at times, and is in need of help, but not so much through any specialized techniques of psychotherapy as through sympathy, listening ability and friendship. It is clear that minor degrees of psychological distress are very widespread, and that qualified psychotherapists are in short supply. The solution may be for the basic techniques of psychotherapy to be more widely practised on a non-professional and semi-professional basis.

Ts prefer and can establish a better relationship with certain kinds of P – those who are middle-class, keen to recover, intelligent, submissive, friendly, and only moderately maladjusted: it is the other Ps who do not recover, and are found difficult by Ts, especially by inexperienced Ts (Luborsky *et al.*, 1971). How far do Ts adapt their approach for different Ps? Apparently very little, since Ts are carefully trained in a particular technique and use it regardless. It seems quite possible that different Ps might profit from differing degrees of directiveness, or different depths of interpretation.

Another feature of skilled behaviour which is important here is the projection of the right image by T. There is a growing body of evidence to show that the T who can make his Ps believe in his therapeutic powers has more success with them. Ps may actually improve before any therapy is received, once T has agreed to treat them. Psychoanalysts may build up the right image by 'heavily laden bookcases ... and usually a large photograph of the leader of their particular school gazing benignly but impressively on the proceedings' (Frank, 1961).

SKILLS WITH GROUPS

Supervision of work groups

We include here not only industrial foremen, but directors of research groups, and leaders of other groups that have a task to do. The primary goal of the supervisor (S) is to get the work done, but an important secondary goal is to keep the team satisfied – otherwise there will be absenteeism, labour turnover, and a general lack of cooperation. Ss may fail in a number of ways of which the most common are: relying too much on formal power; being too authoritative; not giving enough direction, so that other members of the group assume leadership; producing high output but low job satisfaction; producing high job satisfaction but low output. In studies of groups of manual workers it is found that groups under certain supervisors may produce 50 per cent more work than under other supervisors; if the work is machine-paced or under wage-incentives these differences are smaller, though with very bad supervision the difference can be greater (Argyle, 1972). The effects on rates of absenteeism and labour turnover are rather greater – ratios of 4 or even 8:1 have been found; again the worst supervisors produce the most marked effects (Fleishman and Harris, 1962).

A supervisor occupies a position in a hierarchy and possesses formal powers, that is he can make use of sanctions of reward and punishment. In other words he can, up to a point, compel group members to carry out his orders. How much power he has varies between ranks and organizations, and his ability to reward his group contributes a lot to their job satisfaction. Industrial foremen are in a rather awkward position in that they are in the middle of a conflict of interests between management and workers. S has to persuade the men to carry out orders originating from the management, and his formal powers may be opposed by the powers of organized labour. It is for this reason that supervision requires considerable social skill. As well as knowing how to supervise, he must know how to do the job, and his influence will be accepted more readily if it is believed that he really knows his stuff.

A great deal of research has been carried out into the social techniques which are most effective – mainly by comparing the behaviour of Ss in charge of high-output and low-output teams. Similar results have been obtained from research which has been done in a variety of American industries (Likert, 1961), in British electrical engineering factories (Argyle *et al.*, 1958), in Japanese industry, in clerical organizations, in sports teams and in the armed forces. The main findings are as follows:

1. It is essential that the supervisor should really supervise – (1) planning and scheduling the work to be done, and making sure supplies are available, (2) instructing and training subordinates in how to do their work, (3) checking and correcting the work that has been done, (4) giving subordinates feedback on how well they are doing, (5) motivating them to work effectively. If he fails to do these things, it is likely that the group or some of its members will take over these functions. On the other hand, S should do all this with a light hand, since men do not like him breathing down their necks and constantly interfering. He should see them frequently, showing interest, giving help where it is needed, but giving as little direction and criticism as possible. In 'job enrichment' schemes some of S's jobs, such as checking, are delegated to members of the group.

2. Ss are more effective when they look after the needs, interests and welfare of their men. This is particularly true when they are powerful enough to be really able to do something for the men. In matters of discipline they should be persuasive rather than punitive, and try to find out the causes of the offending behaviour. It is interesting that foremen who are more concerned with the welfare of the men than with production usually succeed in getting higher rates of production. On the other hand, a number of studies show that S should be somewhat detached and independent: he should do his own job rather than theirs, and not be afraid of exerting influence over them.

3. Democratic leaders are usually more effective than autocratic ones. A democratic leader does not just rely on his formal

powers, but on (1) motivating people by explanation and persuasion, rather than just giving orders, (2) allowing subordinates
to participate in decisions that affect them, and (3) using techniques of group discussion and group decision. By these skills
the supervisor succeeds in getting the group to set high targets,
and to internalize the motivation to reach them, without exerting pressure himself. There are of course limits to what the
group can decide. It can usually decide about details of administration – who shall work where, how training or holiday
schemes shall be implemented. The group can also make suggestions on more far-reaching matters which S can relay to his
superiors. He exerts real direction and influence but in a way
that does not arouse resentment and antagonism. Autocratic
leaders make more use of their formal power, and give orders
without explanation or opportunity for discussion.

The above findings are of considerable interest, since they
are firmly based on research, and between them define in some
detail the pattern of social techniques of the effective supervisor.
They illustrate the principles about the combination of warmth
and control that we presented earlier (p. 155f.); they illustrate the
importance of sensitivity to feedback both about social events
in the group, and about the work being done; they show that
even when the social-skill performer has power it is better if he
doesn't use it and uses persuasion instead.

So far, we have considered social techniques that are generally
effective. Now we turn to those that are needed in particular
circumstances. The good supervisor should be able to adjust his
style through the operation of 'translation' processes. It has
been found by Fiedler (1964) and others that the democratic–
persuasive style is not always the most effective. It may be
necessary to use different techniques at different times with the
same group: a research group in the planning stage needs permissive handling so that all ideas can come forward, but once the
design has been decided a stricter style is better. Similarly there
are advantages in a more autocratic style when the group is large,
or when the members are themselves authoritarian in personality and accustomed to a strict pattern of leadership.

Another range of problems arises in connection with difficult group members. Sometimes such people are more amenable to group influence than to leaders, e.g. those who are hostile to authority – they should be left to the other group members to control. Another type is more responsive to people in authority – they should be dealt with by the leader privately. The most difficult to deal with are psychopaths, who care neither for leaders nor groups. The only solution is to isolate them as far as possible from the main group activities, to prevent them disrupting the group. Ss also have to deal with interpersonal problems in the group. They will be better able to do so if they understand something of the dynamics of social groups. Sometimes the solution may be to rearrange the workflow system (p. 176f.), to change the membership of sub-groups, to conduct a group discussion, or to interview separately those concerned and work out some solution.

Committee chairmanship

The task of committees and other discussion groups is to solve problems and take decisions in a way that is acceptable to those present, and to those they represent. In some cases the emphasis is on problem-solving and creativity, in others the emphasis is on obtaining consensus. The main value of taking decisions in committee is to find widely acceptable decisions; those present will then be committed to carrying them out. Groups are better than individuals for solving problems if individuals with different skills and knowledge can be combined. Thus, they produce more brain power than any one person. There is also interaction between members, so that one suggests new thoughts to another, and one member's bright ideas are criticized and evaluated by others. These groups usually have a chairman, unless there are only three or four people present. The chairman has a generally accepted social role of controlling discussion and helping the group make decisions. His position is often more temporary than that of other group leaders, and the chairmanship may be rotated so that other committee members take it in turns. Being chairman carries a certain amount of power, but it has to be used with skill. A chairman should see that all members are able to express their views, and that the decisions arrived at are agreeable to as many of them as possible. He should be able to keep control with a light touch, and keep people in order without upsetting them.

A certain amount of research has been done by Maier and Solem (1952) and Hoffman (1965) into which skills of chairmanship produce the best effects. They found, for example, that better and more widely accepted solutions are obtained if minority views can be expressed. Sometimes groups arrive at a solution rather quickly; if the chairman asks them to think of an alternative solution, this is often preferred in the end. The chairman can help the group by focusing on disagreements and searching for a creative solution.

The chairman should study the agenda carefully beforehand, and prepare his introduction to the different items. He should be able to anticipate the items which may cause difficulty; he may speak to some members beforehand if he wants to call on their expertise, or needs their support.

At the beginning of the meeting the chairman should create the right atmosphere, by the use of appropriate non-verbal signals. There are several phases to the discussion of each item on the agenda. First, the chairman introduces the item by outlining the problem to be discussed, summarizing briefly the main background factors, the arguments on each side, and so on. Then the committee is invited to discuss the problem; enough time should be allowed for different views to be expressed, and the chairman should try to keep the discussion orderly, so that different points are dealt with in turn. Now the chairman can help the group to come to a decision, by focusing on disagreements among them and trying to arrive at a creative solution, evaluating different solutions in relation to criteria if these can be agreed, considering sub-problems in turn, or asking the committee to consider two possible solutions. Finally, an attempt is made to secure the group's support for a particular solution. If this is impossible it may be necessary to take a vote; this is unsatisfactory, since it means that some members are not happy about the decision, and will not support it very enthusiastically.

A chairman should be aware of the main processes of behaviour in groups, and be able to prevent these processes interfering with the effective working of the committee. The formation of a status hierarchy will inhibit low-status members from contributing: they should be encouraged to speak. The reason that groups often take riskier decisions than individuals is that, in most situations, risky behaviour is valued in the culture, and it is flattering to the self-image to believe that one is riskier than the other members of the group. As a result, those who discover that they have been making less risky decisions than others shift in the risky direction after group discussion.

Teaching

This section will deal with the teaching of children and adults in classes, i.e. in groups between five and forty in number. Teaching seems to have one primary goal and two subsidiary ones. The primary goal is to increase the knowledge, understanding, or skills of the pupils (Ps). The subsidiary goals are for the teacher (T) to increase the motivation and interest of Ps, and to maintain order and discipline. These goals are subsidiary in the sense that the primary goal cannot be attained without them. Further goals could be listed, e.g. that Ps should enjoy the classes, and that they should develop in mental health, self-control, or other aspects of personality. The commonest source of failure in teaching is in difficulties with discipline: there is evidence that young Ts, especially girls, find this the hardest problem, and this is probably the main reason for their abandoning the profession.

The problems of teaching vary according to the age of the Ps. Younger Ps are usually a captive audience, but are eager to please T; older Ps are less anxious to please, but may be highly motivated for other reasons, especially if they have been successful pupils in the past. In between these groups motivation may be lower, and it is with pupils of fourteen or fifteen that keeping order is most difficult. T usually has some formal power, both disciplinary and in controlling the future progress of Ps.

T may also have power based on his or her expertise and position to help Ps to realize their ambitions.

Some of the social techniques used in teaching will now be discussed in relation to the three main goals.

Maintaining discipline has become a major problem in British and American city schools in recent years. The main solution is probably to get Ps interested in what is being taught, so that any disturbance is felt to be holding up progress, and group support for T can be obtained. Opportunities for disturbance should be avoided – as when there are unfilled pauses, equipment goes wrong, Ps have unclear instructions about what to do. We saw earlier that Ps have their own underworld view of what should happen in school – their own set of 'rules' for teachers. To avoid trouble T should be absolutely fair in dealing with different Ps and not have favourites – a very common source of annoyance. She should not make 'unreasonable' demands – so there must be a certain amount of consultation and negotiation. The warm-and-dominant style of supervision should be used (p. 250f.); she should use firmness and persuasion, in a spirit of support and friendliness, rather than of hostility, and in a confident manner. This is partly done by non-verbal communication – indicating her attitude clearly, and her intention to control the situation. Discipline can be maintained by punitive and threatening methods, but this creates an anxious and unpleasant atmosphere, and makes Ps dislike T, thus hampering the learning process, and discourages a creative, problem-solving approach to the subject studied. A study of Canadian university students found that the teaching techniques which were most disliked were 'ignoring, discouraging and restricting questions; reacting to students' contributions with ridicule, sarcasm, belittlement, hostility, anger and arrogance; squelching students; interrupting students' contributions, or failing to promote discussion or questions' (Crawford and Signori, 1962).

Arousing motivation is more of a problem in teaching than in most other social skills. Ultimately it is a matter of arousing

some drive which most of the Ps have. The need for achievement can be aroused if Ps think there is some probability of success, either in terms of marks, competing against others, or other
forms of recognition. If Ps can have some experience of success,
and receive regular knowledge of results, or if other academic
goals depend on the standard reached, this form of motivation
will be aroused. The need for affiliation can be aroused by letting
Ps work together in small groups on joint cooperative tasks.
When group methods are used, and the group decides what is to
be done, the level of motivation is higher; as in work-groups.
Some Ps may be motivated by the need to be approved by T, a
person in authority; some may identify with T, and assimilate
T's enthusiasm for the subject. If Ps like T they will like the
subject (Oeser, 1955). The curiosity drive, to find out new things
and to solve puzzles, may be aroused by presenting the material
as a set of intriguing and challenging problems. Similarly T can
use material or examples that are dramatic, unusual, funny, or
striking in some other way. Activity methods are one way of
doing this, as are film-strips and other visual aids. Finally, T can
show how the subject-matter is relevant to the needs and
interests of the group.

Conveying information, knowledge or skill. Much of educational
psychology is concerned with the social techniques which are
most effective for this purpose. There are several different types
of activity which can be used: T tells Ps about the material, as in
a lecture; T questions Ps to see how much they have understood; T leads a general discussion of the subject; T gives Ps
work to do, and goes round to check on progress; T uses visual
aids, demonstrations or visits, together with discussion. There
are several basic principles of learning which should be observed. T should get Ps actively involved in the material – by
discussing it, writing about it, doing projects or experiments,
and so on. T should give feedback, both in the form of praise for
success, and of correction for errors. T should try to give Ps
insight and understanding of basic principles.

A lot of research has been done comparing the amount learnt,
or the exam results obtained with different teaching skills

(Rosenshine, 1971). These skills have now been widely incorporated into microteaching programmes (p. 271); this is one of the best examples of social skills training founded on research into which skills produce the best results. The teaching skills which have been found to be most effective are as follows:

1. Introduces (structures) topics or activities clearly.
2. Explains clearly, with examples, and illustrative materials.
3. Systematic and businesslike organization of lessons.
4. Variety of teaching materials and methods.
5. Use of questions, especially higher-order questions.
6. Use of praise and other reinforcement, verbal and non-verbal.
7. Encourages pupil-participation.
8. Makes use of Ps' ideas, clarifies and develops them further.
9. Warmth, rapport and enthusiasm, mainly shown non-verbally.

Teaching consists of cycles of T–P interaction. As we saw earlier, Ts can control these cycles by more or less encouragement of P contributions, more or less use of questions, longer or shorter chunks of explanation, and so on (p. 141f.).

There is some evidence of the need to treat different Ps differently. One interesting example is the finding that introverts respond better to praise and extraverts to blame (Highfield and Pinsent, 1952). There is also evidence that anxious Ps do better under group-centred teaching. It is particularly important for older and more able Ps that T should be seen to be an expert. Teaching illustrates several aspects of social skill in an interesting way – the need to arouse motivation, the importance of the warm and dominant relationship, the presentation of a self-image, and constant scanning for feedback.

Public speaking

The goals of a public speaker (PS) may be to change the attitudes or behaviour of members of the audience (A), or to increase their knowledge and understanding. Often these two aims are combined, but political and religious PSs and other propagandists emphasize the first, while lecturers in educational establishments emphasize the second. The same person may have different goals on different occasions, for example if he gives both sermons and lectures on theology. There is no doubt that PSs can be very effective in attaining these goals. For example, Billy Graham converted 100,000 people during his first three campaigns in Great Britain – about four per cent of those attending; half of these people were still church attenders a year later (Argyle and Beit-Hallahmi, 1975). Graham was exceptionally successful, but many other evangelists are much less effective. In some colleges the public lecture is the main form of instruction, and students acquire most of their education from this source. On the other hand many lecturers are regarded by their students as quite hopeless; if the lectures are not compulsory, few students go, and these learn very little. The main sources of failure in a PS are being inaudible, boring, unconvincing, talking too fast, walking about or having other mannerisms, being nervous, not being able to handle an audience, and presenting the material badly.

There are certain problems requiring special social techniques, which arise with both kinds of PS. First, it is necessary for A to hear him clearly. He should speak loudly and distinctly, with head up, and 'project' his voice to all corners of the audience. He should sound the ends of words, not drop his voice at the ends of sentences, avoid saying 'er', and keep pitch, voice quality, and breathing under control. Elocution teachers can provide help with difficulties in this sphere.

Secondly, it is necessary for PS to have sufficient prestige for A to take him seriously and accept what he has to say. He will have more effect on A if they believe that he is an expert on his subject and is well-intentioned towards them. Such prestige may have been earned by PS's past achievements; it may be built up by the chairman's introduction, or it can be created by PS adopting a confident manner and demonstrating his expertise by the excellence of his presentation.

Thirdly, many PSs are anxious when in front of an audience. Being in front of an audience makes people feel 'observed' and it increases the level of arousal. The performer is aroused and anxious because his esteem and image are exposed to the risk of being damaged. The arousal will be greater the larger and the more important the audience: performance will be most effective at intermediate degrees of such arousal – if the audience is too small he may be too bored to bother with it; if too large his performance becomes disrupted by anxiety (see p. 21). Although stage fright usually becomes less with experience, it declines very slowly.

How can audience anxiety be reduced?

1. It is worth remembering that anxiety is usually greatest before the performance starts; once the performance has started, the performer has to concentrate on the task rather than on himself.

2. The performer should prepare his materials very carefully so that he has confidence in them. He should also have decided on his precise relationship with the audience – is he trying to entertain them, to persuade them to do something, to tell them about some new research? Has he the right, and is he in a position to do this?

3. His self-presentation should be carefully managed, and should be as genuine as possible (p. 198f.).

4. If all else fails, desensitization treatment is very successful (p. 224).

PS must start by establishing rapport with A, and getting its attention and confidence. This may include explaining how he comes to be there, what he is going to talk about and why, and indicating his previous contacts with A or the organization in question. PS should also make certain that he can be clearly heard and that he is not speaking too fast or too softly: for this he can usually rely on visual feedback. In the second phase PS presents the positive case, supported by compelling arguments, clear evidence, good examples and illustrations. Thirdly he should deal with objections, after which the most important conclusions are drawn; finally there may be discussion.

A PS should keep his A under control. He should study its reactions carefully and be on the lookout for people not being able to hear, falling asleep, looking bored, puzzled or cross, or not taking it seriously enough. He should take rapid corrective action, for example, speaking louder, explaining points that are not clear, arousing more interest or quietening them down.

The successful propagandist does not behave when on the platform in a relaxed, informal, and 'familial' style; on the contrary he has 'presence' and dramatizes himself and his message by a certain amount of showmanship. Schizophrenics and hysterics have often been successful in the past as religious leaders, probably because their intense conviction or dramatic self-presentation carried authority with their As. This kind of PS should not allow his A to relax, but should stir it up into a state of emotional arousal. Many studies show that attitude-change takes place more easily when the A is emotionally aroused (Sargant, 1957). Some PSs are adept at arousing the emotions of their As. This is done by the dramatic description of emotively arousing events – such as the horrors of hell, the outrages of the enemy, or the sufferings of the poor. This is combined with an intense manner, conveyed by facial expression and tone of voice, so that A is unable to treat the matter lightly. The experienced PS discovers which examples or stories are the most effective with particular kinds of audience. Having aroused such an emotional state, the classical social technique used by propagandists is then to show that the A can relieve its anxiety, or satisfy its anger, by acting in certain ways. The nineteenth-century revivalists would make their As terrified of going to hell, and then tell them what they must do to be saved; many modern advertisements follow a similar strategy. Research has shown how persuasive messages should be organized to have the maximum effect. One-sided messages are best, unless the A is initially opposed, and educated, in which case objections should be stated and dealt with. If the message is simple and straight-forward, the A should be left to draw the conclusions itself, otherwise PS should do this. Overt behaviour is affected most if specific actions are recommended. Earlier arguments have most effect, so the most appealing part of the argument should come first. It is useful to start with statements with which A will agree, in order to win its confidence.

The social techniques used by a lecturer to convey knowledge and understanding are rather different. He should not adopt the intense manner of the propagandist, which tends to suppress the thinking process. However, successful lecturers have a variety of styles, and it is not possible to prescribe which one is most effective. While lecturers should not arouse the emotions in the same way as propagandists, they should arouse interest, intellectual excitement and curiosity. They should not simply produce a lot of information that nobody wants. So a lecturer should start by stating what problems he is going to deal with, and getting A's attention from the outset. He should follow an intelligible plan, which may be built up on the blackboard or shown in a handout. And he should come to clear conclusions. It is important to accompany the statement of principles by concrete examples. The lecture should be made enjoyable and memorable by the use of materials which are of special interest to the audience, dramatic or simply funny. Particular skill is needed when introducing A to novel ideas or ways of looking at things; it may be necessary to use striking and carefully chosen examples, to jolt A out of its previous ways of thinking. Visual aids such as slides, overhead projector, films and charts can help with the presentation and make it more varied and interesting. The lecturer can keep A's interest by adopting a manner which keeps it involved in the situation – use of eye-contact, and a striking and pleasant style of behaviour. He should spend as little time as possible looking at notes, writing on the blackboard, or otherwise interrupting contact with A. He should show his own enthusiasm for the materials, and a positive attitude to A, by facial expression and tone of voice. Spatial arrangements are important, especially when visual aids are used: choose the best room available, and arrange it to best advantage, so that everyone is comfortable, and can see and hear. The lecturer should be as near as possible, and able to see A. During the discussion the contributions of the audience should be taken seriously and sympathetically, and an effort made to see the points of view expressed. The lecturer should not merely 'deal with' the points made, but use them as an opportunity to explain himself further. He should avoid any confrontation with the audience.

FURTHER READING

Selling
Lombard, G. F. F., *Behavior in a Selling Group*, Harvard University Press, 1955.
Woodward, J., *The Saleswoman*, London: Pitman, 1960.
Selection interview
Fraser, J. M., *Employment Interviewing*, London: MacDonald, 1966.
Ungerson, B., *Recruitment Handbook*, Epping, Essex: Gower Press, 1975.
Social survey interview
Kahn, R. L., and Katz, C. F., *The Dynamics of Interviewing*, New York: Wiley, 1957.
Personnel interview
Sidney, E., and Brown, M., *The Skills of Interviewing*, London: Tavistock, 1961.
Psychotherapy and counselling
Bergin, A. E., and Garfield, S. L., *Handbook of Psychotherapy*, New York: Wiley, 1971.
Supervision of work groups
Argyle, M., *The Social Psychology of Work*, Harmondsworth: Penguin Books, 1972.
Thurley, K., and Wirdenius, H., *Supervision: A Reappraisal*, London: Heinemann, 1973.
Committee chairmanship
Hoffman, L. R., 'Group problem-solving', *Advances in Experimental Social Psychology*, 1965, 2, 99–132.
Teaching
Dunkin, M. J., and Biddle, B. J., *The Study of Teaching*, New York: Holt, Rinehart and Winston, 1974.
Rosenshine, B., *Teaching Behaviour and Student Achievement*, Slough: N.F.E.R., 1971.
Public speaking
Bligh, D. A., *What's the Use of Lectures?*, Harmondsworth: Penguin Books, 1972.

CHAPTER 12

TRAINING IN SOCIAL SKILLS

MANY jobs consist mainly of dealing with people – teaching, interviewing and selling, for example. All jobs involve communication and cooperation, the giving and receiving of orders, maintaining relationships, and other basic social skills. Most of those in the first group get some training, though others have to pick it up on the job. However, some young teachers are not able to keep order, some interviewers get a lot of refusals, and some salesmen sell very little. For all of these people the training has failed. Perhaps a look at the possible methods of training may show how to improve the training of such people. In the modern world an increasing number of jobs consist more of dealing with people than of dealing with things; furthermore the speed of technological change means that many people have to be retrained for a new job once or even twice in the course of their working lives.

Social skills are also needed in everyday life, to deal with family, friends, neighbours, people in shops and offices, and so on. It is difficult to estimate the proportion of the population whose lives are seriously disrupted by the inability to make friends, or deal with other relationships, but our surveys suggest that it is at least seven per cent. Parents implicitly train their children in social skills; perhaps they could do it better. Schools train children in writing and speaking, and sometimes in other aspects of social behaviour; this too could be greatly extended. I believe that it would be possible to train people up to a higher level of sensitivity and competence than is common at present. This could have the effect of making social encounters and relationships far more enjoyable, effective and creative than they often are.

Social skills training has become widely used in recent years. Microteaching has been generally adopted for teacher training; similar kinds of role-playing are often used for social workers, interviewers, salesmen and others. T-groups and encounter groups have also become popular, though their effects are more dubious.

The definition of social competence, and the criteria of successful performance of social skills were discussed earlier (p. 75f.). How can it be decided whether or not a particular form of training works? Experience with various forms of training and therapy shows that while these are often enthusiastically praised by those who have been trained, more careful investigation sometimes shows that there is no real change in behaviour. It is necessary to take measures of performance before and after the training. These measures should not consist just of questionnaires – because people may merely learn what sort of answers to give – but of measures of performance or effectiveness on the job, or objective tests of what they can do. Often ratings by colleagues are used as the criteria; there is a danger that colleagues who believe in a training method will give higher ratings after than before in order to confirm their belief. This can be countered by the use of 'blind' ratings, where the raters do not know which of the individuals they are rating are being trained or belong to a control group. There should be a control group of similar people who are not being trained, in order to allow for improvement with the passage of time, and the effects of practice in doing tests. There should be a greater improvement from before the training to after, for the trained group than for the control group, using some objective index of skill. Wherever possible, studies of this kind will be used below to assess the different methods of training.

LEARNING ON THE JOB

This is probably the commonest form of 'training'. While manual workers are given carefully designed training courses, those who have to deal with people often receive no training at all – because it is so difficult to tell them what they should do. In fact some manual operatives also learn by doing, and learning curves can be plotted which show their rate of progress.

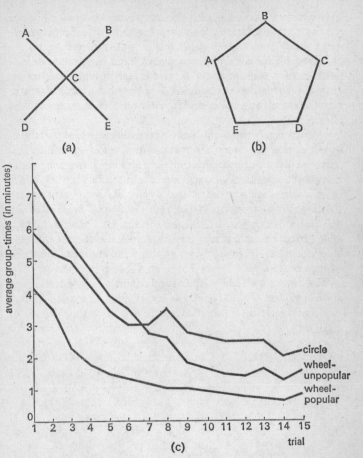

Patterns of communications within the group: (a) the 'wheel' (spokes) pattern – messages passed from member to member via a group leader; (b) the 'circle' pattern – messages passed from member to member round a circle. *Learning curves* (wheel-unpopular = groups where messages were passed via an unpopular leader; wheel-popular = groups where messages were passed via a popular leader): (c) average group-times per trial.

Figure 24. The learning of problem-solving by groups (Mohanna and Argyle, 1960).

Improvement of social skills by experience occurs mainly as a result of trial-and-error processes, together with the development of larger units of response. Rather similar results have been obtained for the joint performance of tasks by groups. An experiment by Mohanna and Argyle (1960) found the learning curves for small groups solving a series of problems, both in terms of the time taken and the number of messages taken (Fig. 24).

Unfortunately this seems to be a very unreliable form of training. A person can do a job for years and never discover the right social skills: some experienced interviewers have great difficulty with candidates who will not talk, for example (p. 235). Or people can somehow learn the wrong skills by experience: Fiedler (1970) found that the more years of experience industrial supervisors had the *less* effective they were. Argyle *et al.* (1958) found that supervisors often learnt the *wrong* things by experience, e.g. to use close, punitive and authoritarian styles of supervision.

The author with Mary Lydall and Mansur Lalljee carried out several studies of the learning of social skills on the job. In one of them an attempt was made to plot the learning curve for

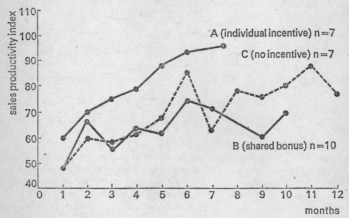

Figure 25. Learning curves for selling (Argyle, Lalljee and Lydall, 1968).

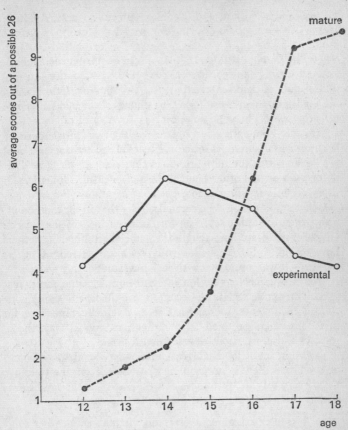

Figure 26. Acquisition of social skills in adolescence (McPhail, 1967).

selling: this task was chosen because there is an objective criterion of success. Annual fluctuations in trade were overcome by expressing the sales of a beginner as a percentage of the average sales of three experienced sellers in the same department. The average results from three shops are shown in Fig. 25; it can be seen that there was an overall improvement, especially where there was an individual incentive scheme. However, individuals responded in a variety of ways, and while on average most improved, some did not, and others got steadily worse. Again it seems that simply doing the job doesn't always lead to improvement.

McPhail (1967) studied the process of acquiring social competence during adolescence. He gave problem situations to 100 males and 100 females aged 12–18. Alternative solutions were selected and these were found to change with age in an interesting way. The younger subjects gave a lot of rather crude, aggressive, dominating responses. McPhail classified these as 'experimental' attempts to acquire by trial and error social skills for dealing with the new situations that adolescents face. The older ones on the other hand used more skilful, sophisticated social techniques, similar to those used by adults (Fig. 26).

Other studies have been carried out by the author to find out how the nature of the social performance changes with practice. In one of these, students taught the game of scrabble, in another how to multiply on a slide-rule, to a succession of other students. It was found that with each new student the 'teacher's' speeches became longer, his interruptions became rarer, his speech errors declined, he became more fluent and confident, and his effectiveness increased. There was clearly some learning in that teachers retained, in a rather stereotyped way, those phrases and illustrations that seemed to work.

Learning on the job has a great advantage over all other forms of training – there is no problem of transfer from the training situation to real life. A number of studies suggest the conditions under which training on the job can be successful.

1. Clear feedback must be given on what the trainee is doing wrong. Gage *et al.* (1960) asked 3,900 school children to fill in rating scales to describe their ideal teacher and how their actual teachers behaved; the results were shown to half of the teachers, who subsequently improved on ten of the twelve scales, compared with the no-feedback group. In most situations this kind of feedback is not available.

2. In order to improve performance new social techniques must be found. The best way of generating new responses is for an expert to suggest them and to demonstrate them. Learning

on the job can be speeded up by imitating successful performers, but it may not be clear exactly what they are doing.

3. Learning on the job will occur if there is a trainer on the spot who frequently sees the trainee in action, and holds regular feedback and coaching sessions. The trainer should be an expert performer of the skill himself, and should be sensitized to the elements and processes of social interaction. The success of such coaching will depend on there being a good relation between the trainee and the supervisor.

ROLE-PLAYING

Most forms of SST (social skills training) are varieties of role-playing. Role-playing consists of trying out a social skill away from the real situation, in the lab, clinic, or training centre, on other trainees or role partners provided for the purpose. The training is usually a series of sessions which may last from one to three hours, depending on the size and stamina of the group. In each session a particular aspect of the skill or a particular range of problem situations is dealt with. There are three main phases to role-playing exercises.

1. There is a lecture, discussion, demonstration, tape-recording, or a film about a particular aspect of the skill. This is particularly important when an unfamiliar skill is being taught or when rather subtle social techniques are involved. The demonstration is particularly important: this is known as 'modelling'.

2. A problem situation is defined, and stooges are produced for trainees to role-play with, for seven to fifteen minutes each. The background to the situation may be filled in with written materials, such as the application forms of candidates for interview, or background information about personnel problems – the stooges may be carefully trained beforehand to provide various problems, such as talking too much, or having elaborate and plausible excuses.

3. There is a feedback session, consisting of verbal comments by the trainer, discussion with the other trainees, and

playback of audio- or video-tapes. Verbal feedback is used to draw attention, constructively and tactfully, to what the trainee was doing wrong, and to suggest alternative styles of behaviour. The tape-recordings provide clear evidence for the accuracy of what is being said.

4. There is often a fourth phase, in which the role-playing, phase 2, is repeated. In microteaching this is known as 'reteaching'.

There are two important preliminary steps to this form of training. Firstly it is necessary to draw up a list of the main problem situations to be faced by those being trained; this can be done by 'critical incident' surveys, or more informally by consulting a number of experienced practitioners – of selling, interviewing, teaching, or whatever is being taught. Secondly it is necessary to find out the best social techniques for dealing with the problem situations.

Interviewer training. One of the first social skills to be taught by role-playing was selection interviewing.

In the course for selection interviewing devised by Sidney and Argyle (1969) some of the exercises are designed to teach participants how to deal with 'awkward' candidates (see p. 237f.). Trainees interview trained stooges who talk too much, too little, are nervous, bombastic, anxious, and so on. Each role-playing session on this course begins with a lecture and a film about the problems to be role-played. There is also training in how to assess stability, judgement, achievement, motivation, etc., in the interview, and how to avoid common errors of person perception.

Role-playing can be conducted without the use of any specialized equipment, but it is greatly assisted if certain laboratory arrangements are available. An ideal set-up for interviewer training is shown in Fig. 27. The role-playing takes place on one side of a one-way screen, and is observed by the trainer and other trainees. A video-tape is taken of the role-playing. The trainer is able to communicate with the role-player through an ear-microphone; the trainer can give comments and suggestions to the trainee while the role-playing is proceeding. (The author

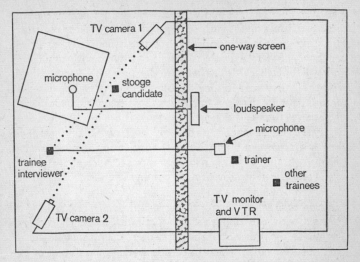

Figure 27. Laboratory arrangements for interviewer training.

once had to advise an interviewer trainee dealing with an over-amorous 'candidate' to move his seat back three feet.)

Microteaching is now widely used for training teachers. A trainee teacher prepares a short lesson, and teaches five or six children for ten to fifteen minutes; this is followed by a video-tape playback and comments by the trainer, after which the trainee teaches the same lesson again. There are usually a number of sessions, each being devoted to one particular teaching skill – asking higher-order questions, encouraging pupil participation, explaining clearly with examples, etc. (p. 257). This form of training is found to be very much faster than alternative forms of training, and is probably the best way of eliminating bad teaching habits (Brown, 1975b; Peck and Tucker, 1973).

Assertiveness training. This was one of the earliest forms of SST; it came from the behaviour therapy tradition, and the rationale was that arousing incompatible (assertive) responses would remove anxious and submissive ones. By assertiveness is meant standing up for your rights, saying No, making requests, initiating conversation and so on. The method of training has consisted of standard role-playing procedures with modelling and VTR playback. It has been widely used with normal adults who think they need it, for example submissive males, and with mental patients. Follow-up studies show a considerable degree of success (Rich and Schroeder, 1976). It is a mistake however to regard assertiveness as the only goal of SST: control of others is important, but then so is the dimension of interpersonal warmth (p. 99), which is probably more important for people who complain that they haven't got any friends.

Heterosexual skills. Many young people suffer from lack of contact with the opposite sex ('minimal dating'), or feel anxious in the presence of the opposite sex. This may be due to lack of social skills, which in turn is usually due to lack of experience, or to anxiety caused by unsuccessful experiences in the past. Training courses have been devised to teach the necessary skills for making dates and for behaviour during dates. Follow-up studies have found these courses to be very successful; one course, for example, increased the average number of dates per week from 0·8 to 1·9 (Curran, 1977).

Social skills training for mental patients has been developed along similar lines. There is usually modelling and role-playing, with video-tape playback, of the skills needed by individual patients, or of skills needed by several patients if done in groups. The form of SST which we have developed at Oxford for neurotic mental patients is based on role-playing. It is different from other forms of training in that we recognize a large number of different kinds of social incompetence, each one corresponding to the break-down of one of the basic processes of social behaviour. Some of these can be corrected by straight role-playing, but others require variations on this theme. Failure of non-verbal communication, for example, needs practice in front of a mirror, or with an audio or video tape-recorder; failure to take the role of the other requires role-reversal practice, for example playing the role of the boss; difficulty with specific situations needs instruction on the basic rules, aims, etc., of each situation. Follow-up studies show that this form of treatment is somewhat better than psychotherapy for patients who are socially inadequate or have social phobias, in terms of self-reported behaviour, performance at laboratory tests of social skill, ratings by friends, and assessment by psychiatrists (Trower, Bryant and Argyle, 1978).

Similar methods have been used for psychotic mental patients. While improved social behaviour has been produced in a number of studies, there has been less evidence of transfer of skills learnt in hospital to other social settings.

Follow-up studies show that role-playing is the most effective form of SST at present available. Experimental comparisons of different procedures show that the full package we described originally is the most effective. It is necessary to include (1) modelling, (2) instructions, (3) role-play practice, (4) an instructor to give the feedback, and (5) realistic stooges, e.g. children for microteaching. However, there is some doubt as to whether the video is necessary, and some trainers have obtained good results without it.

Feedback is one of the crucial components. It can be done in several ways:

1. It may come from the other members of the group, either in free discussion, discussion in smaller groups, questionnaires, or behavioural check lists. This must be done carefully, or it will be disturbing to the recipients of the feedback; on the other hand it is probably a valuable part of the training process for those observing.

2. It may be given by the trainer, who should be in a position to give expert guidance on the social techniques which are effective, and who may be able to increase sensitivity to the subtler nuances of interaction. He may correct errors – such as interrupting, looking or sounding unfriendly. He can suggest alternative social techniques, such as ways of dealing with awkward clients or situations. This has to be done very carefully: the

trainer's remarks should be gentle and kind enough not to upset, but firm and clear enough to have some effect.

3. Sound tape-recordings may be taken and played back to the trainee immediately after his performance. The author's experience is that the trainer's comments should precede the playback, so that trainees know what to look for.

4. Video-tape recordings can be used in a similar way: a television film is played back to the trainee after his performance. This directs the trainee's attention to the behavioural (facial, bodily and gestural) aspects of his performance, as well as to the auditory. It may be useful to play back the sound tape separately to focus attention on sound.

Use of 'homework'. The main difficulty with role-playing is that trainees have to transfer what they have learnt in the training centre to the real world. Some of the best results have been obtained when trainees have been persuaded to try out what they have learnt a number of times between sessions. Gabrielle Maxwell (1976) in New Zealand refused to see her patients again until they had done so. Morton (1965) used role-playing with mental patients on such domestic problems as disciplining children, keeping a budget, and keeping things peaceful. For the role-playing sessions nurses and others were used in the complementary roles; patients returned home at weekends; after the weekend they reported progress at home and this was discussed by the trainer and the group of trainees.

T-GROUP TRAINING

T (training)-groups were first developed in the National Training Laboratories at Bethel, Maine, in 1947, and they have rapidly grown in popularity, first in the U.S.A. and more recently in Europe. The members of a T-group spend their time studying the group and the processes of social interaction that take place in it. The trainer typically starts the group off by saying: 'My name is —, and I am the appointed staff trainer of this group and am here to help you in the study of this group as best I can.' T-groups consist of about twelve trainees who meet for a series of two-hour periods, weekly, or during a residential course. The T-group sessions are often combined with lectures, role-playing and other activities, but the T-group is regarded as central.

The role of the trainer is unusual: he does not take charge or act as a leader, but intervenes from time to time to make interpretations, provide feedback or draw attention to particular problems. He behaves rather like a group therapist, except that he does not discuss the personalities or problems of individuals, but rather the common problems of the group. This abdication of the role of the leader causes some perplexity and annoyance at first: the members are unfamiliar with the situation and seek help from the trainer in coping with it. During the early sessions there is a struggle for dominance, and questions of intimacy and friendship are sorted out. For females in particular it is found that there are problems of dependency – who to be dependent on, and how dependent to be.

Behaviour in T-groups has a strange quality, the conversation is somewhat stilted and embarrassed, and some members either do not take part at all, or engage in irrelevant conversation ('pairing'). A curious pattern of role differentiation has been reported in Harvard T-groups, including 'distressed females', who take little part in the conversation, 'paranoid' and 'moralistic' resisters, who oppose the official task, and 'sexual scapegoats' who present their masculinity problems for the group to study (Mann *et al.*, 1967).

One of the main things that the trainer does is to teach people to give and receive feedback, so that members may become aware of the impact of their behaviour on others and find out how others see them. The trainer shows how to make non-evaluative comments on the behaviour of others, and tries to reduce the defensiveness of those whose behaviour is being commented upon. Feedback is provided in other ways; members may take turns to act as observers who later report back to the group, tape-recordings of previous sessions are studied, and analyses by professional observers may be presented.

Encounter groups use a number of exercises designed to give experience of intimacy and other social relationships. Here are some examples of the exercises used at Esalen (Schutz, 1967).

1. To help people who are withdrawn and have difficulty in making contact with other people:
   (a) 'Blind milling'. Everyone in the room stands up and wanders round the room with their eyes shut; when they meet someone they explore each other in any way they like.
   (b) 'Break in'. Some of the group form a tight circle with interlocking arms. The person left out tries to break through the circle in any way he can.

2. To help people who are unable to express hostility or competition:
   (a) 'The press'. Two people stand facing each other, place their hands on the other's shoulders and try to press the other to the ground.
   (b) 'Pushing'. Two people stand facing each other, clasping their hands, and try to push each other backwards.

3. To help people who have difficulty in giving or receiving affection, who avoid emotional closeness:
   (a) 'Give and take affection'. One person stands in the centre of a circle with his eyes shut; the others approach him and express their feelings towards him non-verbally however they wish – usually by hugging, stroking, massaging, lifting, etc.
   (b) 'Roll and rock'. One person stands in the centre of a circle, relaxed and with his eyes shut; the group pass him round the group from person to person, taking his weight. The group then picks him up and sways him gently backwards and forwards, very quietly.

How successful are T-groups and encounter groups? Those who have been in these groups report that they have been through a powerful experience. Many feel better, but some feel worse. A careful follow-up study was carried out of 206 Stanford students who attended encounter groups, T-groups, etc., and 69 control subjects. Success was estimated by a combination of criteria – self-ratings, ratings by friends, and so on. The results were as follows:

	Percentage group members	Percentage controls
dropouts	13	—
casualties	8	—
negative change	8	23
unchanged	38	60
moderate positive change	20 ⎫	13 ⎫
high positive change	14 ⎭ 34	4 ⎭ 17

About a third of the group members and seventeen per cent of the controls improved, while eight per cent of the group members were harmed by the experience (for example, needing psychiatric help afterwards) in addition to the dropouts and those who showed negative changes. There were no consistent differences between encounter groups and non-touching groups; differences between individual group leaders were more important (Lieberman, Yalom and Miles, 1973).

Similar results have been obtained in a number of other studies – while about a third benefit, something like ten per cent are worse; this is the main focus of criticism of T-groups and encounter groups. A problem with encounter groups which use a lot of bodily contact is that some clients end up with a different spouse than the one they started with. Some people enjoy the groups so much that they lose interest in ordinary life and want to spend all their time having 'deep and meaningful experiences' in groups.

One solution to the emotional stress problem is to do more careful screening of those going on T-group courses or for trainers to be more watchful for signs of distress; however, part of the point of T-groups is to do something about authoritarian or other awkward characters in organizations – just the people who would be screened out. Another solution would be to reduce the level of emotional stress – some T-group practitioners do this, but others believe that the emotional arousal is necessary

– 'It is a matter of what you are prepared to pay for psychically.' It is the author's view that the benefits to be obtained from T-groups can be obtained more painlessly and less dangerously in other ways. However, if there is an insatiable demand for this kind of experience, a rather conservative type of procedure should be followed, in which the following conditions are observed:

1. Screening of trainees likely to be upset.
2. Lowering of the emotional stress.
3. Learning of specific social skills by role-playing or other exercises.
4. Trainers who are very socially skilled and therapeutic.

ALTERNATIVE KINDS OF SENSITIVITY TRAINING

In the training of manual workers in industry, increasing sensitivity is an important part of the process. It involves several different features – learning which cues to look out for at each stage of the process, acquiring increased powers of discrimination between rather similar or very faint cues, and knowledge of their significance (Seymour, 1966).

Finer discrimination and interpretation of physical cues is acquired by doctors – who are able to observe different states of a patient's skin, pupils, and way of walking, and can make deductions about the state of his blood, whether he takes drugs, and the state of his joints. Similar discriminations and interpretations from cues are important to the interactor. He needs to be able to detect another person's emotional state, his interpersonal attitudes, and whether he has understood or agrees with what has been said. For particular social skills there are particular perceptual needs: a salesman needs to know which goods a customer likes; an interviewer needs to know whether a candidate wants the job and is telling the truth. Is it possible to bring about increased sensitivity to the reactions of others by less nerve-racking means than T-groups? Davitz (1964) found that accuracy of identifying emotions from tape-recorded speeches with neutral contents could be improved by training. During the training, groups of three to eight subjects listened to a practice tape in which letters of the alphabet were read with different emotional expressions, and they tried to identify the emotions; during a second playing they were told which emotions were to be expressed before each item; they later tried to express the emotions themselves, and their attempts were discussed by the group. The training occupied several fifteen-minute sessions. An excellent example of an alternative training procedure is given by an experiment in which interpretations of bodily movements were made more accurate. Jecker *et al.* (1965) succeeded in training teachers to perceive more accurately whether or not pupils had understood what they were being taught. The measure consisted of a series of one-minute films showing children being taught; a subsequent question to the child (not shown on the film) found out if he really had understood or not. By showing teachers these films, and by drawing attention to the behavioural cues for comprehension, it was possible to increase their scores on a new set of similar films.

A number of studies of teacher training have found that training in observation skills and practice with the Flanders category scheme (p. 141) improves teaching skills (Peck and Tucker, 1973). This is probably because teachers become sensitized to the importance of pupil participation, and the need to ask questions; they would already be able to perform the skilled moves which are needed.

LECTURES, DISCUSSION, CASE-STUDIES, READING, AND FILMS

It may be possible to teach social skills by more traditional teaching methods. It is important to explore these methods since they are much cheaper and more widely available than those described so far – which need specially qualified trainers or expensive equipment. *Lectures* followed by discussion can be given in which various aspects of skill are explained. They may focus on the basic principles of social behaviour, or on the details of recommended social techniques. The lectures may be followed by discussion among the trainees, or there may be guided discussions without lectures. Experience with management training shows that lectures on 'human relations' are often very popular, and are a good means of conveying knowledge, though not a good way of changing attitudes. Can social skills be taught by means of lectures? Follow-up studies show that lectures on human relations lead to improved scores on questionnaires, but it has not been shown whether any behavioural changes in skill are produced. There are certain difficulties about lectures. They are no good unless the audience is really interested in what the lecturer has to say, or unless he can make them interested by the forcefulness of his presentation, and unless he has a manner and status which make him personally acceptable.*

There is some evidence that *group discussions* on human relations problems, without lectures, lead to changes in questionnaire measures. Group discussion can also be looked at as a kind of role-playing of group problem solving: it has been found that it results in improved committee skills (Maier, 1953). One problem about group methods is that there may be little input of new information to the group. There can be various degrees of feedback, instruction or other guidance from the trainer; probably the more there is the more successful the results. In so far as the method works it is partly due to the better assimilation of material put over in lectures or otherwise, and through practice in group behaviour. It is also possible for a skilful leader to bring about changes in attitudes and values as a result of discussion.

Another group method is the discussion of *case studies*, as is often done in management training. These consist of problem situations to which the group has to find the best solution; they may be presented as film-strips or in written form. Case studies are used for general education in management problems, but can also be focused entirely on the human relations aspects. The main weakness is that trainees do not acquire any general principles, though there can be increased awareness of the human-relations aspects of problems. It might be possible to devise

* See Argyle, Smith and Kirton (1962) for a review of these studies.

case studies in such a way that they would illustrate and draw attention to basic principles; perhaps if a large enough number of cases were used trainees could be helped to make inductive generalizations from them.

This method has recently been used for teaching social skills to school children. A case is presented by the teacher, or from a text book, which illustrates problems such as dealing with authority, emotional problems at home, or moral dilemmas. The case is then discussed by the class under the guidance of the teacher (McPhail, 1972).

Reading is one of the traditional methods of learning, but can social skills be learnt in this way? There are a number of books in this area such as *How to Win Friends and Influence People* (Carnegie, 1936), but there is no evidence about what effect they have. I hope very much that the present book may be helpful in this way, and readers of earlier editions assure me that they found it helpful. There is also the programmed text, in which each section of information is followed by graded problems. The *Culture Assimilator*, based on critical-incident surveys, for training people to cope with other cultures, has shown positive though modest effects (Fiedler *et al.*, 1971). Correspondence courses in conversational skill introduce another element – exercises which the student should carry out before tackling the next lesson. This is an important addition to the readings though we do not know whether people are able to provide their own feedback, i.e. see what they did wrong, when they tried things out in real situations. One solution would be to have a friend who could play the role of trainer and make the helpful comments.

We have already referred to the use of *films* for modelling in connection with role-playing. A number of suitable films are now available, mainly for management skills. Social skills trainers often make up their own video-tapes for modelling behaviour for trainees. However, no follow-up studies are yet available on the use of films for this purpose. Films have been used for training in *manual* skills for some time, and these are found to be successful under certain conditions – if the learner has to try out part of the skill after each piece of film, if there is discussion before or after the film, if the film is shot from his point of view, e.g. over his shoulder, and if appropriate use is made of slow motion, animation and sequences of stills, showing the successive steps in the skill. Again it looks as if films can play an important part in an overall training scheme, but are not much good alone. And so far there are very few suitable films available.

However, there is some evidence that the *combination* of these methods, especially of lectures and group methods, can lead to increases in social skill. Sorenson (1958) studied 205 managers before and after such a course, and 267 controls. Ratings by other managers showed that after the course trainees were rated as more cooperative, self-confident, poised and higher on 'consideration' (i.e. looking after the welfare of subordinates) and delegation. It is quite likely that neither lectures, reading, nor group discussion alone will do the job, but that together they can be very successful, especially in conveying knowledge about translation processes, understanding of social interaction, and general awareness of interpersonal phenomena. On the other hand managers may be better able than other people to apply on the job new principles they have learnt.

METHODS RECOMMENDED FOR DIFFERENT PURPOSES

1. *Professional social skills* were traditionally learnt on the job, but role-playing is now widely used for teachers, interviewers, managers and others. Role-playing, along the lines described above, is the most effective form of training available. It can be supplemented by lectures and discussion, and instructional films where available, on the skill in question. Sensitivity training, as described above, is useful, but T-groups are too dangerous. A trainer is needed who is reasonably experienced and competent at the skill in question himself, and who is familiar with the use of these training methods.

Further problems arise with those people who suffer from more serious interpersonal difficulties at work. They need more specialized forms of treatment, as described in the next section.

2. *Treatment of individuals with interpersonal difficulties.* This includes people who are quarrelsome and difficult at work, those who are anxious in social situations and those who are lonely and isolated, as well as a proportion of mental patients. Some of these come to psychiatrists and some are given SST; more get help from friends, family, doctors and clergy. They are difficult to help, however, without a little knowledge of interpersonal processes. The best treatment is the form of SST described above (p. 272f.) – role playing combined with training in NVC, and other exercises. The treatment is not easy to find, and I would like to see it established in such non-medical settings as community centres or adult education centres.

3. *In schools.* SST is being tried out in a number of schools, as part of English, Social Studies, Moral Education or Biology. Some textbooks and classroom materials are now available (e.g. McPhail, 1972). Video-tape recorders are also available in many schools. It would be quite feasible to teach a new school subject – 'Social Behaviour' – which could be of great practical use to those who studied it.

FURTHER READING

Bradford, L. P., Gibb, J. R., and Bennis, K. D., *T-group Training and Laboratory Method*, New York: Wiley, 1964.

Brown, G., *Microteaching*, London: Methuen, 1978.

Ivey, A. E., *Microcounselling*, Springfield, Ill.: Thomas, 1971.

Trower, P., Bryant, B., and Argyle, M., *Social Skills and Mental Health*, London: Methuen, 1978.

CHAPTER 13

EPILOGUE

I have tried to outline what has been found out, mainly by experimental research, in an important area of human behaviour. Several hundred investigations have been described, and there are several thousand others which have been kept in the background.* The main variables have been introduced, and the main processes behind interpersonal behaviour have been described.

Interpersonal behaviour is a centrally important part of human life. When it goes wrong there is inefficiency, unhappiness and conflict between individuals and groups. Some of the interpersonal aspects of work have been described, together with the social techniques that are found to be most effective in a number of jobs, and the best ways of training people in effective social skills. The character of the most severe breakdowns in social performance – in certain mental disorders – has been discussed, and methods of treatment suggested.

Can the study of interpersonal behaviour make any contribution to everyday social encounters and relationships?

APPLICATIONS OF THE NEW KNOWLEDGE

There are several fields where this new knowledge has already been applied, and where it could be applied more extensively.

1. *Social skills training.* It is no longer necessary for a sizeable proportion of the human race to be lonely, isolated, miserable or mentally ill through lack of social skills. Many thousands have already been trained by one technique or another, and training could easily become available to all. The most useful step would be to include social skills ('human relations') training in the

* Some of the others are reviewed in Argyle (1969, 1975).

school curriculum, and to make SST available to adults in community centres or elsewhere. Through this sort of training, it would be possible to raise the whole *quality* of normal social behaviour so that it is more efficient and more enjoyable, and results in help, cooperation and trust rather than rejection, misunderstanding and social barriers. This would also raise the number of really outstanding performers in the field of social behaviour, which would be of benefit to all.

2. *Re-design of groups and organizations.* A lot is now known about social interaction in various kinds of groups and organizations. It is known that with certain designs there is alienation, frustration, and failure of communication, while other designs work much better. We know for example that there should be small, cooperative teams, under democratic and employee-centred supervisors, and that there should be few levels in the hierarchy, with delegation and representation of junior members. These are not optional extras, which slightly increase job satisfaction, but may be essential if an organization is to survive (Argyle, 1972).

3. *Resolving conflicts between groups.* Some of the most important social problems are due to conflict between people of different races, social classes, ages, and even sexes. Some of these conflicts are due to real differences of wealth or opportunities, but some of the worst conflicts are between groups of very similar affluence. These conflicts are partly due to the difficulties of interacting with people from another culture, who follow different rules and conventions, use different non-verbal signals, and have different ideas. We have seen that a quite short period of training can make people better at dealing with intercultural encounters (p. 186). Such training could be a normal part of the school curriculum.

A NEW MODEL OF MAN

Our research in this area shows that previous psychological

models of man were mistaken or incomplete through not taking account of the interpersonal nature of man.

The latter has as a result remained somewhat mysterious, a fitting domain for theologians, moralists and novelists (not to mention the authors of pop songs and *Mad* magazine). These writers have indeed recognized that relations with others are the most important part of human life, and that most of the essential human characteristics cannot be manifested by a person in isolation. They have rightly been unconvinced of the relevance to human affairs of experiments with people (or rats) studied while they perform laboratory tasks in isolation [Argyle, 1969, pp. 430–31].

Unfortunately, much work in social psychology has been little better – artificial experiments often on one person, sometimes preventing verbal or non-verbal communication, often in a laboratory vacuum resembling no situation in the outside world (Israel and Tajfel, 1972). The formulations of social psychologists have often been highly inadequate – the importance of non-verbal communication and the roles of gaze are recent discoveries; only very recently have social psychologists become aware of the effects of situations and their rules, the way social acts fit together in sequence, or the effect of ideas and language on behaviour.

The model of man we have arrived at is something like this: For the survival of individuals and their genes, for the satisfaction of biological needs and the continuation of the species, cooperation in groups is necessary in animals and men; there are innate tendencies to respond to others, which in man in particular require experiences in the family for their completion; there is a system of non-verbal signals for communicating interpersonal intentions and attitudes; in man there is a second means of communication – language; interaction is conducted by the two channels of vision and hearing, with the verbal and the non-verbal closely coordinated, gaze being the main channel for receiving NVC. Social behaviour is produced as a stream of closely integrated responses, subject to continuous correction as a result of feedback, controlled by more or less conscious plans, and subject to partly verbalized rules derived from the culture. The sequence of events in social behaviour follows a meaningful pattern, in which each act fits those that went before. Individuals perceive and interpret the behaviour of others and the situations they are in, and initiate large and small segments of interaction. Social interaction takes place in a limited range of situations, each with its characteristic structure of rules, roles and purposes.

There is probably one more essential component: there is an innate concern for other members of the immediate family and group, resulting in care for others and restraint of aggression. We have seen that sympathy appears in young children, and that taking account of the point of view of the other is an essential ingredient in interaction. Concern with the views of another takes a second important form: the self-image is largely constructed out of the reactions of others, and leads to self-presentation behaviour to elicit appropriate reactions in later social situations.

This basic equipment, partly innate, partly acquired from the culture, leads to the formation of interpersonal bonds, small social groups and social structures. Relationships between pairs of people are an essential part of human life; they are built up through a gradual process of trial and error, resulting in a synchronizing pattern of interaction, together with intimacy, self-disclosure and attachment. People interact in small social groups, in the family, at work and with friends. Here the interaction patterns are more complex, and groups evolve a stable system with norms and differentiation of roles. In larger groups, the roles become formalized and the whole pattern of interaction follows a regular pattern, which is learnt by new members; this is called a social structure.

The views of social psychologists about the nature of man have also changed in a more fundamental way. We no longer think that man's behaviour is controlled by causal laws, in a deterministic way, or that it is totally predictable. Experiments do, of course, discover regularities, in which one variable is found to affect another. However, when people are told about one of these regularities they are perfectly able to resist it, and thought processes can override reflex responses or similar processes. A number of European 'hermeneutic' social psychologists have argued that the aim of research should be to enable people to free themselves from causal laws by understanding them (Rommetveit, 1972). Linguists make no attempt to predict what anyone will say, and regard this as impossible since most utterances have never been produced before. Similarly, some social psychologists are trying to find the generative rules of social behaviour, which will give understanding but not prediction (Harré and Secord, 1972).

Some recent developments in therapy have been directed towards increasing the individual's power of self-control, i.e. freeing himself from lower-level causal processes (Meichenbaum, 1977). It is hoped that the knowledge contained in this book, and the use of the training techniques described, will increase self-knowledge and understanding in the field of social behaviour.

POSSIBLE DANGERS OF THE NEW KNOWLEDGE

It has been suggested that the new knowledge of interpersonal behaviour might have some undesirable consequences, as well as desirable ones.

1. It is possible that when people become trained to interact better their behaviour may become more contrived and insincere, become more like acting. This is a complex and controversial issue: while authenticity and sincerity are attractive, it may also be argued that civilization depends on the restraint of many interpersonal feelings – aggressive, sexual and disapproving in particular. The most effective and desirable kind of behaviour does not necessarily consist of the direct outward expression of inner feelings.

2. It is objected that people will become self-conscious, awkward and unspontaneous in their social behaviour. As we have seen, much social behaviour has the characteristics of a motor skill. When a person learns a new skill, such as learning the gears of a strange car, he goes through a period when the behaviour is awkward, requires full conscious attention and is accom-

panied by actual or silent speech. This phase rapidly comes to an end as the skill is learnt and becomes habitual, and is done 'without thinking'.

3. If people become more knowledgeable about the non-verbal code these signals may come to acquire much more definite significance: raising the head 10° will be seen as an assertion of status, a shift in orientation as an expression of intimacy, and so on. If this happened the non-verbal code might lose some of its valuable property of vagueness whereby interactors are not committed to a particular relationship.

4. It has been suggested that the discovery of better ways of performing in social situations creates a danger that people may be 'manipulated' by practitioners of the new skills. All scientific discoveries can be used for good or ill, and findings in the field of social interaction are no exception. It need not be assumed that the skilled performer will spend his time outwitting other people and controlling situations to his own advantage. In many situations it is to the advantage of all that people should be socially competent – for example, that a school teacher should be good at teaching. It is in situations of conflict that the more socially skilled person is at an advantage – though the same is true of whoever is most verbally or technically skilled.

RULES AND MORALS

In a previous book it was suggested that the social scientist may,

from time to time, step outside his role of hard-boiled investigation and play the part of the social reformer or critic. His qualification to do so is the insight he gains into new human goals, and new ways of reaching old ones . . . The social scientist is often the critic and guardian of our highest ideals. He may have a further role to play in sensitizing public opinion to new ideals and standards as yet unthought of [Argyle, 1964, p. 203].

What implication does the new knowledge have for how we should conduct our everyday life? The level of social competence could be raised if there were clear social or moral rules indicating which kinds of conduct are to be recommended. There are of course plenty of such rules already, but as was pointed out earlier most moral prescriptions are so vague that it is hard to know precisely what to do in a particular situation. How exactly does one love one's neighbour, or treat people as ends in themselves? What precisely does one do about a naughty child, an incompetent employee, or an uncooperative colleague? The research which has been discussed does suggest the social techniques and relationships which are most effective in some of these situations – and they do not in general consist merely of being nice to people, or behaving in a yielding, unaggressive sort of way. The kinds of behaviour which may be regarded as morally most desirable have to be found out by means of detailed research for each situation. Some of these can be recommended because they enhance the welfare of others, or because they bring about a mutually satisfying relation, or simply because they lead to the efficient execution of cooperative tasks. Several examples have been reported earlier and will be mentioned briefly.

1. Another person's social competence and general personality development can be assisted if he is given feedback about his shortcomings. This is done on social skill training courses and in psychotherapy, but is something from which best friends often shrink. The solution may be to do it via the general non-verbal pattern of response, rather than in words.

2. People are often in trouble and distress, and in need of help. It has been found that much can be done by people who are untrained and unskilled in psychotherapy, provided they can establish a helping relationship. This involves an acceptance of the other, a sympathetic appreciation of his problems, and the provision of a warm and supporting relationship (p. 248).

3. Those who are in charge of others can bring about the greatest satisfaction and the greatest amount of productive effort by establishing a particular kind of relationship. This relationship is not obvious to common sense, and goes beyond traditional moral ideas in some ways. Subordinates should be consulted, and their ideas about the work used as far as possible. They should be helped to set their own goals and evaluate their

own progress; when disciplinary action has to be taken it should be more a matter of discussing such goals and evaluations in a sympathetic, therapeutic, but firm manner. A leader should exercise influence and control, as he thinks right, in a persuasive way (p. 249f.).

4. Parents, teachers, and anyone else in charge of children will be faced by special problems. To exercise effectively the guidance and help the children need requires a combination of warmth and firmness; without warmth the relationship collapses, without control there is no influence. Adults must maintain a certain distance or aloofness, in that they do not share the children's values or point of view, and can only share their activities to a limited extent.

5. People often have doubts and qualms about 'self-presentation' behaviour. However, not only public speakers, and professional social-skill performers, but anyone who takes part in social encounters, must present some kind of 'face' or self-image. If he does not the others will have difficulty in behaving towards him. It does not help for him to be obsequious and self-effacing. On the other hand the image presented should be realistic or there is a danger of it collapsing, which is one of the main causes of embarrassment. He should not be primarily concerned about the image-projection and its success, but about teaching, persuading or whatever he is trying to do. Similarly, it is in the interest of others to be interesting, amusing, nice to look at, and rewarding in other ways.

REFERENCES

Abercrombie, K. (1968), 'Paralanguage', *Brit. J. Dis. Comm.*, 3, 55–9.

Adams, B. N. (1967), 'Interaction theory and the social network', *Sociometry*, 30, 64–78.

Anderson, C. W. (1960), 'The relation between speaking times and decision in the employment interview', *J. Appl. Psychol.*, 44, 267–8.

Argyle, M. (1964), *Psychology and Social Problems*, London: Methuen.

Argyle, M. (1969), *Social Interaction*, London: Methuen.

Argyle, M. (1972), *The Social Psychology of Work*, London: Allen Lane The Penguin Press.

Argyle, M. (1975), *Bodily Communication*, London: Methuen.

Argyle, M. (1976), 'Personality and social behaviour', in R. Harré (ed.), *Personality*, Oxford: Blackwell, 145–88.

Argyle, M., and Beit-Hallahmi, B. (1975), *The Social Psychology of Religion*, London: Routledge and Kegan Paul.

Argyle, M., and Dean, J. (1965), 'Eye-contact, distance and affiliation', *Sociometry*, 28, 289–304.

Argyle, M., Gardner, G., and Cioffi, F. (1958), 'Supervisory methods related to productivity, absenteeism and labour turnover', *Human Relations*, 11, 23–45.

Argyle, M., and Graham, J. A. (1977), 'The Central Europe experiment – looking at persons and looking at things', *J. Env. Psych. and Non-Verbal Beh.*, 1, 6–16.

Argyle, M., and Ingham, R. (1972), 'Gaze, mutual gaze and distance', *Semiotica*, 6, 32–49.

Argyle, M., Ingham, R., Alkema, F., and McCallin, M. (1973), 'The different functions of gaze', *Semiotica*, 7, 19–32.

Argyle, M., and Kendon, A. (1967), 'The experimental analysis of social performance', in L. Berkowitz (ed.), *Advances in Experimental Social Psychology*, 3, 55–98, New York: Academic Press.

Argyle, M., Lalljee, M., and Cook, M. (1968), 'The effects of visibility on interaction in a dyad', *Human Relations*, 21, 3–17.

Argyle, M., Lefebvre, L., and Cook, M. (1974), 'The meaning of five patterns of gaze', *Eur. J. Soc. Psychol.*, 4, 125–36.

Argyle, M., and Little, B. L. (1972), 'Do personality traits apply to social behaviour?', *J. Theory Soc. Beh.*, 2, 1–35.

Argyle, M., and McHenry, R. (1970), 'Do spectacles really increase judgements of intelligence?', *Brit. J. Soc. Clin. Psychol.*, 10, 27–9.

Argyle, M., Salter, V., Nicholson, H., Williams, M., and Burgess, P. (1970), 'The communication of inferior and superior attitudes by verbal and non-verbal signals', *Brit. J. Soc. Clin. Psychol.*, 9, 221–31.

Argyle, M., Shimoda, K., and Little, B. (1978), 'Variance due to persons and situations in England and Japan', *Brit. J. Soc. Clin. Psychol.*, 15, 335–7, 1978.

Argyle, M., Smith, T., and Kirton, M. (1962), *Training Managers*, Acton Society Trust.

Argyle, M., and Williams, M. (1969), 'Observer or observed? A reversible perspective in person perception', *Sociometry*, 32, 396–412.

Austin, J. (1962), *How to do things with words*, Oxford: Oxford University Press.

Ayllon, T., and Azrin, N. (1968), *The Token Economy*, New York: Appleton-Century-Crofts.

Bakan, P. (1971), 'The eyes have it', *Psychology Today*, 4, 64–7.

Bales, R. F. (1950), *Interaction Process Analysis*, Cambridge, Mass.: Addison-Wesley.

Bales, R. F. (1953), 'The equilibrium problem in small groups', in T. Parsons, R. F. Bales, and E. A. Shils (eds.), *Workingpapers in the Theory of Action*, Glencoe, Ill.: Free Press.

Bannister, D., and Salmon, P. (1966), 'Schizophrenic thought disorder: specific or diffuse?', *Brit. J. Med. Psychol.*, 39, 215–219

Barker, R. G., and Wright, H. F. (1954), *Midwest and its Children: the Psychological Ecology of an American Town*, Evanston, Ill.: Row, Peterson.

Baron, R. A., and Byrne, D. (1977), *Social Psychology*, Boston, Mass.: Allyn and Bacon.

Bennis, W. G., *et al.* (1964), *Interpersonal Dynamics*, Homewood, Ill.: Dorsey Press.

Berger, A. (1965), 'A test of the double-bind hypothesis of schizophrenia', *Family Process*, 4, 198–205.

REFERENCES

Bergin, A. E., and Garfield, S. L. (1971), *Handbook of Psychotherapy and Behavior Change*, New York: Wiley.

Berkowitz, L. (1968), 'Responsibility, reciprocity, and social distance in help-giving: an experimental investigation of English social class differences', *J. Exp. Soc. Psychol.*, 4, 46–63.

Berkowitz, L., and Friedman, P. (1967), 'Some social class differences in helping behaviour', *J. Pers. Soc. Psychol.*, 5, 217–25.

Berkowitz, L., and Geen, R. G. (1966), 'Film violence and the cue properties of available targets', *J. Pers. Soc. Psychol.*, 3, 525–30.

Berne, E. (1966), *Games People Play*, London: Deutsch.

Bernstein, B. (1959), 'A public language: some sociological implications of a linguistic form', *Brit. J. Sociol.*, 10, 311–26.

Berscheid, E., *et al.* (1971), 'Physical attractiveness and dating choice: a test of the matching hypothesis', *J. Exp. Soc. Psychol.*, 7, 173–89.

Berscheid, E., and Walster, E. (1974a), 'Physical attractiveness', *Advances in Experimental Social Psychology*, 7, 158–215.

Berscheid, E., and Walster, E. (1974b), 'Romantic love', in T. L. Huston (ed.), *Foundations of Interpersonal Attraction*, New York: Academic Press.

Bion, W. R. (1948–51), 'Experiences in groups', *Human Relations*, 1–7.

Block, J. (1953), 'The assessment of communication role variation as a function of interactional content', *J. Pers.*, 21, 272–86.

Borgatta, E. F., and Bales, R. F. (1953), 'Interaction of individuals in reconstituted groups', *Sociometry*, 16, 302–20.

Bowers, K. S. (1973), 'Situationism in psychology: an analysis and a critique', *Psychol. Rev.*, 30, 307–36.

Brackman, J. (1967), 'The put-on', *New Yorker*, 24 June, 34–73.

Braginsky, B. M., Braginsky, D. D., and Ring, K. (1969), *Methods of Madness. The Mental Hospital as a Last Resort*, New York: Holt, Rinehart and Winston.

Breer, P. E. (1960), 'Predicting interpersonal behavior from personality and role (unpublished), Harvard University Ph.D.

Brown, G. (1975a), *Microteaching*, London: Methuen.

Brown, G. A. (1975b), 'Microteaching: research and developments', in G. Chanan and S. Delamont (eds.), *Frontiers of Classroom Research*, Slough: N.F.E.R.

Brown, R. (1965), *Social Psychology*, New York: Collier-Macmillan.

Brown, G. W., Harris, T. O., and Peto, J. (1973), 'Life events and psychiatric disorders, Part 2: nature of causal link', *Psychol. Med.*, 3, 159–76.

Brown, R., and Lenneberg, E. H. (1954), 'A study in language and cognition', *J. Abnorm. Soc. Psychol.*, 49, 454–62.

Brun, T. (1969), *The International Dictionary of Sign Language*, London: Wolfe Publishing Ltd.

Bruner, J. (1975), 'The ontogenesis of speech acts', *J. Child Lang.*, 2, 1–19.

Bryan, J. H., and Walbek, N. H. (1970), 'Preaching and practising generosity: children's actions and reactions', *Child. Dev.*, 41, 329–53.

Bryant, B., and Trower, P. (1974), 'Social difficulty in a student population', *Brit. J. Educ. Psychol.*, 44, 13–21.

Bryant, B., *et al.* (1976), 'A survey of social inadequacy among psychiatric outpatients', *Psychol Med.*, 6, 101–12.

Bugenthal, D., Kaswan, J. W., and Love, L. R. (1970), 'Perception of contradictory meanings conveyed by verbal and non-verbal channels', *J. Pers. Soc. Psychol.*, 16, 647–55.

Burns, T. (1964), 'Non-verbal communications', *Discovery*, 25 (10), 30–37.

Campbell, D. T. (1975), 'On the conflicts between biological and social evolution and between psychology and moral tradition', *Amer. Psychol.*, 30, 1103–26.

Carment, D. W., Miles, C. G., and Cervin, V. B. (1965), 'Persuasiveness and persuasibility as related to intelligence and extraversion', *Brit. J. Soc. Clin. Psychol.*, 4, 1–7.

Carnegie, D. (1936), *How to Win Friends and Influence People*, New York: Simon and Schuster.

Chapple, E. D. (1956), *The Interaction Chronograph Manual*, Moroton, Conn.: E. D. Chapple Inc.

Chapple, E. D., and Donald, G. (1947), 'An evaluation of department store salespeople by the interaction chronograph', *Journal of Marketing*, 13, 173–85.

Chaikin, A. L., and Derlega, V. J. (1976), 'Self disclosure', in J. W. Thibaut, J. T. Spence and R. C. Carson (eds.), *Contemporary Topics in Social Psychology*, Morristown, N.J.: General Learning Press.

Clancy, H., and McBride, G. (1969), 'The autistic process and its treatment', *J. Child Psych. Psychiat.*, 10, 233–44.

Clarke, D. (1975), 'The use and recognition of sequential

structure in dialogue', *Brit. J. Soc. Clin. Psychol.*, 14, 333–9.

Cline, V. B., and Richards, J. M. (1960), 'Accuracy of interpersonal perception – a general trait?', *J. Abnorm. Soc. Psychol.*, 60, 1–7.

Clore, G. L., and Gormly, J. B. (1974), 'Knowing, feeling, and liking: a psychophysiological study of attraction', *J. Res. Pers.*, 8, 218–30.

Clore, G. L., Wiggins, N. H., and Itkin, S. (1975), 'Judging attraction from nonverbal behavior: the gain phenomenon', *J. Consult. Clin. Psychol.*, 43, 491–7.

Collett, P. (1971), 'On training Englishmen in the non-verbal behaviour of Arabs: an experiment in intercultural communication', *Int. J. Psychol.*, 6, 209–215.

Collett, P. (ed.) (1977), *Social Rules and Social Behaviour*, Oxford: Blackwell.

Collett, P., and O'Shea, G. (1976), 'Pointing the way to a fictional place: a study of direction-giving in Iran and England', *Eur. J. Soc. Psychol.*, vol. 6, no. 4, 43–54.

Cooper, J. E., *et al.* (1972), *Psychiatric Diagnosis in New York and London*, Oxford University Press.

Cottrell, N. B., *et al.* (1968), 'Social facilitation of dominant responses by the presence of an audience and the mere presence of others', *J. Pers. Soc. Psychol.*, 9, 245–50.

Cranach, M. von, and Ellgring, J. H. (1973), 'The perception of looking behaviour', in M. von Cranach and I. Vine (eds.), *Social Communication and Movement*, London: Academic Press.

Crawford, D. G., and Signori, E. I. (1962), 'An application of the critical incident technique to university teaching', *Canadian Psychologist*, vol. 3a, no. 4.

Crook, J. H. (1970), 'The socio-ecology of primates', in J. H. Crook (ed.), *Social Behaviour in Birds and Mammals*, London: Academic Press, 103–166.

Curran, J. P. (1977), 'Skills training as an approach to the treatment of heterosexual-social anxiety', *Psychol. Bull.*, 84, 140–57.

Davitz, J. R. (1964), *The Communication of Emotional Meaning*, New York: McGraw-Hill.

Dawkins, R. (1976a), *The Selfish Gene*, Oxford University Press.

Dawkins, R. (1976b), 'Hierarchical organization: a candidate principle for zoology', in P. P. G. Bateson and R. A. Hinde (eds.), *Growing Points in Ethology*, Cambridge University Press.

Deutsch, H. (1955), 'The imposter: contribution to ego psychology of a type of psychopath', *Psychoanalytic Quarterly*, 24, 483–505.

Dickman, H. R. (1963), 'The perception of behavioral units', in R. G. Barker (ed.), *The Stream of Behavior*, New York: Appleton-Century-Crofts.

Dion, K., Berscheid, E., and Walster, E. (1972), 'What is beautiful is good', *J. Pers. Soc. Psychol.*, 24, 285–90.

Doob, A. N., and Wood, L. (1972), 'Catharsis and aggression: the effects of hurting one's enemy', *J. Pers. Soc. Psychol.*, 22, 156–62.

Duck, S. W. (1973), *Personal Relationships and Personal Constructs*, London: Wiley.

Duncan, S., and Fiske, D. W. (1977), *Face-to-Face Interaction*, Hillsdale, N. J.: Erlbaum.

Dutton, D. G., and Aron, A. P. (1974), 'Some evidence for heightened sexual attraction under conditions of high anxiety', *J. Pers. Soc. Psychol.*, 30, 510–17.

Duval, S., and Wicklund, R. A. (1972), *A Theory of Objective Self Awareness*, New York: Academic Press.

Eibl-Eibesfeldt, I. (1972), 'Similarities and differences between cultures in expressive movements', in R. A. Hinde (ed.), *Non-Verbal Communication*, Cambridge: Royal Society and Cambridge University Press.

Ekman, P., Friesen, W. V., and Ellsworth, P. (1972), *Emotions in the Human Face*, Elmsford, N.Y.: Pergamon.

Ellsworth, P. (1975), 'Direct gaze as a social stimulus: the example of aggression', in P. Pliner, L. Kramer, and T. Alloway (eds.), *Nonverbal Communication and Aggression*, New York: Plenum.

Endler, N. S. (1965), 'The effects of verbal reinforcement on conformity and deviant behavior', *J. Soc. Psychol.*, 66, 147–54.

Endler, N. S., and Magnusson, D. (eds.) (1976), *Interactional Psychology and Personality*, Washington: Hemisphere.

Erikson, E. H. (1956), 'The problem of ego identity', *American Journal of Psychoanalysis*, 4, 56–121.

Etzioni, A. (1961), *A Comparative Analysis of Complex Organizations*, Glencoe, Ill.: Free Press.

Exline, R. V. (1963), 'Explorations in the process of person perception: visual interaction in relation to competition, sex and need for affiliation', *J. Pers.*, 31, 1–20.

Exline, R. V. (1971), 'Visual interaction: the glances of power and preference', *Nebraska Symposium on Motivation*, University of Nebraska Press, 163–206.

Exline, R. V., Ellyson, S. L., and Long, B. (1975), 'Visual behavior as an aspect of power role relationships', in P. Pliner, L. Kramer, and T. Alloway (eds.), *Nonverbal Communication of Aggression*, New York: Plenum.

Exline, R. V., and Winters, L. C. (1965), 'Affective relations and mutual glances in dyads', in S. Tomkins and C. Izard (eds.), *Affect, Cognition and Personality*, New York: Springer.

Exline, R. V., *et al.* (1970), 'Visual interaction in relation to Machiavellianism and an unethical act', in R. Christie and F. L. Geis, *Studies in Machiavellianism*, New York: Academic Press.

Exline, R. V., and Yellin, A. (1969), 'Eye contact as a sign between man and monkey', cited in Exline (1971).

Eysenck, H. J. (1957), *The Dynamics of Anxiety and Hysteria*, London: Routledge and Kegan Paul.

Eysenck, H. J., and Eysenck, S. B. G. (1969), *Personality Structure and Measurement*, London: Routledge and Kegan Paul.

Fairweather, G. W., *et al.* (1969), *Community Life for the Mentally Ill*, Chicago: Aldine.

Fiedler, F. E. (1953), 'Quantitative studies on the role of therapists' feelings towards their patients', in O. H. Mowrer (ed.), *Psychotherapy, Theory and Research*, New York: Ronald.

Fiedler, F. E. (1964), 'A contingency model of leadership effectiveness', *Advances in Experimental Social Psychology*, 1, 150–191.

Fiedler, F. E. (1970), 'Leadership experience and leader effectiveness – another hypothesis shot to hell', *Org. Beh. and Hum. Perf.*, 5, 1–14.

Fiedler, F. E., Mitchell, R., and Triandis, H. C. (1971), 'The culture assimilator: an approach to cross-cultural training', *J. Appl. Psychol.*, 55, 95–102.

Flanders, N. A. (1970), *Analyzing Teaching Behavior*, Reading, Mass.: Addison-Wesley.

Fleishman, E. A., and Harris, E. F. (1962), 'Patterns of leadership behaviour related to employee grievances and turnover', *Personnel Psychol.*, 15, 43–56.

Forgas, J., Argyle, M., and Ginsburg, G. (in press), 'Person perception as a function of the situation: the fluctuating structure of an academic group', *J. Soc. Psychol.* (in press).

Frank, J. D. (1961), *Persuasion and Healing*, Baltimore: Johns Hopkins Press.

Freedman, J. L., and Fraser, S. C. (1966), 'Compliance without pressure: the foot-in-the-door technique', *J. Pers. Soc. Psychol.*, 4, 195–202.

Gage, N. L., Runkel, P. J., and Chatterjee, B. B. (1960), *Equilibrium Theory and Behavior Change: an experiment in feedback from pupils to teachers*, Bureau of Educational Research, Urbana, Illinois.

Garfinkel, H. (1963), 'Trust and stable actions', in O. J. Harvey, *Motivation and Social Interaction*, New York: Ronald.

Garvey, C. (1974), 'Some properties of social play', *Merrill-Palmer Quart.*, 20, 163–80.

Gergen, K. J., and Morse, S. J. (1967), 'Self-consistency: measurement and validation', *Proc. Amer. Psych. Assoc.*, 207–8.

Gibbins, K. (1969), 'Communication aspects of women's clothes and their relation to fashionability', *Brit. J. Soc. Clin. Psychol.*, 8, 301–12.

Giles, H., and Powesland, P. F. (1975), *Speech Style and Social Evaluation*, London: Academic Press.

Goffman, E. (1955), 'On face-work: an analysis of ritual elements in social interaction', *Psychiatry*, 18, 213–31.

Goffman, E. (1956), *The Presentation of Self in Everyday Life*, Edinburgh University Press.

Goffman, E. (1961), *Encounters*, Indianapolis: Bobbs-Merrill.

Goffman, E. (1963), *Behavior in Public Places*, Glencoe, Ill.: Free Press.

Goffman, E. (1971), *Relations in Public*, London: Allen Lane The Penguin Press.

Goldstein, A. J. (1973), *Structured Learning Therapy: Toward a Psychotherapy for the Poor*, New York: Academic Press.

Goldthorpe, J., *et al.* (1969), *The Affluent Worker in the Class Structure*, Cambridge University Press.

Gordon, R. L. (1976), *Interviewing Strategy, Techniques and Tactics*, Homewood, Ill.: Dorsey.

Gorer, G. (1965), *Death, Grief and Mourning*, Garden City, New York: Doubleday.

Gough, H. G. (1957), *Manual for the California Psychological Inventory*, Palo Alto: Consulting Psychologists Press.

Graham, J. A., and Argyle, M. (1975), 'A cross-cultural study of the communication of extra-verbal meaning by gestures', *Int. J. Psychol.*, 10, 57–67.

Graham, J. A., Ricci Bitti, P., and Argyle, M. (1975), 'A cross-cultural study of the communication of emotion and gestural cues', *J. Hum. Mov. Stud.*, 1, 68–77.

Griffitt, W., and Veitch, R. (1971), 'Hot and crowded: influences of population density and temperature on interpersonal affective behavior', *J. Pers. Soc. Psychol.*, 17, 92–8.

Griffitt, W., and Veitch, R. (1974), 'Ten days in a fall-out shelter', *Sociometry*, 37, 163–173.

Gross, E., and Stone, G. P. (1964), 'Embarrassment and the analysis of role requirements', *Amer. J. Sociol.*, 70, 1–15.

Hall, E. T. (1955), 'The anthropology of manners', *Scientific American*, 192, April, 84–90.

Hall, E. T. (1966), *The Hidden Dimension*, Garden City, N.Y.: Doubleday.

Harlow, H. F., and Harlow, M. K. (1965), 'The affectional systems', in A. M. Schrier *et al.* (eds.), *Behavior of Non-human Primates*, New York and London: Academic Press.

Harré, R. (1976), 'Living up to a name', in R. Harré (ed.), *Personality*, Oxford: Blackwell, 44–60.

Harré, R., and Secord, P. (1972), *The Explanation of Social Behaviour*, Oxford: Blackwell.

Hastorf, A. H., and Cantril, H. (1954), 'They saw a game: a case study', *J. Abnorm. Soc. Psychol.*, 49, 129–34.

Haynes, E. T., and Phillips, J. P. N. (1973), 'Inconsistency, loose construing and schizophrenic thought disorder', *Brit. J. Psychiat.*, 123, 209–17.

Haythorn, W. (1956), 'The effects of varying combinations of authoritarian and equalitarian leaders and followers', *J. Abnorm. Soc. Psychol.*, 52, 210–19.

Heckhausen, H. (1967), *The Anatomy of Achievement Motivation*, New York: Academic Press.

Hersen, M., and Bellack, A. S. (1976), 'Social skills training for chronic psychiatric patients: rationale, research findings, and future directions', *Comprehensive Psychiatry*, 17, 559–80.

Highfield, M. E., and Pinsent, A. (1952), *A Survey of Rewards and Punishments in Schools*, London: Newnes.

Hoffman, L. R. (1965), 'Group problem-solving', *Advances in Experimental Social Psychology*, 2, 99–132.

Hokanson, J. E., and Burgess, M. (1962), 'The effects of three types of aggression on vascular processes', *J. Abnorm. Soc. Psychol.*, 64, 446–9.

Hollander, E. P. (1958), 'Conformity, status and idiosyncrasy credit', *Psychol. Rev.*, 65, 117–27.

Horner, M. (1970), 'Femininity and successful achievement: a basic inconsistency', in J. Bardwick *et al.* (eds.), *Feminine Personality and Conflict*, Belmont, Calif.: Brooks-Cole.

Hurlock, E. B. (1929), 'Motivation in fashion', *Arch. Psychol.*, 111, 1–72.

Hyman, H. H., *et al.* (1955), *Interviewing in Social Research*, University of Chicago Press.

Israel, J., and Tajfel, H. (eds.) (1972), *The Context of Social Psychology: A Critical Assessment*, London: Academic Press.

Izard, C. E. (1971), *The Face of Emotion*, New York: Appleton-Century-Crofts.

Izard, C. E. (1975), 'Patterns of emotions and emotion communication in "hostility" and aggression', in P. Pliner, L. Kramer, and T. Alloway (eds.), *Nonverbal Communication of Aggression*, New York: Plenum.

Jacob, T. (1975), 'Family interaction in disturbed and normal families: a methodological and substantive review', *Psychol. Bull.*, 82, 33–65.

Jecker, J. D., Maccoby, N., and Breitrose, H. S. (1965), 'Improving accuracy in interpreting non-verbal cues of comprehension', *Psychology in the Schools*, 2, 239–44.

Jennings, H. H. (1950), *Leadership and Isolation*, New York: Longmans Green.

Jones, E. E. (1964), *Ingratiation: a Social Psychological Analysis*, New York: Appleton-Century-Crofts.

Jones, E. E., Davis, K. E., and Gergen, K. J. (1961), 'Role playing variations and their informational value for person perception', *J. Abnorm. Soc. Psychol.*, 63, 302–10.

Jones, E. E., and Davis, K. E. (1966), 'From acts to dispositions', *Advances in Experimental Social Psychology*, 2, 220–67.

Jones, E. E., and Gerard, H. B. (1967), *Foundations of Social Psychology*, New York: Wiley.

Jones, E. E., Gergen, K. J., and Jones, R. G. (1963), 'Tactics of ingratiation among leaders and subordinates in a status hierarchy', *Psychol. Monogr.*, 77.

Jones, E. E., and Nisbett, R. E. (1972), 'The actor and the observer: divergent perceptions of the causes of behavior', in E. E. Jones *et al.* (eds.), *Attribution: Perceiving the Causes of Behavior*, Morristown, N.J.: General Learning Press.

Jourard, S. M. (1964), *The Transparent Self*, Princeton, N.J.: Van Nostrand.

Jourard, S. M. (1966), 'An exploratory study of body-accessibility', *Brit. J. Soc. Clin. Psychol.*, 5, 221–31.

Jourard, S. M. (1971), *Self-Disclosure*, New York: Wiley-Interscience.

Jourard, S. M., and Secord, P. F. (1955), 'Body-cathexis and personality', *Brit. J. Psychol.*, 46, 130–38.

Kahn, R. I., and Cannell, C. F. (1957), *The Dynamics of Interviewing*, New York: Wiley.

Kahn, R. L., Wolfe, D. M., Quinn, R. P., and Snoek, H. D. (1964), *Organizational Stress*, New York: Wiley.

Katz, D., and Braly, K. W. (1933), 'Racial prejudice and racial stereotypes', *J. Abnorm. Soc. Psychol.*, 30, 175–93.

Kazdin, A. E., and Wilcoxon, L. A. (1976), 'Systematic desensitization and non-specific treatment effects: a methodological evaluation', *Psychol. Bull.*, 83, 729–58.

Kelley, H. H. (1950), 'The warm–cold variable in first impressions of persons', *J. Pers.*, 18, 431–9.

Kelley, H. H. (1967), 'Attribution theory in social psychology', *Nebraska Symposium on Motivation*, University of Nebraska Press, 15.

Kelly, G. A. (1955), *The Psychology of Personal Constructs*, New York: W. W. Norton.

Kendon, A. (1967), 'Some functions of gaze direction in social interaction', *Acta Psychologica*, 28 (1), 1–47.

Kendon, A. (1972), 'Some relationships between body motion and speech: an analysis of an example', in A. Siegman and B. Pope (eds.), *Studies in Dyadic Communication*, Elmsford, New York: Pergamon.

Kendon, A. (1975), 'Some functions of the face in a kissing round', *Semiotica*, 15, 299–334.

Kendon, A. (1977), *Studies in the Behavior of Social Interaction*, Bloomington, Indiana: Indiana University Press.

Kendon, A., and Cook, M. (1969), 'The consistency of gaze patterns in social interaction', *Brit. J. Psychol.*, 60, 481–94.

Kendon, A., and Ferber, A. (1973), 'A description of some human greetings', in R. P. Michael and J. H. Crook (eds.), *Comparative Ecology and Behaviour of Primates*, London: Academic Press.

Krasner, L. (1958), 'Studies of the conditioning of verbal behavior', *Psychol. Bull.*, 55, 148–79.

Krebs, D. L. (1970), 'Altruism – an examination of the concept and a review of the literature', *Psychol. Bull.*, 73, 258–302.

Krech, D., Crutchfield, R. S., and Ballachey, E. L. (1962), *Individual in Society*, New York: McGraw-Hill.

Kuhn, M. H., and McPartland, T. S. (1954), 'An empirical investigation of self-attitudes', *Amer. Sociol. Rev.*, 19, 68–76.

Labov, R. (1964), 'Phonological correlates of social stratification', supplement to *American Anthropologist*, 66, 164–76.

Laing, R. D., Phillipson, H., and Lee, A. R. (1966), *Interpersonal Perception*, London: Tavistock.

Laird, J. D. (1974), 'Self-attribution of emotion: the effects of expressive behavior on the quality of emotional experience', *J. Pers. Soc. Psychol.*, 29, 475–86.

Latané, B. (ed.) (1966), 'Studies in social comparison', *J. Exp. Soc. Psychol.*, Supplement 1.

Lefebvre, L. (1975), 'Encoding and decoding of ingratiation in modes of smiling and gaze', *Brit. J. Soc. Clin. Psychol.*, 14, 33–42.

Lemmert, E. M. (1962), 'Paranoia and the dynamics of exclusion', *Sociometry*, 25, 2–20.

Lennard, H. L., and Bernstein, A. (1960), *The Anatomy of Psychotherapy*, Columbia University Press.

Lenrow, P. D. (1965), 'Studies of sympathy', in S. S. Tomkins and C. E. Izard (eds.), *Affect, Cognition and Personality*, London: Tavistock.

Lett, R. E., Clark, W., and Altman, I. (1969), *A propositional inventory of research on interpersonal space*, Washington: Naval Medical Research Institute.

Leventhal, H. (1974), 'Emotions: a basic problem for social psychology', in C. Nemeth (ed.), *Social Psychology: Classic and Contemporary Integrations*, Chicago. Ill.: Rand McNally.

Levine, M. H., and Sutton-Smith, B. (1973), 'Effects of age, sex, and task on visual behavior during dyadic interaction', *Dev. Psychol.*, 9, 400–405.

Lieberman, M. A., Yalom, I. D., and Miles, M. B. (1973), *Encounter Groups: First Facts*, New York: Basic Books.

Likert, R. (1961), *New Patterns of Management*, New York: McGraw-Hill.

Lombard, G. G. F. (1955), *Behavior in a Selling Group*, Harvard University Press.

Lott, A. J., and Lott, B. E. (1960), 'The formation of positive attitudes towards group members', *J. Abnorm. Soc. Psychol.*, 61, 297–300.

Lott, A. J., and Lott, B. E. (1965), 'Group cohesiveness as interpersonal attraction: a review of relationships with antecedent and consequent variables', *Psychol. Bull.*, 64, 259–309.

Luborsky, L., *et al.* (1971), 'Factors influencing the outcome of psychotherapy: a review of quantitative research', *Psychol. Bull.*, 75, 145–85.

McDavid, J., and Schroder, H. M. (1957), 'The interpretation of approval and disapproval by delinquent and non-delinquent adolescents', *J. Pers.*, 25, 539–49.

McPhail, P. (1967), 'The development of social skill in adolescents', paper to B.P.S. (unpublished), Oxford Department of Education.

McPhail, P. (1972), *Moral Education in Secondary Schools*, London: Longmans.

Mahannah, L. (1968), 'Influence of clothing color on the perception of personality', M. A. thesis, University of Nevada, Reno, cited by Secord and Backman (1974).

Maier, N. R. F. (1953), 'An experimental test of the effect of training on discussion leadership', *Hum. Relat.*, 6, 161–73.

Maier, N. R. F., and Solem, A. R. (1952), 'The contribution of a discussion leader to the quality of group thinking: the effective use of minority opinion', *Hum. Relat.*, 5, 277–88.

Mann, L. (1970), 'The social psychology of waiting lines', *Amer. Sci.*, 58, 390–98.

Mann, R. D., *et al.* (1967), *Interpersonal Styles and Group Development*, New York: Wiley.

Marcia, J. E. (1966), 'Development and validation of ego-identity status', *J. Pers. Soc. Psychol.*, 3, 551–8.

Marsh, P., Harré, R., and Rosser, E. (1978), *The Rules of Disorder*, London: Routledge and Kegan Paul.

Maxwell, G. M. (1976), 'An evaluation of social skills training', unpublished, University of Otago, Dunedin, New Zealand.

May, P. R. A. (ed.) (1968), *Treatment of Schizophrenia*, New York: Science House.

Mehrabian, A. (1969), *Tactics in Social Influence*, Englewood Cliffs, New Jersey: Prentice-Hall.

Meichenbaum, S. (1977), *Cognitive-Behavior Modification*, New York: Plenum.

Meldman, M. J. (1967), 'Verbal behavior analysis of self-hyperattentionism', *Dis. Nerv. Syst.*, 28, 469–73.

Melly, G. (1965), 'Gesture goes classless', *New Society*, 17 June, 26–7.

Merton, R. K., *et al.* (1957), *The Student-Physician*, Harvard University Press.

Milgram, S. (1974), *Obedience to Authority*, New York: Harper & Row.

Milgram, S., Bickman, L., and Berkowitz, L. (1969), 'Note on the drawing power of crowds of different sizes', *J. Pers. Soc. Psychol.*, 13, 79–82.

Miller, D. T., and Ross, M. (1975), 'Self-serving biases in the attribution of causality: fact or fiction?', *Psychol. Bull.*, 82, 213–25.

Miller, N. E. (1944), 'Experimental studies of conflict', in J. McV. Hunt (ed.), *Personality and the Behavior Disorders*, New York: Ronald.

Minsky, M. (1975), 'A framework for representing knowledge', in P. H. Winston (ed.), *The Psychology of Computer Vision*, New York: McGraw-Hill.

Mohanna, A. I., and Argyle, M. (1960), 'A cross-cultural study of structured groups with unpopular central members', *J. Abnorm. Soc. Psychol.*, 60, 139–40.

Moos, R. H. (1968), 'Situational analysis of a therapeutic community milieu', *J. Abnorm. Psychol.*, 73, 49–61.

Moos, R. H. (1969), 'Sources of variance in responses to questionnaires and in behavior', *J. Abnorm. Psychol.*, 74, 405–12.

Morley, I. E., and Stephenson, G. M. (1977), *The Social Psychology of Bargaining*, London: Allen and Unwin.

Morton, R. B. (1965), 'The uses of the laboratory method in a psychiatric hospital', in E. H. Schein and W. G. Bennis (eds.), *Personal and Organizational Change through Group Methods*, New York: Wiley.

Moscovici, S. (1976), *Social Influence and Social Change*, London: Academic Press.

Mussen, P., and Distler, L. (1964), 'Child-rearing antecedents of masculine identification in kindergarten boys', *Child. Dev.*, 31, 89–100.

Muuss, R. E. (1962), *Theories of Adolescence*, New York: Random House.

Naegele, K. D. (1958), 'Friendship and acquaintance: an exploration of some social distinctions', *Harvard Educ. Rev.*, 28 (3), 232–52.

Newtson, D. (1977), 'The objective basis of behavior units', *J. Pers. Soc. Psychol.*, 35, 847–62.

Nisbett, R. E., and Wilson, T. D. (1976), 'Telling more than we know: verbal reports on mental processes', *Psychol. Rev.*, 84, 231–59.

Oeser, O. A. (1955), *Teacher, Pupil and Task*, London: Tavistock.

Osgood, C. E., Suci, G. J., and Tannenbaum, P. H. (1957), *The Measurement of Meaning*, University of Illinois Press.

Paivo, A. (1965), 'Personality and audience influence', *Progress in Experimental Personality Research*, 2, 127–73.

Parnell, R. W. (1958), *Behaviour and Physique*, London: Arnold.

Patterson, M. L. (1976), 'An arousal model of interpersonal intimacy', *Psychol. Rev.*, 83, 235–45.

Paul, G. L. (1966), *Insight v. Desensitization in Psychotherapy*, Stanford University Press.

Peck, R. F., and Tucker, J. A. (1973), 'Research on teacher education', in R. M. W. Travers (ed.), *Second Handbook of Research on Teaching*, Chicago: Rand McNally.

Phares, E. (1976), *Locus of Control in Personality*, Morristown, N.J.: General Learning Press.

Piliavin, I. M., Rodin, J., and Piliavin, J. A. (1969), 'Good Samaritanism: an underground phenomenon?', *J. Pers. Soc. Psychol.*, 13, 289–99.

Potter, S. (1952), *One-Upmanship*, Hart-Davis.

Price, R. H., and Bouffard, D. L. (1974), 'Behavioral appropriateness and situational constraint as dimensions of social behavior', *J. Pers. Soc. Psychol.*, 30, 579–86.

Rapoport, R., and Rapoport, R. H. (1964), 'New light on the honeymoon', *Human Relations*, 17, 33–56.

Regan, D. T. (1971), 'Effects of a favor and liking on compliance', *J. Exp. Soc. Psychol.*, 7, 627–39.

Rich, A. R., and Schroeder, H. E. (1976), 'Research issues in assertiveness training', *Psychol. Bull.*, 83, 1081–96.

Richardson, A. (1961), 'The assimilation of British immigrants in a Western Australian community – a psychological study', *Research Group for European Migration Problems*, vol. 9, nos. 1–2.

Riesman, D., Potter, R. J., and Watson, J. (1960), 'Sociability, permissiveness, and equality', *Psychiatry*, 23, 323–40.

Robson, R. A. H. (1966), 'Group Structure in Mixed Sex Triads', (unpublished), Department of Sociology, University of British Columbia.

Rogers, C. R. (1942), *Counselling and Psychotherapy*, Boston: Houghton Mifflin.

Rommetveit, R. (1972), 'Language games, syntactic structures and hermeneutics', in J. Israel and H. Tajfel (eds.), *The Context of Social Psychology: A Critical Assessment*, London: Academic Press.

Rommetveit, R. (1974), *On Message Structure. A Conceptual Framework for the Study of Language and Communication*, London: Wiley.

Rosenberg, M. (1965), *Society and the Adolescent Self-image*, Princeton University Press.

Rosenfeld, H. M. (1967), 'Non-verbal reciprocation of approval: an experimental analysis', *J. Pers. Soc. Psychol.*, 3, 102–11.

Rosenshine, B. (1971), *Teaching Behaviours and Student Achievement*, Slough: N.F.E.R.

Rubin, Z. (1973), *Liking and Loving*, New York: Holt, Rinehart and Winston.

Runyan, W. M. (1976), 'The life course as a theoretical orientation: sequences of person × situation interaction' (unpublished), Institute of Human Development, University of California, Berkeley.

Rutter, D. (1976), 'Visual interaction in recently admitted and chronic long-stay schizophrenic patients', *Brit. J. Soc. Clin. Psychol.*, 15, 295–303.

Sahlins, M. D. (1965), 'On the sociology of primitive exchange', in *The Relevance of Models for Social Anthropology*, A.S.A. Monographs I, London: Tavistock Publications.

Sarason, I. G., and Ganzer, V. J. (1971), *Modeling: an approach to the rehabilitation of juvenile offenders*, U.S. Dept of Health, Education and Welfare.

Sarbin, T. R., and Hardyk, C. D. (1953), 'Contributions to role-taking theory: role-perception on the basis of postural cues', unpublished, cited by T. R. Sarbin (1954), 'Role theory', in G. Lindzey (ed.), *Handbook of Social Psychology*, Cambridge, Mass: Addison-Wesley.

Sarbin, T. R., and Jones, D. S. (1956), 'An experimental analysis of role behavior', *J. Abnorm. Soc. Psychol.*, 51, 236–41.

Sargant, W. (1957), *Battle for the Mind*, Heinemann.

Schachter, S. (1959), *The Psychology of Affiliation*, Stanford University Press.

Schachter, S., and Singer, J. (1962), 'Cognitive, social, and physiological determinants of emotional state', *Psychol. Rev.*, 69, 379–99.

Schaffer, H. R., and Emerson, P. E. (1964), 'The development of social attachments in infancy', *Monogr. Soc. Res. Child Dev.*, 29(3).

Scheflen, A. E. (1965), *Stream and Structure of Communicational Behavior*, Eastern Pennsylvania Psychiatric Institute.

Scherer, K. R. (1974), 'Acoustic concomitants of emotional dimensions: judging affect from synthesized tone sequences', in S. Weitz (ed), *Nonverbal communication*, New York: Oxford University Press, 105–11.

Schofield, W. (1964), *Psychotherapy, the Purchase of Friendship*, New Jersey: Prentice-Hall.

Schutz, W. C. (1958), *FIRO: A three-dimensional theory of interpersonal behavior*, New York: Holt, Rinehart and Winston.

Schutz, W. C. (1967), *Joy*, New York: Grove Press.

Secord, P. F., and Backman, C. W. (1974), *Social Psychology*, New York: McGraw-Hill.

Seligman, M. E. P. (1975), *Helplessness*, San Francisco: Freeman.

Seymour, W. D. (1966), *Industrial Skills*, London: Pitman.

Sherif, M., *et al.* (1961), *Intergroup conflict and cooperation: The Robbers Cave Experiment*, Norman: University of Oklahoma Book Exchange.

Shimoda, K., Argyle, M., and Ricci Bitti, P. (1978), 'The intercultural recognition of emotional expressions by three national groups – English, Italian and Japanese', *Eur. J. Soc. Psychol.*, 8, 169–79.

Short, J., Williams, E., and Christie, B. (1976), *The Social Psychology of Telecommunications*, London: Wiley.

REFERENCES

Shouby, E. (1951), 'The influence of the Arabic language on the psychology of the Arabs', *Middle East Journal*, 5, 284–302.

Shrauger, J. S. (1975), 'Responses to evaluation as a function of initial self-perceptions', *Psychol. Bull.*, 82, 581–96.

Sidney, E., and Argyle, M. (1969), *Training in Selection Interviewing*, London: Mantra.

Simon, A., and Boyer, E. G. (eds.) (1974), 'Mirrors for Behavior', Third Edition, *Classroom Interaction Newsletter*, Wyncote, Penn.: Communication Materials Center.

Singer, J. E. (1964), 'The use of manipulation strategies: Machiavellianism and attractiveness', *Sociometry*, 27, 138–50.

Sissons, M. (1971), 'The psychology of social class', *Money, Wealth and Class*, 115–31, The Open University Press.

Slater, P. E. (1955), 'Role differentiation in small groups', in A. P. Hare *et al.* (eds.), *Small Groups*, New York: Knopf.

Sommer, R. (1965), 'Further studies of small group ecology', *Sociometry*, 28, 337–48.

Sorensen, O. (1958), *The Observed Changes Enquiry*, New York: G.E.C.

Spielberger, C. D. (ed.) (1966), *Theory and Research on Anxiety*, New York: Academic Press.

Stone, G. C., Gage, N. L., and Leavitt, G. S. (1957), 'Two kinds of accuracy in predicting another's responses', *J. Soc. Psychol.*, 45, 245–54.

Subotnik, L. (1972), 'Spontaneous remission: fact or artifact?', *Psychol. Bull.*, 77, 32–48.

Sundberg, N. D., and Tyler, L. E. (1962), *Clinical Psychology*, New York: Appleton-Century-Crofts.

Sydiaha, D. (1961), '"Bales" interaction process analysis of personnel selection interviews', *J. Appl. Psychol.*, 45, 393–401.

Sykes, G. M., and Matza, D. (1957), 'Techniques of neutralization: a theory of delinquency', *Amer. Sociol. Rev.*, 22, 667–89.

Szasz, T. S. (1961), *The Myth of Mental Illness*, London: Secker and Warburg.

Tagiuri, R. (1958), 'Social preference and its perception', in R. Tagiuri and L. Petrullo (eds.), *Person Perception and Interpersonal Behavior*, Stanford University Press.

Tajfel, H. (1970), 'Experiments in intergroup discrimination', *Sci. Amer.*, vol. 223, no. 5, 96–102.

Taylor, D. A. (1965), 'Some aspects of the development of inter-personal relationship: social penetration processes', Washington: Naval Medical Research Institute.

Thayer, S., and Schiff, W. (1969), 'Stimulus factors in observer judgment of social interaction: facial expression and motion pattern', *Amer. J. Psychol.*, 82, 73–85.

Thibaut, J., and Riecken, H. W. (1955), 'Some determinants and consequences of the perception of social causality', *J. Pers.*, 24, 113–33.

Thomas, E. J., and Fink, C. F. (1963), 'Effects of group size', *Psychol. Bull.*, 60, 371–84.

Trist, E. L., *et al.* (1963), *Organizational Choice*, London: Tavistock.

Trower, P., Bryant, B., and Argyle, M. (1978), *Social Skills and Mental Health*, London: Methuen.

Truax, C. B., and Mitchell, K. M. (1971), 'Research on certain therapist interpersonal skills in relation to process and out-come', in A. E. Bergin and S. L. Garfield, *Handbook of Psychotherapy and Behavior Change*, New York: Wiley.

Tuckman, B. W. (1965), 'Developmental sequence in small groups', *Psychol. Bull.*, 63, 384–99.

Turner, R. H. (1956), 'Role-taking, role standpoint, and reference group behavior', *Amer. J. Sociol.*, 61, 316–28.

Ulrich, L., and Trumbo, D. (1965), 'The selection interview since 1949', *Psychol. Bull.*, 63, 100–116.

Valins, S. (1966), 'Cognitive effects of false heart-rate feedback', *J. Pers. Soc. Psychol.*, 4, 400–408.

Van Gennep, A. (1908), *The Rites of Passage*, University of Chicago Press, 1960.

Van Hooff, J. A. R. A. M. (1972), 'A comparative approach to the phylogeny of laughter and smiling', in R. A. Hinde (ed.), *Non-verbal Communication*, Cambridge: Royal Society and Cambridge University Press.

Videbeck, R. (1960), 'Self-conception and the reactions of others', *Sociometry*, 23, 351–9.

Von Cranach, M., and Ellgring, J. H. (1973), 'Problems in the recognition of gaze direction', in M. von Cranach and I. Vine (eds.), *Social Communication and Movement*, London: Academic Press.

Wachtel, P. (1973), 'Psychodynamic behavior therapy, and the implacable experimenter: an inquiry into the consistency of personality', *J. Abnorm. Psychol.*, 82, 324–34.

Walster, E. (1966), 'Assigning responsibility for an accident ', *J. Pers. Soc. Psychol.*, 3, 73–9.

Walster, E., *et al.* (1966), 'Importance of physical attractiveness in dating behavior', *J. Pers. Soc. Psychol.*, 4, 508–16.

Walters, R. H., and Parke, R. D. (1964), 'Social motivation, dependency, and susceptibility to social influence', in L. Berkowitz (ed.), *Advances in Experimental Social Psychology*, vol. 1, 232–76, New York: Academic Press.

Warr, P. B. (1965), 'Proximity as a determinant of positive and negative sociometric choice', *Brit. J. Soc. Clin. Psychol.*, 4, 104–9.

Watzlawick, P., Beavin, J. H., and Jackson, D. D. (1967), *Pragmatics of Human Communication*, New York: W. W. Norton and Co.

Weiner, B. (1974), *Achievement Motivation and Attribution Theory*, Morristown, N.J.: General Learning Press.

Weitz, S. (1972), 'Attitude, voice and behavior', *J. Pers. Soc. Psychol.*, 24, 14–24.

Wicklund, R. A. (1975), 'Objective self-awareness', *Advances in Experimental Social Psychology*, 8, 233–75.

Williams, E. (1974), 'An analysis of gaze in schizophrenia', *Brit. J. Soc. Clin. Psychol.*, 13, 1–8.

Wilson, E. O. (1975), *Sociobiology: The New Synthesis*, Cambridge, Mass.: Harvard University Press.

Wilson, G., and Nias, D. (1976), *Love's Mysteries: the Psychology of Sexual Attraction*, London: Open Books.

Wing, J. K. (1967), 'Institutionalism in mental hospitals', in T. Scheff (ed.), *Mental Illness and Social Processes*, New York: Harper & Row.

Wish, M. (1975), 'Role and personal expectations about interpersonal communication', U.S.–Japan seminar, roneoed, University of California, San Diego.

Wolpe, J. (1958), *Psychotherapy by Reciprocal Inhibition*, Stanford University Press.

Woodward, J. (1960), *The Saleswoman*, Pitman.

Wortman, C. B., and Brehm, J. (1975), 'Responses to uncontrollable outcome: an integration of reactance theory and the learned helplessness model', *Advances in Experimental Social Psychology*, 8, 278–336.

Wylie, R. C. (1961), *The Self Concept*, Lincoln, Nebraska: University of Nebraska Press.

Zajonc, R. B. (1965), 'Social facilitation', *Science*, 149, 269–74.

Zigler, E., and Child, I. L. (1969), 'Socialization', chapter 24 in G. Lindzey and E. Aronson (eds.), *Handbook of Social Psychology*, 3, Reading, Mass.: Addison-Wesley.

Ziller, R. C. (1964), 'Individuation and socialization', *Human Relations*, 17, 341–60.

Zimbardo, P. G. (1969), 'The human choice: individuation and order versus deindividuation, impulse and chaos', *Nebraska Symposium on Motivation*, University of Nebraska Press, 17.

Zimbardo, P. G. (1973), 'A Pirandellian prison', *New York Times Sunday Magazine* 8 April, 38–60.

INDEX OF NAMES

SUBJECT INDEX

319